Building
Struggling Students'
Higher Level Literacy

Practical Ideas,
Powerful Solutions

James L. Collins & Thomas G. Gunning, EDITORS

INTERNATIONAL
Reading Association
800 BARKSDALE ROAD, PO BOX 8139
NEWARK, DE 19714-8139, USA
www.reading.org

The International Reading Association attempts, through its publications, to provide a forum for a wide spectrum of opinions on reading. This policy permits divergent viewpoints without implying the endorsement of the Association.

Executive Editor, Books   Corinne M. Mooney
Developmental Editor   Charlene M. Nichols
Developmental Editor   Tori Mello Bachman
Developmental Editor   Stacey L. Reid
Editorial Production Manager   Shannon T. Fortner
Design and Composition Manager   Anette Schuetz

Project Editors   Tori M. Bachman and Rebecca A. Stewart

Cover   Design, Linda Steere; Photograph © Shutterstock Images

Library of Congress Cataloging-in-Publication Data

Building struggling students' higher level literacy : practical ideas, powerful solutions / James L. Collins and Thomas G. Gunning, editors.

    p. cm.

Includes index.

ISBN 978-0-87207-687-7

1. Reading--Remedial teaching. I. Collins, James L. II. Gunning, Thomas G.

LB1050.5.B855 2009

372.43--dc22

2009040621

CONTENTS

 **James L. Collins** is a professor in the Graduate School of Education at The State University of New York's University at Buffalo. He regularly teaches courses on reading–writing–thinking relations and how reading and writing can be brought together to improve reading comprehension; formative and design research in the English language arts; language variation and literacy; and discourse analysis. Throughout his teaching, as in his research, Jim places emphasis on helping students who have difficulty with school-sponsored learning, especially literacy learning.

Jim's master's degree at the University of Massachusetts was supported by a fellowship on Teaching English to the Urban Disadvantaged, and this was the start of his career-long interest in helping students in low-performing schools. Jim developed a strong interest in literacy and the teaching of literacy during his 10 years as a high school English teacher, and this interest has supported his research ever since. Jim taught in a large city in Massachusetts, and just about daily he would wonder why his students had so much difficulty using reading and writing as instruments of thought and expression. Since coming to the University at Buffalo in 1979, his pursuit of answers to that question has resulted in 7 books and almost 200 chapters, articles, papers, and research reports.

Increasingly over the past decade Jim has focused his research on reading–writing relations, and especially on how writing can be used to enhance reading comprehension. With his colleague Jaekyung Lee, he received a grant from the Institute of Education Sciences, U.S. Department of Education, for a three-year study called "Writing Intensive Reading Comprehension" (WIRC) to examine the efficacy of using writing to improve reading comprehension in low-performing urban schools. This research, and its meaning for teaching, is the subject of Jim's own chapter in this volume.

What excites Jim most about his work is getting into schools and helping teachers solve real problems with the teaching and learning of literacy skills. Throughout his research and teaching, Jim has worked with teachers who are focused and energetic, and the research problems he has targeted have been anchored in real classroom issues and concerns and real difficulties students encounter, exactly like the questions about literacy instruction that have driven the writing of this book.

 **Thomas G. Gunning** is a professor emeritus at Southern Connecticut State University, where he was department chairperson and director of the Reading Clinic. He is currently an adjunct professor in the Reading/Language Arts Department of Central Connecticut State University, where he teaches courses in assessment and intervention. Tom has been a secondary English teacher, a secondary school reading specialist, and an elementary school reading consultant. Tom was also the editor of *Know Your World Extra*, a periodical for struggling readers.

Tom has conducted research on group reading inventories, severe reading disabilities, intervention programs, readability, response to intervention, decoding processes and strategies, and literacy skills needed to cope with high-stakes tests. Tom has been a consultant for elementary schools in areas that include improving the core curriculum, implementing Response to Intervention, and planning programs for severely disabled readers. Tom has been trained as a Junior Great Books discussion leader and has tried out this approach with students in an urban elementary school. Recently, Tom served as a hands-on consultant for a Reading First school.

Tom is the author of a number of professional books for educators. He also was a contributing editor for *My Friend,* a nonprofit magazine for students in grades 1–8, and a member of *Sports Illustrated for Kids'* panel of experts to advise the editorial staff on readability and suitability of this magazine's articles. Tom is a past president of the IRA Readability Special Interest Group and is currently the group's membership chairperson.

Tom has bachelor's and master's degrees from Loyola University (Baltimore, Maryland) and earned a doctorate in the Psychology of Reading from Temple University (Philadelphia, Pennsylvania). Tom was a Mellon Visiting Fellow at Yale University (New Haven, Connecticut), where he studied brain development and its implications for literacy instruction.

The impetus for this book grew out of Tom's lifelong work with struggling readers, recent work with struggling comprehenders in a Reading First school, and current work with students who are proficient decoders but poor comprehenders.

CONTRIBUTORS

Nancy N. Boyles
Professor of Reading, Graduate
  Reading Program
Southern Connecticut State
  University
New Haven, Connecticut, USA

James L. Collins
Professor
University at Buffalo, The State
  University of New York
Buffalo, New York, USA

Kathleen F. Clark
Assistant Professor and Director,
  Hartman Literacy and Learning
  Center
Marquette University
Milwaukee, Wisconsin, USA

Emily Phillips Galloway
Michael Pressley Memorial Fellow
Benchmark School
Media, Pennsylvania, USA

Irene W. Gaskins
Founder and Head of Benchmark
  School, Emerita
Director of Research and Professional
  Development
Benchmark School
Media, Pennsylvania, USA

Thomas G. Gunning
Adjunct Professor
Central Connecticut State University
New Britain, Connecticut, USA

Timothy P. Madigan
Head of School
Stratford Friends School
Philadelphia, Pennsylvania, USA

Diane R. Phelps
Research Assistant and Adjunct
  Instructor
University at Buffalo, The State
  University of New York
Buffalo, New York, USA

Kristin Bourdage Reninger
Assistant Professor of Education
Otterbein College
Westerville, Ohio, USA

Karen C. Waters
Clinical Assistant Professor and
  Director, Connecticut Literacy
  Specialist Program
Sacred Heart University
Fairfield, Connecticut, USA

Ian A.G. Wilkinson
Associate Professor
The Ohio State University
Columbus, Ohio, USA

PREFACE

This is a book for teachers who believe that struggling students can learn to do advanced reading and writing tasks if they are provided the right kinds of learning experiences, assistance, and support. Too often programs for struggling readers and writers emphasize decoding and lower level literacy skills because the focus is on what students can do by themselves, without new learning and without assistance from teachers or support from parents and the community. Such programs treat reading and writing as if they were always demonstrations of what one already knows, even if that means limiting struggling students to low-level literacy tasks. This book takes the opposite approach. Each chapter provides concrete evidence that struggling students can make substantial, and sometimes even remarkable, progress toward higher level literacy if we help them learn higher order skills and knowledge rather than focusing instruction and assessment only or primarily on lower level tasks. The book is designed so that each of the chapters offers practical advice on helping students overcome particular difficulties with literacy learning. The chapters are composed and arranged so that they offer key elements in what adds up to a comprehensive program for developing struggling students' higher level literacy.

The initial impetus for the book grew out of a year Tom Gunning spent working with students in an urban school. Although most students did well in classroom discussions of texts they had read, many did poorly when asked to put their thoughts down on paper. A smaller number of students—about one in five—had difficulty both with classroom discussions and with providing written responses. An examination of the program the school was using, which was a typical basal reading series, revealed that there was inadequate instruction and practice for struggling readers. Discussions with colleagues, an examination of the research literature on higher level literacy skills, and an analysis of results on national and state tests revealed that the problem witnessed in the urban school was widespread. A search for solutions brought together other professionals who had direct experience fostering the higher level literacy skills of struggling readers. The professionals shared their experience and expertise in an institute entitled "Developing Struggling Students' Higher Level Reading and Writing Skills and Strategies," held in 2007 at the International Reading Association Convention in Toronto. This book grew out of that institute.

Based on the premise that developing higher level literacy in struggling readers requires a systematic effort, this book takes a multipronged approach that integrates reading, writing, and talk as well as affective factors, such as engagement and persistence. An essential part of the approach is providing adequate professional development and enlisting parental and community support. Although grounded in research and practice, the recommendations provided are also based on the realities of today's classrooms. Each of the contributors writes from direct hands-on experience with struggling readers and writers and their teachers. And, to enhance your own experience in the classroom and with this book, each contributor has provided an Action Plan segment to help you implement ideas immediately, as well as a list of Questions for Study and Reflection you can use as part of a self-directed study or for school-based professional development.

In the first chapter of the text, "Struggling Readers and Higher Level Literacy," Gunning provides some statistics on the number of students who struggle with higher level literacy but discusses some studies that show that struggling readers can and do learn. The introductory chapter also lays out a theory of higher level comprehension and lists the skills and strategies included in higher level comprehension.

In Chapter 2, "Assessment-Based Instruction in Developing Higher Level Literacy," Gunning and Diane R. Phelps discuss ways to assess higher level literacy, with an emphasis on formative assessment. The chapter discusses a range of formal and informal assessments and includes reading inventories, running records, think-alouds, think-alongs, observations, work samples, discussions, and tests. The chapter presents evidence that some assessments might be underestimating students' comprehension and are painting a picture that is bleaker than it needs to be. Also discussed are ways to modify assessments so that they are more reader friendly and more accurate.

Chapter 3, "Using Discussions to Promote Striving Readers' Higher Level Comprehension of Literary Texts," is the first of two chapters in the book to discuss implications of major literacy studies funded by the Institute of Education Sciences, U.S. Department of Education. In it, Kristin Bourdage Reninger and Ian A.G. Wilkinson present their experience and research with striving fifth-grade readers using discussion frameworks. The chapter provides a foundation for instruction in higher level literacy by describing a highly successful approach for promoting higher level talk. Reninger and Wilkinson describe and give examples of genuine classroom discussions, those which encourage students to be active and responsive during the conversation, talking and listening to one another, asking and answering questions, building on one another's responses, and even controlling much of the flow of the discussion. They then describe characteristics of genuine discussions and show how they support striving students' higher level thinking.

In Chapter 4, "Shifting Talk About Text: Developing Struggling Readers' Comprehension Processes During Talk About Text," Kathleen F. Clark builds on the discussion in Chapter 3 by using her research with teachers to explain and illustrate how strategy instruction can be integrated with discussions about texts. Clark emphasizes the importance of making explicit for students the processes they are using in understanding the texts being discussed so that these processes can be called on for comprehending other texts, thus developing comprehension abilities. She describes and exemplifies two key components in comprehension strategy instruction: direct explanation and scaffolding. Clark shows how teachers may shift their instructional language to make comprehension strategies accessible to students, and she presents seven procedures for shifting instructional language with examples for each procedure. Throughout, the emphasis is on making comprehension strategies explicit for students who have not already acquired them.

In Chapter 5, "Using Writing to Develop Struggling Learners' Higher Level Reading Comprehension," James L. Collins and Timothy P. Madigan report the results and practical implications of a three-year study in multiple urban classrooms called the Writing Intensive Reading Comprehension (WIRC) project. They describe how assisted writing in the form of interactive thinksheets can be used to develop reading comprehension. A thinksheet consists of several pages of questions and answer spaces that help students write about the reading they are doing. An interactive thinksheet is one that the writer uses in collaboration with teachers and peers. Collins and Madigan make the case that interactive thinksheets scaffold higher order thinking by helping struggling learners write about their reading, and they offer guidelines and examples for teachers who want to develop thinksheets to use with their own students.

Building on Chapter 5, Nancy N. Boyles provides a practical program for building students' ability to construct high-quality, higher level written responses in Chapter 6, "Teaching Struggling Readers to Respond in Writing to Open-Ended Questions: Making the Writing *and* Reading Strategic." The chapter first describes how to make writing about text strategic in four key steps: explaining criteria, modeling processes, providing guided practice, and then moving to independent application. Similarly, Boyles describes how to make the reading strategic in a series of steps, from choosing texts to gradually releasing responsibility to students. The chapter uses answer organizers and planning templates, which are similar to the thinksheets in Chapter 5.

Chapter 7, "A Step-by-Step Program for Developing Higher Level Skills in Struggling Readers," is based on Gunning's work with struggling readers in classrooms and literacy clinics. The chapter explains an approach that builds subskills and proceeds in step-by-step fashion to foster struggling readers' abilities to use higher level skills and strategies. The chapter recommends finding out where students are and moving forward from there. A series of suggested techniques and activities for fostering higher level literacy is presented in approximate order of difficulty so that the skills taught build on one another. Included are intriguing and highly effective techniques, such as using imaging, graphic organizers, and manipulatives, to develop the comprehension ability of the readers who struggle most.

In Chapter 8, "Beyond Strategy Instruction: Looking at Person, Situation, Task, and Text Variables," Irene W. Gaskins and Emily Phillips Galloway draw on experience with struggling readers at the Benchmark School and considerable research on psychological, social, and contextual variables beyond decoding skills and comprehension strategies. They offer practical recommendations for assessing and fostering personal characteristics, habits, and behaviors using an instrument called the Interactive Learner Profile (ILP). They illustrate the usefulness of ILP for understanding the full complexity of learning difficulties by discussing the case of Liam, a 9-year-old who appeared lazy and disinterested in reading, but who had other learner characteristics and difficulties as revealed by the ILP. The chapter shows how teachers can match learner characteristics to interventions, thus establishing the kinds of instructional settings and conditions that are essential for the acquisition of higher level literacy.

Chapter 9, "Strategy Instruction and Lessons Learned in Teaching Higher Level Thinking Skills in an Urban Middle School Classroom," is an account of how Karen C. Waters won over a class of reluctant struggling learners. Her focus is on the critical importance of mediated dialogue in the classroom, that is, on scaffolding discussions so that struggling students have the same opportunities to engage in rich talk as do their higher performing peers. Waters shows how teacher-scaffolded, rich classroom discourse supports the achievement of independent problem solving and comprehension, and she illustrates her methods with examples from her class of reluctant seventh graders. Like other authors in this book, Waters used a gradual release model with emphasis on modeling, guided practice, and increasingly independent applications. She describes using this model with several specific strategies, including Story Impressions, Probable Passage, Tea Party, Discussion Web, Pointed Reading, Concept of Definition, and Semantic Feature Analysis.

In Chapter 10, "Literacy Initiatives in the Urban Setting That Promote Higher Level Thinking," we hear again from Waters, but this time her voice is that of the literacy director for her urban district. Waters recounts her experience developing a higher level literacy program in a large urban school district. She describes the personnel, resources, data, and methods she and her colleagues used to transform the literacy program. Of course, she includes the classroom discussion, the subject of Chapter 10, in her design for moving from what she calls an outdated curriculum to a comprehensive literacy plan. Her discussion of the steps taken to meet the challenges of establishing the program can serve as a blueprint for others faced with similar program revisions.

Chapter 11, "School, Home, and Community: A Symbiosis for a Literacy Partnership," explains steps Waters took to spread the comprehensive literacy program in her district into homes in the community. She describes how she and her staff enlisted the involvement of parents in fostering higher level literacy through family literacy programs. These were monthly meetings of school personnel, children, and their parents. Waters tells how she organized the meetings around simple meals, good books, and literacy activities in which children could scaffold their parents' reading and learning, thus exemplifying methods used for literacy learning in the district. The chapter includes numerous examples of parents' writing to illustrate strategies Waters offers for making such programs a success. The major benefit, of course, is that parents become more actively involved in their children's literacy learning.

The book concludes with Chapter 12, "Next Steps: Implementing a Program of Higher Level Literacy for Struggling Readers and Writers." This final chapter highlights recommendations for carrying out the assessment and instructional practices featured in the text. A self-assessment chart is featured to assist with implementation of a program of higher level literacy for struggling students.

Based on cutting-edge research and firmly grounded in hands-on and minds-on experience, *Building Struggling Students' Higher Level Literacy: Practical Ideas, Powerful Solutions* embodies highly effective techniques and approaches for setting up and implementing an in-depth program designed to foster the higher level literacies of struggling students. It is an all-out effort to meet one of the most pressing challenges in the field of education—bringing struggling readers and writers to full literacy.

—James L. Collins and Thomas G. Gunning

CHAPTER 1

Struggling Readers and Higher Level Literacy

Thomas G. Gunning

W hat percentage of fourth graders do you think would be able to answer this question, which is based on the excerpt below?

Explain why Rosa visits the ducks at the beginning of the story. Use details from the story in your answer.

Dishpan Ducks

By Margaret Springer

Rosa walked home from school slowly. The rows of apartment buildings and the streets full of cars looked all the same. And it was cold.

Rosa missed her country. She had begun to learn some English, but she did not know what to say or what to do when other kids were around. They were friendly, but Rosa felt safer being alone.

Behind Rosa's brick apartment building was a special place, a small creek where Rosa always stopped after school. There were ducks there, and she could speak to them in her language. The ducks seemed to understand.

Every afternoon Rosa sat on a concrete slab above the creek and watched the ducks until Mama came home from work.

Rosa did not feed them. She knew that most "people food" was not right for ducks. But she watched them swim and feed and walk up to her, quacking. Once they even walked over Rosa's tummy as she lay with her feet stretched out on the bumpy grass. They like me, Rosa said to herself. (Lee, Grigg, & Donahue, 2007, p. 22)

Only 54% of U.S. fourth graders received full credit for their responses to this question, which was drawn from a recent National Assessment of Educational Progress (NAEP) reading test. Some 34% received partial credit and 12% received no credit. The text is straightforward, as is the question. According to the Dale-Chall Readability formula, the text is on a 2–3 readability level (Chall & Dale, 1995). Yet nearly half the fourth graders who took the test were unable to answer the question fully.

In a sense, the students' response to the question is the reason this text was written. Living as we do in the information age with its rapid advances in technology, proliferation of knowledge, and ever-increasing demands for higher levels of literacy, this text and other examples that abound—whether one is looking at national, state, or local tests—highlight the need for developing the higher level literacy skills of all students, but especially those who struggle. Efforts to develop higher level skills need to be made early and sustained throughout the grades.

Actually, as one long-term study suggests, schools in the United States do a remarkable job of developing basic literacy but fall short when it comes to building higher level comprehension skills. Beginning in the fall of 1998, researchers began a long-term study titled the Early Childhood Longitudinal Study (ECLS), in which they followed the progress of a representative sample of kindergarteners as they made their way though the grades. Data on comprehension were collected in third, fifth, and eighth grades. By the end of third grade, almost all children could read sentences (Rathbun & West, 2004). Seventy-eight percent could make literal inferences based on text (e.g., recognize the comparison being made in a simile). However, only 46% were able to use cues to derive meaning from text (e.g., use background knowledge combined with sentence cues to understand the use of homonyms). And just 29% were able to make interpretations beyond what was stated in text (e.g., make connections between problems in a narrative and similar problems in their own lives).

Fifth graders performed better but still fell short on higher level tasks. Some 97% of fifth graders were proficient in sentence comprehension, 87% in making literal inferences, and 70% in making and supporting inferences (Princiotta, Flanagan, & Germino Hausken, 2006). However, only 44% were proficient in making connections or evaluating the author's craft. And just 7% were able to identify the author's purpose or give evidence for and against a position.

As a group, the eighth graders also did well on literal and basic inferential comprehension (Walston, Rathbun, & Germino Hausken, 2008). Some 91.7% of eighth graders demonstrated proficiency in this area. However, as the level of comprehension increased, scores decreased. The percentage for extrapolation (making higher level inferences and justifying inferences) was 81.1. For evaluation of fiction, which consists of judging the author's craft and making connections between elements in a story and one's own life, the percentage was 64.4. At all grade levels, students living in poverty, members of minority groups,

English-language learners, and students whose mothers have limited education had even lower percentages of achievement.

In summary, as the students progressed through the grades, they acquired basic comprehension skills. However, as the comprehension tasks grew more complex and involved higher level cognitive processes, the percentage of students who were proficient decreased. At every level, there is a significant difference between students' literal and higher level comprehension.

Results from the NAEP tests paint an even bleaker picture (Lee, Grigg, & Donahue, 2007) than that depicted by the Early Childhood Longitudinal Study. Some 67% of fourth graders achieved at the basic level on the NAEP. However, only 33% of students performed at the proficient level. At the eighth-grade level, 74% of students scored at the basic level, with just 31% scoring at the proficient level. At the twelfth-grade level, percentages at the basic and proficient levels were 73 and 35 (Grigg, Donahue, & Dion, 2007). Overall, most students at every level can construct a literal understanding of text, but a significant percentage have difficulty constructing a higher level understanding. The results from both the NAEP and ECLS indicate a need for systematic instruction in higher level skills for the millions of students at every level who have difficulty with higher level literacy.

This data on students' higher level literacy comes with a caveat. Observations and anecdotal data (see Chapters 2 and 6 for details) suggest that tests that contain constructed responses might be masking students' comprehension abilities. There are a number of students who do well when asked comprehension questions orally but who have difficulty when required to compose a written response. This doesn't mean that there isn't a problem, but it might not be as extensive as is sometimes suggested.

The Nature of Higher Level Comprehension

Before embarking on a program to develop higher level comprehension, it is important to come to an agreement about what comprehension is and, of course, what is encompassed by higher level comprehension. The mental model, as explained by Kintsch and Kintsch (2005) and discussed below, is a widely accepted theory of how readers construct meaning. The 2009 NAEP Framework for reading (National Assessment Governing Board, 2008) has been adopted for use in this text as a basis for a listing of comprehension skills. NAEP is considered to be the gold standard of reading assessment, and its current framework fits in with a mental model theory of reading comprehension.

Mental Model Theory of Reading Comprehension

Theoretically, comprehension consists of a textbase and mental model (Kintsch & Kintsch, 2005). The textbase is composed of a series of idea units known as propositions that are based on decoding the printed words that express these ideas. The propositions are interrelated in a microstructure and also in an overall macrostructure. The microstructure links the propositions. Propositions might be linked by connecting words, such as *and* or *but*, or by pronouns and antecedents. In the sentences, "The platypus has the bill of a duck, the fur of a bear, and the tail of a beaver. It also has had webbed feet," there are four propositions: (1) The platypus has the bill of a duck, (2) The platypus has the fur of a bear, (3) The platypus has the tail of a beaver, (4) The platypus has webbed feet. The first three propositions are linked with the connector *and*. The fourth proposition is linked to the other three with the connecting word *also* and the pronoun *it*, which refers back to the antecedent *platypus*. Students get lost in the microstructure if they are unable to read the words or if they fail to link up the propositions.

The macrostructure is hierarchal so that it might be organized according to main idea and supporting details, cause and effect, or in some other way. Constructing a macrostructure means that the students must grasp the main idea of the passage, "The platypus is a strange animal," and the details that support that idea.

As its name suggests, the textbase, which may include some low-level inferences, is a representation that is closely based on the text. In addition to activating schema, constructing a textbase requires four key processing abilities: understanding essential details at a literal level; integrating text across sentences and paragraphs; making low-level, text-based inferences; and monitoring for meaning. Working memory is also an integral element (Cain, Oakhill, & Bryant, 2004). Students might not be able to hold all the key ideas in mind and thus might have difficulty constructing a textbase.

A mental model is constructed when the textbase is integrated with the reader's prior knowledge, goal for reading, and other reader factors. A mental model is a model of the situation expressed in the text. Adept readers reading the same passage would construct a similar textbase, but their mental models might differ because their backgrounds and goals for reading vary. In constructing a mental model, the reader goes beyond the text. Whereas the textbase is verbal—it consists of word meanings combined into propositions—the mental model can include imagery and even an emotional component. As theoreticians Kintsch and Kintsch (2005) explain:

There is no uniform comprehension to be assessed. Instead comprehension involves different levels and a variety of skills: the extraction of meaning from the text, the construction of the situation model, and the integration of the reader's prior knowledge and the goals with the information provided by the text. (p. 87)

In other words, there is not one particular correct mental model for a text. Because readers differ in their backgrounds, purposes for reading, and perspectives, mental models will vary. However, they should have a solid foundation in the textbase.

As summarized by Hampton and Resnick (2009), comprehension consists of the following:

- **Developing a textbase: making connections within the text.** In this process, readers work with the information and ideas presented by the text. They develop a textbase, which is a network of ideas that links the meaning drawn from phrases, clauses, and sentences into larger ideas.

- **Building a mental model: making meaning from the text.** In this process, readers build a world or create an image in their minds of the situation described by the text, using the related knowledge, experiences, and purposes they already have. They build a mental model, which is a representation of the ideas in the textbase that is enriched by the reader's knowledge. (p. 22)

As Hampton and Resnick further explain,

Readers move back and forth between the textbase and mental model. As they read, strong readers continually check their mental model against the textbase to make certain that the mental model accurately reflects what the text says and is consistent with their knowledge base. (p. 23)

Comprehension Skills and Strategies

What skills and strategies are included in the textbase and mental model? Strategies are deliberate, planned procedures designed to help the reader reach a goal (Afflerbach, Pearson, & Paris, 2008). Previewing, predicting, summarizing, visualizing, connecting, and questioning are strategies. In contrast to strategies, skills are automatic processes, such as noting sequence or cause–effect relationships, that are usually performed without conscious control. When strategies are applied automatically, they become skills. In this volume, the emphasis is on teaching students to use strategies so that they will become skilled readers. Often, strategies and skills are taught at the same time, so in some instances the combination term *strategies/skills* will be used.

The 2009 NAEP Framework (National Assessment Governing Board, 2008) has divided skills and strategies into three components: Locate and Recall, Integrate and Interpret, and Critique and Evaluate (see Table 1.1). The first component, Locate and Recall, is a textbase. The other two represent mental models. In this text, higher level strategies and skills are defined as those that are included in the mental model levels.

Locate and Recall

Locate and Recall consists of building a textbase. For fiction, it consists of being able to identify the main elements of a story: the characters, setting, and plot. For expository text, it entails grasping the main idea and supporting details. Although it is primarily literal, some low-level inferences are included. Monitoring for meaning is also included as students note whether what they are reading makes sense. However, not all Locate and Recall tasks are of equal difficulty. Selecting or deriving a main idea can be quite challenging.

Integrate and Interpret

The distinctive feature of this stage is that readers integrate their knowledge with that of the text. They use both their knowledge of the content of the text and their knowledge of text structure and literary elements. Based on their knowledge and information in the text, they interpret what they read. As the National Assessment Governing Board (2008) explains,

> When readers engage in behaviors involving integrating and interpreting, they make comparisons and contrasts of information or character actions, examine relations across aspects of text, or consider alternatives to what is presented in text. This aspect of the reading is critical to comprehension and can be considered the stage in which readers really move beyond the discrete information, ideas, details, themes, and so forth presented in text and extend their initial impressions by processing information logically and completely. As readers integrate information and interpret what they read, they frequently form questions, use mental images, and make connections that draw on larger sections of text, often at an abstract level. (p. 37)

Table 1.1. Comprehension Skills and Strategies

Cognitive Dimension	Skills/Strategies
Locate and Recall	**Details** Recalling details Locating details Recognizing details that answer questions Locating supporting details Recognizing/determining important details Locating and describing explicit details in narratives, such as plot, setting, characters, story problem Making simple inferences
	Main idea/supporting details Recognizing stated main idea Recognizing implied main idea Constructing main idea (stated) Constructing main idea (implied) Noting supporting details
	Summarizing Retelling Summarizing orally Recognizing best summary Composing written summary Polishing written summary by combining and condensing
Integrate and Interpret	**Inferring/concluding** Recognizing inference Recognizing support for inference Given inference, locating support Given support, making inference Constructing inference and providing support Explaining support Judging inferences, conclusions
	Predicting Using background and text to predict Revising predictions Supporting predictions
	Imaging Constructing partial image Constructing fuller image Constructing concrete image Constructing abstract image

(continued)

Table 1.1. Comprehension Skills and Strategies (*continued*)

Cognitive Dimension	Skills/Strategies
Integrate and Interpret (*continued*)	**Questioning** Constructing general questions Constructing specific questions Constructing literal-level questions Constructing higher level questions
	Comparing/contrasting Noting differences Noting similarities Noting differences and similarities Determining key similarities and differences Comparing texts Comparing ideas across texts
	Connecting Noting general connections Noting key connections Justifying/explaining connections
Critique and Evaluate	**Identifying author's purpose** Identifying stated purpose Identifying implied purpose Identifying dual purpose
	Judging fairness/accuracy Distinguishing between facts and opinions Noting biased language Identifying biased/slanted language Identifying persuasive techniques Identifying assumptions Judging credibility of source
	Judging literary quality Identifying/evaluating elements of author's craft Judging effectiveness of literary techniques

Adapted from Gunning, T.G. (2008). *Developing higher level literacy in all students: Building reading, reasoning, and responding.* Boston: Allyn & Bacon, and National Assessment Governing Board (2008). *Reading Framework for the 2009 National Assessment of Educational Progress.* Washington, DC: Author.

Critique and Evaluate

The distinctive feature of this stage is that readers stand back from text and examine it with a critical eye. They might judge the quality of the writing and credibility of the plot in a piece of fiction or the accuracy and fairness of information in an expository piece. They might look at the language of a piece as well as what the piece says. Given the availability of masses of information in the media and the ability of anyone to post information on the Internet without going through the reviewing and editing checks of traditional publishing, it is more important than ever that students learn to evaluate information.

Building Struggling Readers' Higher Level Comprehension

One reason why struggling readers have a difficult time with higher level comprehension is that, all too often, their instruction focuses on lower level skills. Struggling readers spend less time reading silently and more time reading orally, are asked a greater proportion of low-level questions, and are given fewer prompts and less time to respond (Allington, 1983; Barr & Dreeben, 1991). Struggling readers also are frequently given materials that are well beyond their reading ability, so they have little chance of getting much meaning out of their texts (Allington, 2009). As Resnick (1999) explains, struggling readers need to be taught higher level skills and need to read widely so they have topics to which they can apply these higher level skills:

> Children who have not been taught a demanding, challenging, thinking curriculum do poorly on tests of reasoning or problem-solving... In experimental programs and in practical school reforms, we are seeing that students who, over an extended period of time are treated *as if* they are intelligent, actually become so. If they are taught demanding content, and are expected to explain and find connections as well as memorize and repeat, they learn more and learn more quickly. They think of themselves as learners. (n.p.)

Teaching Higher Level Literacy to All Learners

In research conducted more than four decades ago, Wolf, King, and Huck (1968) found that higher level thinking and reading skills can be taught to students beginning in grade one and that students of all ability levels learn the skills. These researchers concluded, "Children of all intelligence levels who receive instruction can learn to read critically" (p. 489). The key phrase is "who receive instruction." In study after study, struggling readers who receive instruction achieve, sometimes at surprisingly high levels. In one experiment, students who were good decoders but poor comprehenders did so well on their content area tests after being taught a series of comprehension strategies that they were accused of cheating (Pearson, 1986). In their study of exemplary teachers, Pressley et al. (2001) found that the most effective teachers provided extra instruction and practice to students who needed it so that, by year's end, the poorest readers in the exemplary teachers' classrooms read as well as the average students in the average teacher's classroom. This is easier to do at the lower levels. For students in the middle grades and beyond who are adequate decoders but poor comprehenders, added instruction by the classroom teacher and also the content area teachers should go a long way toward building higher level skills. However, for students who are poor decoders and who read significantly below grade level, a more extensive effort will need to be made (Allington, 2009).

An essential element in the building of higher level thinking skills is the development of background knowledge. As Resnick (1999) cautions,

> Thinking and problem-solving will be the "new basics" of the 21st century, but the common idea that we can teach thinking without a solid foundation of knowledge must be abandoned. So must the idea that we can teach knowledge without engaging students in thinking. Knowledge and thinking must be intimately joined. (n.p.)

Cognitive psychologist Willingham (2009) concurs:

> Research from cognitive science has shown that the sorts of skills that teachers want for students—such as the ability to analyze and think critically—require extensive factual knowledge.... The implication is that facts must be taught, ideally in the context of skills, and ideally beginning in preschool and even before. (p. 19)

The good news is that progress is being made in developing the comprehension abilities of low-achieving students. According to a comparison of NAEP Reading Tests, the comprehension scores of the lowest achieving students are improving. From 2000 to 2007, the lowest tenth percentile increased by 17 points. With the passage of No Child Left Behind and reform efforts that preceded and accompanied it, increased attention has been paid to struggling learners. As Finn and Petrilli (2008) comment, "Low achieving students made solid progress on the National Assessment of Educational Progress (NAEP) from 2000 to 2007 (an accomplishment surely worth celebrating, even though these students are far, far behind)" (p. 8). The remainder of this book is devoted to an exploration of approaches and techniques designed to move struggling readers as far as possible along the pathway to higher level literacy.

ACTION PLAN

- Using Table 1.1 as a framework, examine the strategies and skills you are teaching your struggling readers. Which strategies and skills from the Integrate and Interpret and Critique and Evaluate levels are you teaching? How balanced is your program? Which higher level skills, if any, might need more attention? Draw up a scope and sequence of strategies and skills for your struggling readers.

- Also look at the content that you are teaching. What major topics and concepts will you be presenting? Are there other topics that might be added? What plans do you have for covering the content in such a way that it builds on and enriches students' background knowledge? What other steps might you take to increase students' background knowledge?

QUESTIONS FOR STUDY AND REFLECTION

1. What is your theory of reading comprehension? How does it compare with the mental model theory?

2. How can you use your theory of comprehension instruction to plan a program of higher level literacy for struggling readers?

3. What is the overall status of comprehension achievement in your class (or school)?

4. What programs are in place for fostering the higher level literacy of struggling readers in your school?

REFERENCES

Afflerbach, P., Pearson, P.D., & Paris, S.G. (2008). Clarifying differences between reading skills and reading strategies. *The Reading Teacher, 61*(5), 364–373

Allington, R.L. (1983). The reading instruction provided readers of differing reading ability. *The Elementary School Journal, 83*(5), 548–559. doi:10.1086/461333

Allington, R.L. (2009). *What really matters in response to intervention: Research-based designs.* Boston: Allyn & Bacon.

Barr, R., & Dreeben, R. (1991). Grouping students for reading instruction. In R. Barr, M.L. Kamil, P. Mosenthal, & P.D. Pearson (Eds.), *Handbook of reading research* (Vol. 2, pp. 885–910). New York: Longman.

Cain, K., Oakhill, J., & Bryant, P. (2004). Children's reading comprehension ability: Concurrent prediction by working memory, verbal ability, and component skills. *Journal of Educational Psychology*, 96(1), 31–42. doi:10.1037/0022-0663.96.1.31

Chall, J.S., & Dale, E. (1995). *The new Dale-Chall readability formula*. Cambridge, MA: Brookline.

Finn, C.E., Jr., & Petrilli, M.J. (2008). Foreword. In A. Duffett, S. Farkas, & T. Loveless (Eds.), *High-achieving students in the era of NCLB* (pp. 8–12). Washington, DC: Thomas B. Fordham Institute. Available at www.fordhaminstitute.org

Grigg, W., Donahue, P., & Dion, G. (2007). *The nation's report card: 12th-grade reading and mathematics 2005* (NCES 2007-468). U.S. Department of Education, National Center for Education Statistics. Washington, DC: U.S. Government Printing Office.

Gunning, T.G. (2008). *Developing higher level literacy in all students: Building reading, reasoning, and responding*. Boston: Allyn & Bacon.

Hampton, S., & Resnick, L.B. (2009). *Reading and writing with understanding*. Washington, DC: National Center on Education and the Economy.

Kintsch, W., & Kintsch, E. (2005). Comprehension. In S.G. Paris & S.A. Stahl (Eds.), *Current issues in reading comprehension and assessment* (pp. 71–92). Mahwah, NJ: Erlbaum.

Lee, J., Grigg, W., & Donahue, P. (2007). *The nation's report card: Reading 2007* (NCES 2007-496). Washington, DC: National Center for Education Statistics, Institute of Education Sciences, U.S. Department of Education.

National Assessment Governing Board. (2008). *Reading framework for the 2009 National Assessment of Educational Progress*. Washington, DC: Author.

Pearson, P.D. (1986, March). *Advances in reading comprehension*. Paper presented at a meeting of the Connecticut Association for Reading Research, New Britain, CT.

Pressley, M., Wharton-McDonald, R., Allington, R., Block, C.C., Morrow, L., Tracey, D., et al. (2001). A study of effective first-grade literacy instruction. *Scientific Studies of Reading*, 5(1), 35–58. doi:10.1207/S1532799XSSR0501_2

Princiotta, D., Flanagan, K.D., & Germino Hausken, E. (2006). *Fifth grade: Findings from the fifth grade follow-up of the Early Childhood Longitudinal Study, kindergarten class of 1998–99* (NCES 2006-038). Washington, DC: National Center for Education Statistics.

Rathbun, A., & West, J. (2004). *From kindergarten through third grade: Children's beginning school experiences* (NCES 2004-007). Washington, DC: National Center for Education Statistics, U.S. Department of Education.

Resnick, L.B. (1999, June 16). Making America smarter. *Education Week Century Series*, 18(40), 38–40. Retrieved September 9, 2009 from http://ifl.lrdc.pitt.edu/ifl/index.php?section=articles

Walston, J., Rathbun, A., & Germino Hausken, E. (2008). *Eighth grade: First findings from the final round of the Early Childhood Longitudinal Study, kindergarten class of 1998–99* (NCES 2008-088). Washington, DC: National Center for Education Statistics, Institute of Education Sciences, U.S. Department of Education.

Willingham, D. T. (2009). *Why don't students like school? A cognitive scientist answers questions about how the mind works and what it means for the classroom*. San Francisco, CA: Jossey-Bass.

Wolf, W., King, M.L., & Huck, C.S. (1968). Teaching critical reading to elementary school children. *Reading Research Quarterly*, 3(4), 435–498. doi:10.2307/747152

CHAPTER 2

Assessment-Based Instruction in Developing Higher Level Literacy

Thomas G. Gunning and Diane R. Phelps

Fifth grader Eduardo was a puzzle to his teacher. Although his decoding skills were excellent and his oral reading was smooth and expressive, his retellings were sketchy and his responses to comprehension questions were frequently lacking in detail and accuracy. The first step in helping Eduardo was to determine his basic reading level. The teacher needed to know at what level Eduardo would be able to construct a textbase. Once that had been established, assessments would be directed to discover Eduardo's ability to construct a situation model, which involves comprehending at higher levels.

Determining the Textbase

Informal reading inventories (IRIs) and running records are frequently used to estimate students' reading levels (Gunning, 2010). In an IRI, students read a series of increasingly difficult passages to determine at what level students can read on their own (usually 98 to 99% word recognition and 90% comprehension) and at what point they need instruction (usually 95 to 98% word recognition and 70 to 89% comprehension). Because many high-stakes tests are written on grade level, struggling students, who by definition are reading below grade level, are sometimes given test-prep materials and other texts that are on grade level. However, an overwhelming body of research indicates that students do best when they experience a high rate of success (Allington, 2009). Struggling readers who are given material at their reading level rather than at their grade level make significantly greater gains in word recognition, fluency, and comprehension over peers who are merely provided with grade-level material.

Most commercial IRIs focus on the textbase. In their study of eight IRIs, Applegate, Quinn, and Applegate (2006) report that more than 91% of the test items required only simple recall or low-level inferences. They concluded that the IRIs they examined were unable to "distinguish between readers who could *remember* what they read and those who could *think about it*" (p. 5, emphasis in original). However, in the Qualitative Reading Inventory (Leslie & Caldwell, 2006), 20% of the questions were classified as being higher level. In the Critical Reading Inventory, which Applegate, Quinn, and Applegate (2004) authored, three kinds of questions are asked: textbased, inference, and critical response. Of course, because IRIs are informal assessments, users can add higher level questions if they wish.

Running records are similar to IRIs. As a student reads one or a series of passages, her or his reading performance is recorded. Although running records tend to focus on word recognition and have a more lenient standard (95 to 99% word recognition is the independent level as opposed to 98 to 99% on IRIs; 90 to 94% is the instructional level as opposed to 95 to 97% on IRIs), they serve a similar function. Two commercial assessments that use a running record format are the Developmental Reading Assessment (published by Pearson) and The Fountas and Pinnell Benchmark Assessment System (published by Heinemann).

Analyzing Assessment Results to Plan Instruction

If carefully analyzed, individual reading assessments (such as running records or IRIs) can yield valuable information about the processes the student is using. Dewitz and Dewitz (2003) carefully analyzed IRI results to determine why Mark, a sixth grader with excellent decoding skills, was having difficulty comprehending passages at the sixth-, fifth-, and even fourth-grade levels. Through analyzing Mark's responses and using probing questions, Dewitz and Dewitz determined that Mark was able to respond to questions in which the answer was contained in a single sentence but had difficulty when he had to combine information from two or more sentences. He also had difficulty with segments that contained advanced vocabulary or complex syntax. These are all textbase issues. However, Mark also had difficulty constructing an accurate mental model.

Mark used an ineffective strategy that many struggling students use when they encounter challenging reading. He used background information rather than information from the selection to answer questions. Key causes of faulty comprehension and probing questions that might be used to reveal these factors are listed below (based on Dewitz and Dewitz, 2003):

- Inadequate background knowledge. Ask questions designed to probe students' background knowledge. Probe areas that you believe might be weak: "What can you tell me about fables? What is a continent? Have you ever seen a microscope?"

- Difficulty with vocabulary. Go back to the passage, point to a key word that you judge may be unfamiliar to the student, and ask, "What does this word mean?"

- Difficulty with syntax. Go back to the sentence containing complex syntax, and ask questions about it: "Which animal does *it* refer to?"

- Overuse of background knowledge. Ask, "What makes you think that the United States is a continent? Is that in the article?"

- Failure to recall or comprehend directly stated information. Ask, "Can you find the answer to that in the article?"

- Failure to link ideas in a passage. Ask, "What happened because the plates rubbed against each other? What other possessions did Jason give away? To whom did Jason give his possessions?"

- Failure to make inferences. Ask, "Why do you think Rosa disliked lunch time? What do you think the islanders will do now that the homes have been flooded?"

Oral Retellings

Running records typically rely upon retellings (sometimes supplemented with questions) to assess comprehension. Conversely, IRIs typically use questions as the main way to assess and quantify comprehension but use retellings as a supplement. Retellings can provide information about the students' grasp of the textbase and also provide some insight into the students' ability to construct a mental model. As its name suggests, in a retelling, students are asked to retell a story or informational piece that they have read. Retellings are scored according to the idea units recalled. A retelling provides the opportunity to note how many details the students recalled and also how the details are organized. Questions guide students to a particular aspect of the text; they help to determine the nature of the response. Retellings are a way of gaining insight into what the student thinks is important and the processes used to organize and formulate a response. Retellings can indicate whether the information is organized sequentially or hierarchically, whether it is a summary or an unorganized recitation of all the details. In general, students recall more idea units from a narrative text than they do from an expository text. In their study of retellings, Leslie and Caldwell (2006) report that, on average, students recalled one-third or less of the idea units in a selection.

When assessing comprehension with IRIs or running records, the question is often asked, Should students be allowed to look back in the test passage? Leslie and Caldwell (2006) report that at the third-grade level and beyond, students often increased their scores by 20% or more when allowed to look back to find answers to questions that they were not able to answer initially. In most cases, the questions had to do with explicitly stated details. In many instances, these were complex details that posed memory problems. Allowing lookbacks provides information as to whether inability to answer a question is a comprehension or a memory problem.

Prompting a Retelling

Retellings may be scored informally. However, using a checklist or retelling guide can provide more accurate and more comprehensive insight. In general, the following question can be used to assess a retelling: Does the retelling follow the structure of the piece? In retelling a fictional narrative, the retelling would include the setting, main characters, story problem, key events, resolution of the problem, and ending. In a nonfiction piece, the selection would include the main ideas and supporting details. The most important ideas would be included. The retelling would be sequential. The retelling might also use language from the text and words used to structure the retelling, such as *first, next, then,* and *last.* Also to be noted are inferences or conclusions that the reader constructs, or connections that are drawn between this text and other texts or personal experiences. Finally, note evaluative statements.

Prompts can be used to get a retelling started or to help a student continue. For fiction, these might be, What happened at the beginning of the story? What happened next? What did the main character do then? For nonfiction, prompts might include the following: What did the author tell you? The title of this article is "Electric Cars of Tomorrow." What did the author tell you about electric cars of tomorrow? What else did you learn? What is the most important thing that you learned?

Analyze the retelling. Note what the student did well and what caused the student difficulty and how this information might be used to plan instruction. You might note, for instance, that the student is able to describe the main character's actions but does not infer why the main character acted in a certain way. If, even with prompting, the student is unable to conclude why the character acted in a certain way, then this is a sign that the student needs work on making inferences about character motivation. Note the following excerpt from a retelling by a third grader of a fable titled "The Hen and the Tree."

Teacher: Now that you've read the story, I want you to tell it to me. Tell me the whole story. Pretend that I have not read the story and don't know anything about it.

Tyanna: Well, the story is about this hen. She sees an apple tree growing in her yard. And the hen starts talking to the tree. And the hen tells the tree that it looks funny. It has furry toes.

Teacher: Can you tell me more?

Tyanna: Yes, the hen tells the tree that it has pointed ears. And the tree says that it is a special kind of tree.

Teacher: Do you think the tree is really a tree?

Tyanna: Yes.

Teacher: What is strange about the tree?

Tyanna: It has furry toes and pointed ears.

Teacher: Why do you think it has furry toes and pointed ears?

Tyanna: It is a special kind of tree.

The student has constructed a reasonable textbase but fails to realize that the tree is a wolf in disguise, despite the fact that the teacher asks why the tree has furry toes and pointed ears. The student, a third grader with good decoding skills, might have limited experience with fables and trickster tales and so might lack a schema for animals that use disguises or other devices to trick other animals. Instruction for her should include reading and discussing traditional tales.

In the following excerpt about the Boston Tea Party, a student named Darryl is retelling a segment from a history text:

The Boston Tea Party, um, they threw more than three hundred bags of tea and some of it was left to rot and, um, the action, what they were doing, was called the Boston Tea Party, 'cause nobody was buying the tea so they just threw it away and let it rot. (Beck & McKeown, 2006, p. 18)

Darryl recalled some of the details of the activities of the Boston Tea Party but did not understand its purpose. He believed that the tea was thrown away because it wasn't selling. He did not see the action as a protest against taxes on tea. His textbase was both inaccurate and incomplete. Before he could make inferences about the Boston Tea Party, it would be necessary to build a better textbase.

Oral retellings have some shortcomings. They may underestimate the ability of shy children, English learners, and students who have difficulty expressing themselves orally. In addition, students who have limited experience with retellings might be penalized. At the primary level, Leslie and Caldwell (2006) describe a weak relationship between retelling skill and ability to answer questions. They conjecture that some children have had little or no experience with retelling. Being more accustomed to answering questions, they do better with questions than retelling. In addition, younger students may have a less well-developed schema for text and so have more difficulty organizing a retelling. At the middle and higher levels, there is a stronger relationship between the quality of retellings and performance on questions. However, the authors conclude that although there is a commonality between retelling and answering questions, there are some differences.

The Fountas and Pinnell Benchmark Assessment System (published by Heinemann) has an IRI/running record format and a retelling component called the Comprehension Conversation, which does a particularly good job of providing follow-up prompts. In the Comprehension Conversation, the teacher provides the prompt, "Talk about what you learned in this book." Expected Key Understandings are listed for each selection. These include Understandings that are Within the Text (literal textbase), Beyond the Text (implied meaning and synthesizing information), and About the Text (author's craft, characteristics of the text). Each Key Understanding is accompanied by a prompt so that if the student fails to include an element in her or his retelling, the teacher can prompt it: "Why do you think dogs are so important to people?" With the scaffolding provided by the prompts, the Comprehension Conversation should elicit a great deal of insight about the student's comprehension.

Written Retellings

Although oral retellings are valuable, they are time consuming. With older students, written retellings might be used. One advantage of written retellings is that they provide students with more time to organize their thoughts. However, written retellings may penalize students who have difficulty expressing themselves in writing.

Despite limitations, written retellings can be a means of monitoring students' comprehension. Lipson and Wixson (2008) explain that brief written recalls that focus on specific but important story components can be used to assess the results of instruction. They can also be used to highlight ongoing needs and thus help provide a framework for instruction. Assessment passages can be drawn from materials similar to those that students are reading and can be used to assess skills and strategies that are the focus of current instruction. After a biography unit, for instance, students might be provided with a segment of a biography drawn from a trade book. The written retelling might focus on students' abilities to summarize and make inferences about a key incident in the subject's life.

Group Inventories

Three widely used tests that function as group inventories include the Degrees of Reading Power (published by Questar), the Scholastic Reading Inventory, and STAR (published by Advantage Learning Systems). All three use a modified cloze format in which students choose from among four or five words the one that best replaces a deleted word. Instead of yielding a grade-level score, the Degrees of Reading Power provides a DRP score. The DRP score indicates what level of material the student should be able to read. A complementary readability formula is used to indicate the difficulty level of books in DRP units so that students can be matched with appropriate materials. The Scholastic Reading Inventory yields Lexile scores, so that students can be matched with materials whose difficulty has been estimated in Lexile units. Scholastic's inventories come in levels for each grade. Students reading significantly below grade level may need to be reassessed on a lower level test than the one provided for their grade level. STAR, which uses vocabulary and modified cloze, is administered and scored by a computer. The STAR assessment has an adaptive feature: If students do well they are given higher level passages, but they are given lower level passages if a certain number of responses are incorrect. The group inventories only yield information about the textbase; they do not provide information about the situation or mental model.

Maze Tests

An easy-to-give test that takes little instructional time but provides information about the students' grasp of the textbase is the maze test. Similar to modified cloze, maze provides a quick assessment of students' ability to understand at a textbase level. In a maze test, students replace words that have been deleted from a text by selecting from three possible choices. The choices include the deleted word and two distracters. One distracter may be the same part of speech as the deleted word but would not fit the sense of the sentence. The other distracter is neither the same part of speech nor an appropriate fit semantically. The distracters should have approximately the same number of letters as the answer and, if possible, should be selected from the words in the text. The distracters should be on the same approximate difficulty level as the correct answer.

The first sentence is left intact. After that, every seventh word is deleted. The three answer choices are placed in parentheses in the blank left by the omitted word, as in Figure 2.1. Students respond by choosing the word that best fits the sense of the passage. Passages can vary in length from 150 to 400 words. Students are given two-and-a-half or three minutes to circle as many answers as they can. Students should be provided with passages that are on their reading level.

Maze tests for grades 4 to 6 are available from the University of Southern Maine (www.usm.maine.edu/cehd/Assessment-Center/CBM.htm). A series of 18 maze passages, 2 at each level from grades 2 to 10, can be found in *Assessing Reading: Multiple Measures: For All Educators Working to Improve Reading*

Figure 2.1. Sample Maze Passage

The longest living animal is slow moving. And it eats mostly grass and (**has, other, name**) plants. Although it's slow moving, the (**longest, hard, crawl**) living animal has a good way (**and, to, is**) protect itself. It can crawl into (**its, for, or**) hard shell. That might sound like (**by, can, a**) turtle. Box turtles can live for 120 (**holds, years, slow**) or more. The longest living land (**animal, good, grass**) is actually a tortoise. A tortoise (**and, shell, is**) a turtle that lives on land. (**A, By, On**) tortoise by the name of Harriet (**lived, might, hard**) to be 175 years old. But (**is, a, for**) tortoise by the name of Tui Mali (**way, holds, more**) the record for living the longest. She lived for 188 years.

Achievement (2nd ed.; Diamond & Thorsnes, 2008). Mazes are also available from AIMSweb (www.aimsweb.com) and System to Enhance Educational Performance (www.isteep.com). Mazes can be given quarterly, monthly, or even more frequently and so can be used to monitor student ability to construct a textbase. One limitation of maze passages is their relative insensitivity to growth. Students making average progress only gain about a half replacement per month (AIMSweb, 2006, as cited in Hosp, Hosp, & Howell, 2007).

Assessing Students on Their Level

Once you have established a student's textbase, you can make sure that the student is assessed on the appropriate level. A large number of high-stakes tests fail to provide an adequate range of items and so provide little or no useful information on the literacy skills of struggling readers and writers. Reading and writing abilities vary greatly. As a rule of thumb, the variability in reading levels in a class beyond second grade is equal to the number of years represented by the grade level (Bond, Tinker, Wasson, & Wasson, 1994). This means that in a typical sixth-grade class, reading levels will range from grade 3 to grade 9. However, many high-stakes tests are written on grade level and do not include below-grade-level passages for the large number of students reading below grade level. For instance, test specifications for the state of Connecticut call for construction of passages at grade level and slightly above. Nationwide, English-language learners (ELLs) who have been attending schools in the United States for at least 10 months are required to take state tests.

Tests have a bottom and a ceiling. The bottom is the lowest level passage; the ceiling is the highest. Tests that have a number of below-level passages will provide information about struggling readers. Another solution is to test students on their reading level, not their grade level. Although this practice is not allowed in many high-stakes tests, it should be implemented whenever possible. Besides providing useful information on those students most at risk, it is also more humane, because it does not put struggling readers or ELLs in the position of coping with a test that is far too difficult. A first principle of assessment, especially when working with struggling readers, is to provide tests on the appropriate level. As Pearson and Hamm (2005) comment,

> It might be...that students have a lot more to say when it is relatively easy for them to read, digest, think about, and even critique the texts they encounter. It might also turn out that difficulty interacts with student achievement level in such a way

that easy passages provide opportunities for low-achieving students to shine whereas hard passages provide just the challenge that high-achieving students need to get involved in the assessment. (p. 59)

Unit Tests

Good sources of information about students' abilities to respond to higher level questions are the assessments that accompany basal reading and other commercial reading programs. All the major basal programs introduce higher level reading and responding skills and include tests and other measures to assess students' grasp of these skills. You might also create your own tests. Although this can be a daunting task, you might join with other teachers in your grade or department and divide up the task. This is what teachers in the Chittenango Central School District in New York State did. They mirrored the format of the state test on their tests. However, their unit tests assessed the strategies they had focused on during the unit (Athans & Devine, 2008). The assessments included multiple-choice questions, brief constructed-response items, and an extended essay.

Sample Tests and Released Tests

Another source of comprehension assessment measures are practice tests and released items offered by the federal government, states, and individual school districts. The National Association of Educational Progress (NAEP) offers high-quality released test items for grades 4, 8, and 12 that can be used for assessment. Many states also offer released test items for practice or assessment. For instance, Wisconsin offers the Wisconsin Knowledge and Concepts Examinations Criterion-Referenced Test at dpi.wi.gov/oea/readingptri.html. Items are available for grades 3 to 8 and 10. In addition, there are a number of online sites that include tests. Online practice reading tests for grades 2 to 8 can be found at www.pearsonlongman.com/ae/marketing/sfesl/practicereading.html.

Commercial Tests

Most reading tests indicate the general level of students' comprehension and highlight which students are having difficulty but don't tell why the students are having difficulty. One commercial test that attempts to go beneath the surface is the Test of Reading Comprehension (TORC; published by Pearson), which can be administered to students from ages 7 to 17. The TORC includes the following subtests:

- **General Vocabulary**—measures the reader's understanding of sets of vocabulary items that are all related to the same general concept
- **Syntactic Similarities**—measures the reader's understanding of meaningfully similar but syntactically different sentence structures
- **Paragraph Reading**—measures the reader's ability to answer questions related to story-like paragraphs
- **Sentence Sequencing**—measures the reader's ability to build relationships among sentences, both to one another and to a reader-created whole

Conducting an Item Analysis

After administering an assessment, conduct an item analysis (Winters, 2009). In an item analysis, all the test items are listed and the number of incorrect responses is tallied for each item. However, before tallying the number of incorrect responses, note any items that are not aligned with your curriculum. If an item assesses a skill that you don't teach and don't believe should be taught, ignore the item. If your item analysis reveals that an unusually high number of students got an item wrong, take a careful look at the item. It might be poorly worded or misleading, or it might be assessing a skill that was not effectively taught. An item analysis can indicate neglected areas. If many students are getting a valid item wrong, it could be indicating a weakness in instruction. Also look at the performance of individuals on the assessment and note areas of strength and weakness. Most important of all, use the analysis to plan instruction.

Assessing Cognitive Complexity

In addition to assessing and regulating the difficulty of materials that struggling readers encounter, also assess and control the cognitive complexity of the questions or other comprehension tasks to which they are asked to respond. The NAEP 2009 Framework (National Assessment Governing Board, 2008), as explained in Chapter 1, provides a hierarchy of skills and strategies that represent comprehension tasks that increase in cognitive complexity: Locate and Recall, Integrate and Interpret, and Critique and Evaluate. The Web Alignment Tool (WAT) is a more formal and highly developed system for judging the cognitive complexity required by comprehension objectives and questions (Web, Alt, Ely, & Vesperman, 2005). Cognitive complexity in the WAT system is defined as the depth of knowledge required by comprehension tasks. Extensive guidance is provided at the WAT website, wat.wceruw.org/index.aspx. A third system, which is adapted from WAT, is used by the Florida Department of Education (2008) to assess and control the cognitive complexity of questions posed on the Florida Comprehensive Assessment Test. Items are judged to be of low, medium, or high cognitive complexity. A description of the levels and sample items is available at fcat.fldoe.org/fcatpub2.asp. As a word of caution for all three systems, expect some overlap. Some tasks classified as being lower level might be more difficult in some situations than some tasks designated as being at a higher level.

Using one of these systems or one that you adapt or devise, determine the cognitive complexity of comprehension tasks that students encounter. Then determine how well prepared students are to meet the cognitive demands of these comprehension tasks. Using the results of formal and informal assessments as described later in this chapter, determine the kinds of cognitive tasks that students can handle. They might be able to handle tasks on the Locate and Recall level but have difficulty with tasks at the Integrate and Interpret level. They might have difficulty with complex inferences or contrasting two characters or events. After determining the level of cognitive complexity that students can handle, use that information to plan a program that builds the skills and strategies necessary to move into higher levels. For instance, if students are having difficulty making comparisons, you might teach them how to determine essential similarities. Developing needed reasoning processes is the often-neglected foundation for building higher level literacy.

Going Beyond the Textbase

Grasping the textbase is a necessary but not sufficient condition for inferencing and other higher level processes. Without an adequate textbase, students have difficulty making inferences. In a study by Kintsch and Kintsch (2005), one of four students tested had difficulty making inferences despite having constructed an adequate textbase. Assessment needs to go beyond the textbase and provide information about the situation model. An especially effective device for going beyond the textbase is the think-aloud, which can be used in conjunction with an IRI or similar test.

Think-Alouds

Although we can view the products of comprehension in the form of test results (written and oral responses), it would be helpful to gain insight into the processes of comprehension. One way of gaining insight into the way students process written text is through think-alouds. In a think-aloud the reader tells what is going on in her or his mind as she or he reads. To create think-alouds, select passages that are about 200 words in length and that are complex or challenging enough to lend themselves to thoughtful examination but that are on the students' instructional reading level. Decide on stopping places. Stopping places should be after a logical break: at the end of a paragraph, after a description, or after a listing of supporting details. Don't make the stopping parts too far apart, or students will have difficulty recalling what they read. Try out the think-aloud and make adjustments as necessary.

Prompts are typically open-ended: "Tell me what you were thinking as you read this section." To get the best results, model the think-aloud process. In your modeling, include a variety of different types of think-aloud comments so that students have a better sense of the ways in which they might respond. Table 2.1 presents a series of possible think-aloud prompts.

In their think-alouds, most students paraphrase or summarize information (Leslie & Caldwell, 2006). However, students indicate understanding in a variety of ways: They make inferences or draw conclusions, comment that they understand what they are reading, make a connection between what they are reading and background knowledge or experience, or pose questions that indicate an understanding of the selection. Students' think-aloud statements or questions might also indicate a lack of understanding. Think-alouds don't work for all students. Leslie and Caldwell (2006) find that some students made no think-aloud comments despite the invitation to do so.

Stopping to think about text that one has read is an effective strategy for enhancing comprehension. Sixth graders who were assessed with think-alouds recalled more than sixth grader who read the same passage silently (Loxterman, Beck, & McKeown, 1994). Leslie and Caldwell (2006) report that think-alouds fostered increased comprehension when the materials being read were especially challenging. Using think-alouds can help students discover where they need help to comprehend better and what kinds of strategies they might use (Israel & Massey, 2005). Think-alouds also help students use self-talk so that they can better regulate their use of strategies: "I'll turn the heading into a question. Then I'll read to answer the question I made." Although time-consuming to give,

Table 2.1. Think-Aloud Prompts

Type of Prompt	Think-Aloud Prompt	Features to Note
Before reading (Note whether student engages in any pre-reading activities, such as surveying the text.)	What do you think this selection might be about? What makes you think so?	Does the student survey before reading? Does the student make predictions? Are predictions based on the survey? Does student activate background knowledge? What is the extent of student's background knowledge?
During reading (Note whether student is using titles, headings, illustrations, and other text features or rereading portions of the text.)	What was going on in your mind as you read the selection? What were you thinking about?	Does student use text features, such as headings and illustrations? Does the student paraphrase or summarize?
	What do you think will happen next in the selection? What makes you think so?	Does the student make inferences and ongoing predictions or use imaging? Does the student make connections? Does the student evaluate or judge the information?
	Were there any parts that were confusing? What did you do when you came across parts that were confusing?	Does student reread or use other fix-up strategies when a passage is puzzling?
After reading (Have the student summarize the selection.)	(For nonfiction) What was this selection mainly about? What did the author tell you about (topic)? (For fiction) What happened in the story?	Does the student include most of the main points in the summary? If the summary is incomplete, you can encourage the student to tell you more.
(Have the student evaluate the selection.)	(For nonfiction) Is the information in the selection accurate? Is it up to date? Was the information presented fairly? (For fiction) Was the story interesting? What did the author do to make it interesting? Did the characters seem like real people?	Does the student have and apply a set of criteria for judging the accuracy and fairness of a piece of informational text and the quality of a narrative piece?

(continued)

Table 2.1. Think-Aloud Prompts *(continued)*

Type of Prompt	Think-Aloud Prompt	Features to Note
Connections (Ask the student to make connections.)	(For nonfiction) How does the information in this passage fit in with what you already know? Is there anything in this passage that makes you think of something that you read about or heard about? (For fiction) Is there anything in this passage that reminds you of someone that you know or something that has happened in your life?	What kinds of connections does the student make? Are the connections substantive? Do the connections deepen the student's understanding or appreciation of the selection?

Adapted from Gunning, T.G. (2008). *Developing higher-level literacy in all students: Building reading, reasoning, and responding.* Boston: Allyn & Bacon.

think-alouds actually have the potential to improve comprehension even when they are only being used for assessment purposes. Although they might distort students' normal reading processes, think-alouds indicate how well students could comprehend if they became more aware of their reading processes and stopped periodically to reflect upon what they had read.

Published Think-Alouds

Think-alouds are available for students reading on a sixth-grade level and above in the Qualitative Reading Inventory-4 (Leslie & Caldwell, 2006). The TARA: Think-Aloud Reading Assessment (Monti & Cicchetti, 1996), which can be used with students in any grade, combines interviews and think-alouds. Designed to provide information about the textbase and situation model, TARA assesses fluency, reading rate, miscues, prereading strategies, prior knowledge, comprehension monitoring, fix-up strategies, and retelling. Assessment starts with the establishment of the student's instructional reading and fluency levels. Students are then assessed at the level at which their accuracy is above 95%, their retellings are adequate, and their reading rate is adequate. To be judged as being average, a retelling must contain 70% of the main ideas and supporting details in the passage.

Monti and Cicchetti (1996) report that struggling readers tended to have difficulty at the textbase level. The struggling readers they assessed focused on decoding and pronunciation, rarely activated background knowledge or raised questions about the selections they were reading, and did not monitor their comprehension.

Prompted Think-Alouds

Klingner, Vaughn, and Boardman (2007) use a prompted think-aloud procedure, which starts with the following explanation: "I am going to ask you to read a page from a magazine. While you are reading, I'm going to ask you to tell me what you are thinking. You can tell me what you're thinking in either Spanish or English" (p. 43). The text is marked off by asterisks. Whenever the student comes to an asterisk (usually after reading a brief paragraph), the student stops and is asked to tell what she or he is thinking. After the student finishes responding, the teacher prompts for added details by asking, "Anything else?" (p. 43). Just before the student begins reading the first segment, the teacher probes to see what the student does before reading: "When I give you this to read, what is the first thing you do?" (p. 43). After the initial response, the teacher asks, "Anything else?" (p. 43). At the end of the reading, the student is asked to tell what she or he does to remember what has been read and to make sure it has been understood: "What do you do to help yourself remember what you have read? Anything else? What do you do to make sure you understand everything you have read? Anything else? What do you do when you do not understand a word or an idea the first time you read it?" (p. 44).

A rubric is used to analyze the Prompted Think-Aloud. Students are given credit on the prereading questions if responses include brainstorming what they already know and predicting what they think they will learn. The student also gets credit for mentioning use of text features or graphics, such as headings, charts, graphs, and italicized or boldfaced words. For the during-reading portion, students are given credit for a gist or main idea statement or a retelling. After-reading statements are given credit if they fall into one of the following categories: testing, summarizing, questioning, understanding, or making an outline. Mentioning a rereading is given partial credit.

Higher Level Thinking Think-Alouds

In an intriguing activity virtually guaranteed to assess students' ability to hypothesize and justify their hypotheses, Wade (1990) presents think-alouds in which the main idea or topic is not revealed until the last sentence—an inverted passage think-aloud—as in the following selection, which is read in segments:

- It is really colorless but when light reflects off its surface, it looks white.
- Sometimes it can turn black or brown when it mixes with factory dust, or yellow when it mixes with airborne pine tree pollen.
- Sometimes it looks light and delicate. A cubic foot of it may weigh only 6 pounds. But when it is compressed it can weigh up to 30 pounds a cubic foot, powerful enough to crush buildings.
- It is one of nature's best insulators. Hold a thermometer just above it and look at the temperature. Now push the thermometer inside of it and see how much warmer it reads.
- Farmers know that snow holds heat in the ground and keeps their seeds from freezing. (Wade, 1990, p. 446)

Before beginning to read the think-aloud passage, students are told that they will be reading a story in segments, and that after reading it they will be asked to tell what the segment is about. The think-aloud passage is read in portions consisting of one to four sentences. After each segment the students are asked, "What do you think this is about?" The responses are followed by the prompt, "What makes you think that?" After students have worked her or their way through the passage, the student is asked to reread the passage before engaging in the retelling of the whole passage. Results of the think-aloud can be analyzed with the following questions:

- How well were readers able to hypothesize the topic of the passage?
- How well did readers support their hypotheses with reasons, inferences, or predictions?
- At what point did the readers guess the topic?
- What information from the text did the readers use?
- How did the readers make use of background knowledge?
- What strategies did the readers use?
- How did the readers handle unfamiliar words or puzzling portions of the text?

A think-aloud passage should be from 80 to 200 words in length and on the student's instructional level. It should be about a familiar topic. Otherwise, the student will lack the background needed to predict the topic of the passage.

Students to whom the think-aloud was administered fell into five main categories, as follows (Wade, 1990):

Good comprehenders. Good comprehenders use information from text and background knowledge to generate and support their hypotheses. They are flexible and change their hypotheses when a change is indicated by new information in the text.

Nonrisk takers. Nonrisk takers stick closely to the text and are hesitant to offer a hypothesis. They fail to make use of background knowledge. Nearly 1 in 5 students was a nonrisk taker. Most were younger readers or struggling readers.

Nonintegrators. As their label suggests, this group of students fails to put together information from various segments of the text. They pose a new hypothesis based on the current segment of text without regard to previously read segments.

Schema imposers. The schema imposer holds onto her or his initial hypothesis. The information in succeeding passages is altered to fit the reader's schema. About 1 in 10 students is a schema imposer. Schema imposers might over-rely on background knowledge because of difficulty they have processing the text.

Storytellers. These readers rely heavily on background knowledge to create a plausible scenario that might have little to do with the text. As with schema imposers, they may have difficulty processing text and find it easier to create their own meaning rather than to construct meaning from the text. About 1 student in 12 is a storyteller.

When assessed with an inverted passage think-aloud, Eduardo (the student described at the beginning of this chapter) was judged to be a mixed non-integrator and storyteller. This information was used to provide a series of strategy lessons, which proved to be highly effective. Along with being an excellent assessment device, the use of inverted passages, which were dubbed "mystery passages," for think-alouds can also be a good instructional activity for building student ability to construct meaning. (An example of an instructional application of mystery passages can be found in Chapter 7 of this volume.)

Think-Alongs and Read-Alongs

In another adaptation of think-alouds, Farr (2009) uses a written version called think-alongs. The teacher, after demonstrating thinking aloud, has students engage in think-alouds. Students are then asked to record their thinking in writing. Boxes inserted in the text at appropriate points ask students to record what they are thinking about at that moment. Although they might not elicit the same depth or quantity of information as oral think-alouds do, written think-alongs make it possible to assess the whole class at one time and on a continuing basis. Farr (2009) provides the following steps for constructing a think-along:

1. Model thinking aloud as students follow along with a copy of the text. Ask students to keep a list of the things you do to help you understand the text. Discuss students' responses and record them on the board. Compose a list of key strategies.

2. In preparation for a second think-aloud, tell students that now they will be doing the thinking aloud. Explain that you will stop and ask, "What are you thinking about now?" Do a brief sample passage cooperatively; provide prompts and explanations as needed. You might start off with a passage that lends itself to a relatively easy-to-use strategy, such as visualizing, and later work on passages in which multiple strategies might be used. Discuss the strategies used.

3. Provide additional guided practice with varied texts.

4. Prepare materials in which students can compose written think-alongs. Indicate stopping points. Select stopping points that lend themselves to a think-aloud. You might go through the passage and note the kinds of strategies you use and what might be the most appropriate stopping points. Insert writing boxes into the text. Explain to students that they will be writing their think-alongs in the boxes. Discuss students' think-alongs and the strategies used. Probe for greater depth in responses. Collect students' written think-alongs, analyze the results, and use the results to help plan instruction.

Sticky Notes as Think-Alouds

Another way to gain insight into the processes students are using is to have them use sticky notes to record their thinking. Using sticky notes, students can periodically tell what was going on in their minds as they were reading or note passages that were confusing or places where they used strategies. Students might be asked to post a sticky note at the end of each section, when they encounter a confusing passage, or whenever they have an idea they wish to share or something in the text stands out. As one teacher commented, "I have them do the sticky notes first because that's the immediate conversation that we would be having...I love to hear them verbalize [their thinking]" (Fiene & McMahon, 2007, p. 409).

The teacher in Fiene & McMahon's (2007) study requested that her students use sticky notes to reflect on their reading and raise questions. The teacher then collected the notes and used them to plan instruction. She noted that some students were having difficulty making inferences; another group was having difficulty making comparisons. Instruction was planned for the groups. The sticky notes, which represented the students' immediate reactions to the text, were used as the basis for composing extended responses in their journals. Both the sticky notes and the journal entries became rich sources of data for planning instruction.

Questionnaires

Because they can be given to groups, questionnaires can be an economical device for gathering information about students' awareness of and use of strategies. The Metacognitive Strategy Index (MSI; Schmitt, 1990) is designed to assess the following higher thinking processes of middle and upper elementary school students: use of predicting and verifying, previewing, purpose setting, self-questioning, drawing from background knowledge, summarizing, and applying fix-up strategies. The questionnaire can be read silently by students or, if you suspect students might have difficulty reading it themselves, you can read the statements and possible responses to students. As Schmitt (1990) notes, the MSI can be used to identify students' awareness of strategies, indicate which strategies students consider to be important, and evaluate students' awareness of the appropriate time to use strategies.

For secondary students, the Metacognitive Awareness of Reading Strategies (MARS; Mokhtari &.Reichard, 2002) can be used to assess strategy awareness. In addition to providing information about the students' use of strategies, questionnaires such as the MSI and MARS can be used to build students' awareness of strategies (Klingner et al., 2007). One problem with questionnaires is that it is possible that students might answer according to teacher expectation. To find out if students actually do what they say they do, observations can be helpful (Klingner et al., 2007).

Question–Answer Relationships (QAR)

Observations can be spontaneous or planned. Some planned observations that can be especially revealing are situations in which students are using Question–Answer Relationships. Although it is primarily a teaching technique, QAR can also be used to assess comprehension. Pearson and Johnson (1978) classify comprehension questions according to the source of the answers. Answers are said to be text explicit, text implicit, or script implicit. Text explicit questions refer to information directly stated in the text. Text implicit questions require the readers to use information from the text and inferences. Script implicit questions depend on the reader's background knowledge or script. The following classification system is incorporated in QAR (Raphael, 1984, 1986):

Right There: Answer is contained within a single sentence in the text.

Putting It Together (Think and Search): It is necessary to put together information from several sentences to obtain an answer.

Writer and Me: The reader must combine personal knowledge with information from the text to construct an inference.

On My Own: The answer is part of the student's prior knowledge.

Inferring What's Missing

One way to assess students' abilities to make inferences is to ask them to tell what's missing. Students are given a story and asked to fix what is wrong with it. A crucial literal sentence is covered up with a sticky note and students write what the sentence should be. An adaptation of this technique is known as macro-cloze. In macro-cloze, students use their background of experience and inferential reasoning to supply a missing sentence (Yuill & Oakhill, 1991) as in the following example:

The dog was charging at me with its fangs bared. _____.
I breathed a deep sigh of relief.

Classroom Discussions and Responsive Elaboration

Classroom discussions can provide valuable information about students' comprehension and reasoning processes and background knowledge. As Hampton and Resnick (2009) note, "Classroom talk is a habit that provides a window into comprehension and knowledge, allowing teachers to monitor how well students understand what they read and offer guidance when they experience difficulty" (p. 10). However, asking probing questions designed to reveal students' thought processes provides greater insight and increased opportunity for helping students. Duffy and Roehler (1987) have successfully used a technique known as "responsive elaboration." They use prompts based on the students' responses to help readers correct and elaborate on those responses, as in the following exchange, which took place after the student provided a main idea statement that did not include all the details in the selection:

Teacher: Well, let's test it. Is the first sentence talking about new words from the Indians?

Student: Yes.

Teacher: Is the next?

Student: Yes.

Teacher: How about the next?

Student: No.

Teacher: No. It says that Indians also learned new words from the settlers, right? Can you fit that into your main idea?

Student: The Indians taught the settlers words and the settlers taught the Indians words.

Teacher: Good. You see, you have to think about all the ideas in the paragraph to decide on the main idea. (Duffy & Roehler, 1987, p. 517)

As part of responsive elaboration, the teacher analyzes the student's response. She looks for where it has gone off track, if it is erroneous, or where it needs to be elaborated upon if it is incomplete. She then uses that analysis to guide the student to a correct or more elaborated response, hence the term "responsive elaboration."

When assessing student discussions, note how they do with different levels of questions. Intentionality is a key factor in assessment (Winters, 2009). You must intend to assess higher level literacy and make specific provision for it. In a discussion, for instance, you must be sure to pose questions at varying levels and note student performance. You might use a group observation guide such as the one presented in Figure 2.2.

Observe students when they are working with a partner, involved in peer tutoring, or engaging in a cooperative learning activity. As Klingner et al. (2007) note, "Listening to how a tutor describes strategy implementation to another student, for example, can provide useful information regarding what the student knows and can do" (p. 31).

Recording Observations

Because memories of interactions can be fleeting and interactions themselves can be sporadic, it is helpful to use some sort of observation guide to facilitate observations and record responses. A group observation guide such as the one in Figure 2.2, which is adapted from Bookshop (Mondo, 2004), might be used.

Figure 2.2. Group Observation Guide

Names					
Focuses					
Draws logical conclusions					
Is able to justify conclusions with supporting details					

Key: S = satisfactory   N = needs additional instruction

Needs and notes for future instruction _____

_____

_____

Adapted from Bookshop (Mondo, 2004)

The teacher records one or more focus areas, which in this session is student ability to draw conclusions and support them. The names of students in the group being observed are recorded along with any needs noted. Focus might be placed on key higher level skills and strategies that pose problems for struggling readers.

Anecdotal Records

Anecdotal records are brief descriptions of key events or incidents that might provide insight into a student's comprehension, work habits, interests, attitude, or other related areas. Anecdotal records should include a variety of observations and not just those that occur when the student is having a particularly good or bad day. Positive as well as negative occurrences should be recorded. The setting of the event should be described. The anecdotal record should be written in a neutral style. Judgments or interpretations should be placed in a separate section of the record. In a QAR lesson, for instance, noting that the student did not know that the sun set in the west might be recorded as an anecdotal record. If other records indicate gaps in knowledge, then you have evidence for areas that need work.

Journals, Logs, and Work Samples

If students reflect on their reading and compose responses, these can be invaluable sources of information about their comprehension. Teachers in the Chittenango Central School District in New York State created a series of read-along guides to help students apply strategies as they read high-interest materials (Athans & Devine, 2008). Teachers periodically checked students' read-along guides to monitor progress and, in many cases, were able to supply on-the-spot assistance if a difficulty was evident. Performance on the guide was used to provide individual help as needed or group assistance if the difficulty was shared by all the students in the group. As part of a reading guide or as one of your purpose questions or prompts for journal entries, ask students to note how they used the particular strategy, such as visualizing, that is the current focus of instruction. Did you visualize any parts of the article? If you did, how did visualizing help you to better understand the story?

You might also use brief writing activities to gauge students' grasp of strategies and concepts. For instance, at the end of a class period, you might have students complete a quickwrite or exit slip designed to assess their learning. Provide prompts that elicit various levels of thought.

- What did I learn today?
- What did I do well?
- What am I confused about?
- What questions do I have?
- How does what I learned fit in with what I already know?
- How might I use this information?
- How might I use the strategy that we learned today?

Rubrics

Although often thought of as being scoring guides for writing assignments, rubrics can be devised for virtually any learning task. Rubrics have the power to guide and foster learning. A well-constructed rubric specifies the key elements in a task so that the teacher and the students have a clear idea of what is expected. Rubrics result in more specific feedback. If students are involved in the construction of a rubric, they also gain a sense of ownership as well as a clearer understanding of the learning task.

The construction of a rubric begins with a description of the key characteristics of the task to be completed. For a rubric on a constructed response that involves making and supporting an inference, the key elements might simply be making an inference and providing support, as in Figure 2.3. Explain each item in the rubric so that it will be understandable to students. For instance: what is involved in providing support for an inference? Criteria to be considered should be limited to three to five. The criteria should also be teachable. If a student has shortcomings in an area, the rubric can be used as a basis for instruction. If the student has not provided adequate support for an inference, for example, then this skill can be taught. Show the rubric to colleagues and invite their suggestions. Also try it out with students and make revisions as called for.

Creating a Sensitive Rubric. Rubrics should be sensitive to growth. Phelps and Collins (2008) present results of the use of a six-level rubric to assess and compare the essays of struggling readers whose writing had been judged by New York State's four-level rubric. As depicted by Table 2.2, the six levels are (1) some incoherence or an incomplete written response; (2) coherent and repetitive

Figure 2.3. Rubric on a Constructed Response

Skill	Needs Work	Exploring	Developing	Proficient
Making an Inference	No response	Draws an inference unrelated to the information in the selection	Draws a logical but unimportant inference	Draws a logical, important inference
Providing Support	No response	Provides no support for the inference or the support does not come from the selection	Provides limited support for the inference	Provides two or more supporting details from the selection

Suggestions _____

_____

Table 2.2. Observations and Categorization of Written Responses

6-point rubric	4-point rubric
Some incoherence or an incomplete written response	1
Coherent and repetitive writing	1
Coherent, repetitive, very little detail, may be retelling the story	1
Coherent, repetitive or not, some detail, may be retelling the story	2
Coherent, repetitive or not, detailed	3
Coherent and very detailed	4

writing; (3) coherent, repetitive, with very little detail, may be retelling the story as a default writing strategy; (4) coherent writing that may or may not be repetitive, some detail, may be retelling the story; (5) coherent writing, repetitive or not, detailed; and (6) coherent and very detailed writing. According to New York State scoring guidelines (New York State Department of Education, 2000), three of the six distinctive levels of emergent writing are all given the score of one out of four possible points on the rubric. However, an application of the six-level rubric revealed that although some students at the lowest level made substantial gains and moved up on the six-level scale, their gains weren't enough to move them into level two of the state's rubric. The four-point rubric lacked the sensitivity to fully detect the writing gains of struggling and emergent writers.

When students understand rubrics and especially when they have been involved in creating them, rubrics can help build their awareness of task demands and help them to self-assess. Checklists might be used instead of rubrics. Checklists, if filled out by students, can also build awareness of task demands and foster self-assessment. As part of a rubric or checklist, where feasible, include provisions for higher level literacy.

Beyond Strategies

Although research clearly indicates that using strategies results in increased comprehension, comprehending a passage is more than just using strategies. Comprehension also depends on background knowledge. In fact, background knowledge might be a more important factor than strategies. Students read more slowly and comprehend less when reading about unfamiliar topics (Hirsch, 2006). In their tryouts of the Qualitative Reading Inventory, Leslie and Caldwell (2006) found a strong relationship between their assessments of students' prior knowledge and comprehension. In fact, prior knowledge predicted passage comprehension more frequently than did a general measure of reading achievement. As Hirsch (2006) points out, reading tests typically contain selections on varied topics. To attain high scores, students must have broad general knowledge. As part of your assessment, note the breadth and depth of students' background knowledge. To assess background knowledge, Leslie and Caldwell use concept questions and predictions. From three to five concept questions are asked before students read a test selection. Students are told, "Before you read, I want to know what you already know about some ideas in the text. I will ask you a few questions to find out" (p. 55). Sample questions include, What do flowers need to grow? What are pyramids? Why do people work? What is a biography? What do you do to take care of a pet? Responses to concept questions are then used to set up a prediction. Responses to the concept questions are included in the prediction prompt: "Given that the title to this selection is 'The Trip to the Zoo' and it has the ideas 'class trip,' 'taking notes,' and 'why people use maps,' what do you think the story will be about?" (p. 59). The prediction task is scored by counting the number of ideas that actually occur in the selection. Predictions are judged on the degree to which they integrate information from the concepts with the title.

Prereading discussions and encouraging students to make predictions can provide valuable insight into students' background knowledge. Brainstorming techniques are also effective for revealing students' background knowledge. Use brainstorming techniques such as KWL to get a sense of students' background knowledge.

One indirect measure of background knowledge is the quality and quantity of the students' vocabularies. Words are markers of how much we know. In general, the more words we know, the more knowledge we have. Obtain information from any vocabulary tests that your students have taken. Many norm-referenced standardized reading tests have a vocabulary subtest. Or your students may have been given an individual vocabulary test, such as the Peabody Picture Vocabulary Test. If formal test data are not available, note the level of vocabulary that your students use in discussions and the kinds of words that pose problems for them in their reading.

The Role of Written Responses

Although reading and writing are related, they are not the same. While visiting a second-grade class in an urban elementary school, I (first author) noticed that one of the students was still working on the end-of-unit test that accompanied the school's newly purchased basal reading series. It was obvious that she was feeling some distress. Tears began to flow. When I asked her what was wrong, she replied, between sniffles, "I don't know how to do this." The question that prompted her tears was a constructed-response query that asked, "Could this story have happened in real life the way it is told here?" (Valencia, 2001, p. 10). Wondering whether she had a decoding problem and was unable to read the question, I asked her to read it. She read it flawlessly. I then asked her to read the first paragraph of the story. Her oral reading was fluent. Wondering if perhaps she was a good decoder but poor comprehender, I then asked her a few questions about the story. The story, *Who Took the Farmer's Hat* (Nodset, 1963), was about a farmer who was searching for his hat, which had blown off his head. I asked her if that could happen in real life. She said that it could. We then discussed the segment of the story in which the farmer seeks help from a squirrel, but the squirrel replies that it hadn't seen the farmer's hat. The student said that couldn't happen in real life because animals can't talk. She explained that the story was a fantasy. I suggested that she write down what she had just told me. However, her answer stated, "The story couldn't happen in real life. It is a fantasy." I was about to ask her to justify her circular answer by explaining what specifically made it a fantasy when the classroom teacher reminded me that the student was taking a test and that I should not be giving her help. Although I wasn't able to help the distraught student, I had learned a real-life lesson that perhaps could be used to help other struggling students (Gunning, 2007).

This real-life lesson was that the assessment was masking the student's grasp of the selection. I had only asked her questions. I had not supplied any information or given any hints or clues, beyond a few prompts. It was apparent that the second grader's comprehension of the story was at least adequate. However, she was having difficulty articulating a written response. Without my prompting, the student would probably not have written any response, and the teacher would have assessment data indicating, erroneously, that the child was lacking in higher level comprehension. The fault was not in the student but in the assessment process. I couldn't help wondering how many other students there are who have adequate comprehension but are unable to express it. A few days later, I had an experience that suggested that there were a large number of students whose comprehension was being underestimated because they had difficulty formulating responses.

The third-grade teachers explained that there was a problem with the end-of-unit tests. They complained that the tests were indicating that the students' comprehension was inadequate. However, based on classroom discussions, the students evidenced a depth of understanding. Fearing that the tests were poorly constructed, I examined them and the students' responses. The test questions were clear and straightforward and assessed skills and strategies taught during the unit. However, the students' responses were, for the most part, inadequate. To determine whether students' inadequate answers were due to poor comprehension or underdeveloped responding skills, I interviewed students, observed them as they responded to constructed responses, and discussed selections with them. For the most part, the teachers' observations were accurate. Most students had adequate comprehension but inadequate constructed responses. There were a smaller number whose deficient responses were caused by a failure to understand the test selections (Gunning, 2007).

Members of the Writing Intensive Reading Comprehension research team have also noted a disparity between what struggling students can do in the classroom and their performance on high-stakes tests. Writing Intensive Reading Comprehension (WIRC), which is described in Chapter 5, uses a series of written prompts contained on thinksheets to scaffold the comprehension of fourth and fifth graders in a large urban district. There was a marked contrast between the students' thinksheet writing and posttest writing on the reading test. In general, the thinksheet writing was much more connected, coherent, and lengthy than the posttest writing. To a certain extent, the essential difference between formative thinksheet writing and summative assessment writing would account for an increase in quality of coconstructed thinksheet writing over the timed and independently written assessment writing. Yet this phenomenon does not fully explain why the struggling and emergent writers of the WIRC experiment were able to excel at thinksheet writing and then so often fail miserably on the intervention posttest, which was patterned after New York State's English Language Arts (ELA) exam.

As I looked at the research in this area, it became clear that difficulty responding in writing to comprehension questions isn't limited to elementary school students. Calder and Carlson (2002) report, in their study of college freshmen, that many of the middle-level students' oral responses were superior to their written answers. They conclude that

> for them, deep understandings seemed to evaporate when they tried to wrestle their thoughts to paper. This told us that we had work to do if we wanted to distinguish between assessing understanding and assessing students' ability to communicate their understanding. (p. 2)

To gather added information about this issue, I examined 200 constructed responses from past NAEP tests. An analysis of constructed responses on the NAEP suggests that for many students there is a gap between what students comprehend and their ability to express their understanding. As Pearson and Hamm (2005) warn,

> For years, we have asked students to write in response to reading, generally regarding it as a useful approach to comprehension assessment for more complex reading tasks, such as critical response to literature and critical evaluation of ideas and arguments. Yet we also know that the writing requirements can obscure some children's ability to understand and interpret text because of their poor motor skills development, inadequate spelling, and underdeveloped writing dispositions. (p. 53)

The implications of the gap between what students understand and their ability to express it or our ability to assess it are a bit staggering. They would seem to suggest that many students who are assessed with tests containing constructed responses comprehend far better than we have given them credit for.

A second implication is that students need to be taught how to respond to test questions. A third implication is that we need to take another look at assessment of higher level literacy. Although I had overstepped my bounds as guest observer in the second-grade teacher's class, she had missed an opportunity to obtain information that would have empowered her teaching. Had I been able to continue to ask probing questions, I believe I would have been able to get enough of a sense of how the student was processing her response so that I would have been able to make suggestions to the teacher that would have enabled the student to learn effective responding strategies.

Considering the Context

Because literacy is a social activity, it is important to consider the context of the assessment task. A response written at home to a self-selected text might provide a different and more valid glimpse into a student's literacy development than a response written to a test passage under time constraints. At present, socially constructed aesthetic writing done in the classroom throughout the school year does not even factor into the formula for standardized writing assessment. The WIRC team suggests future research on assessment enhancement to include a portfolio-based assessment for a percentage of scores on the ELA and similar high-stakes assessments.

Because comprehension is a complex activity, it is essential that a broad sample of activities and tasks be included in the assessment. As Gaskins and Galloway discuss in Chapter 8, it is also important to go beyond the cognitive domain and look at students' motivation, volition, and other personal characteristics.

Assessment Context: Strategically Constructing Assessments

Some assessment contexts are more conducive to eliciting students' best performance than others. Context is especially important when assessing struggling readers and writers. In addition to making sure that struggling readers are administered assessments that are on the proper level, high-stakes assessments can be modified to make them more reader friendly. The better constructed the exam, the more efficiently the student is able to work to demonstrate her or his understanding. In one assessment, many struggling students from two fifth-grade experimental classrooms were confused when the reference text for a particular writing question did not immediately precede the question (Phelps,

2008). Two contrasting paintings of an ocean had been inserted between the text and the corresponding writing prompt. This confusion was reflected in students' written responses. Students described the illustrations rather than referencing the text to answer the question.

Using Word Banks to Overcome Strategic Vocabulary Deficits

Unfamiliar vocabulary can also hinder responding. In one fourth-grade classroom, many struggling writers demonstrated a distinct problem with making a connection between the text and the writing prompt (Phelps, 2008). One question asked the writer to identify three symbols from the text and to tell what each meant. Although this question adequately scaffolds back to connect with the reading passage, several struggling writers manifested difficulty with the meaning of the word *symbol* as it pertained to the reading passage. Although the verb *symbolizes* is provided in the word bank, many students did not seem to know what the word *symbol* means and so apparently were unsure as to what evidence to look for in the reading passage. This assessment test might better facilitate the student construction of a macrostructure if the meaning of the key word *symbol* were to be provided in the word bank. As demonstrated by the WIRC student posttest data, struggling writers have also demonstrated a strategic vocabulary deficit. It appears that these students rely upon using the word bank and that they need to be provided with more information about text-based strategic vocabulary words (Kintsch & Kintsch, 2005) to make the inferences necessary to correctly answer writing prompts.

Making the Planning Page Count

It is accepted practice to include a planning page in a standardized writing assessment with the hope that the student will use it in constructing extended writing responses. Because the planning page often does not assist with the structure or organization of the writing task, chances are good that it will end up being used as scrap paper. The inclusion of a thinksheet style graphic organizer planning page could be an additional component for process evaluation and would serve as a link from the reading of a single passage to a simple deductive writing task. Such a planning page would not hinder the confident writer but could assist the struggling writer in organizing his or her thoughts. Figure 2.4 shows a planning page with a question about an article on the languages of art. Figure 2.5 shows a slightly modified planning page, with a writing question

Figure 2.4. Example Planning Page About Art Article

Directions: You may use this page to prepare your answer to the question on the next page. Do not write your final answer on this page. Write your final answer on the next page.

Complete the chart below in the following two steps:
• Go back to the article and underline three things art tells you by using pictures instead of words.
• In each box, write one thing that art tells you by using pictures instead of words.

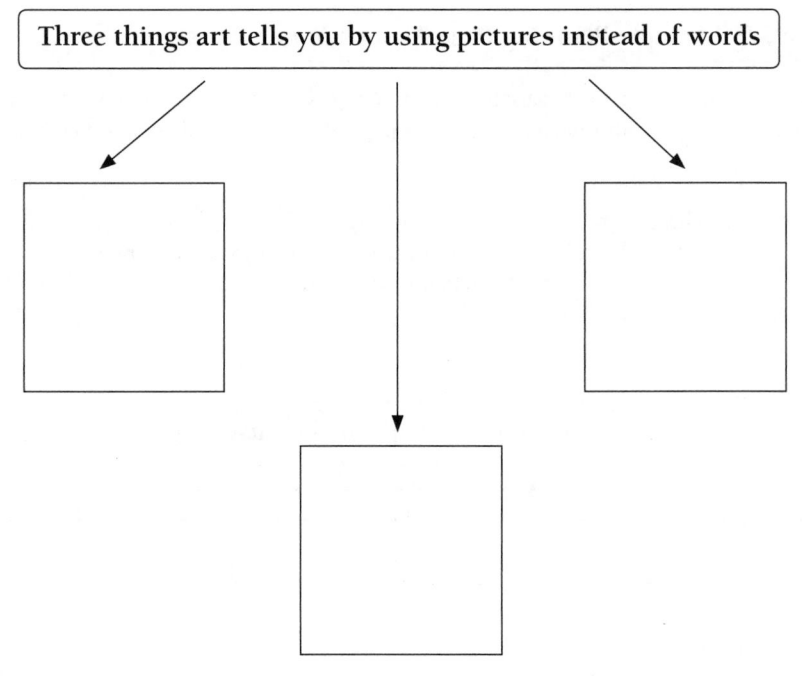

Writing Question:
This article tells us that artists create many artistic languages. According to the author, what are three things that art tells you about by using pictures instead of words?

Essay Writing Guidelines:
Introduction: Tell what you are going to write about.
Body: Explain three things that art tells you by using pictures instead of words.
Conclusion: Tell why artists use different kinds of pictures.
Continue on another page if you need to.

based on an article about a young artist. Questions that require students to use two sources of information are especially challenging. The overall assessment and the planning page would be enhanced if an extended writing question—which asks the student to respond based on the reading of the two articles—clearly connected the two passages. Figure 2.6 shows a planning page that connects the two passages that are the basis for a constructed response. Figures 2.4–2.6 are revisions of a writing task on the New York State English language arts assessment (CTB McGraw-Hill, 2004). Content is as important as reading

Figure 2.5. Example Planning Page About a Young Artist

Directions: You may use this page to prepare your answer to the question on the next page. Do not write your final answer on this page. Write your final answer on the next page.

Complete the chart below in the following two steps:
• Go back to the article and underline three reasons why Alexandra is inspiring.
• In each box, write one reason that tells why Alexandra is inspiring.

Alexandra is inspiring because…

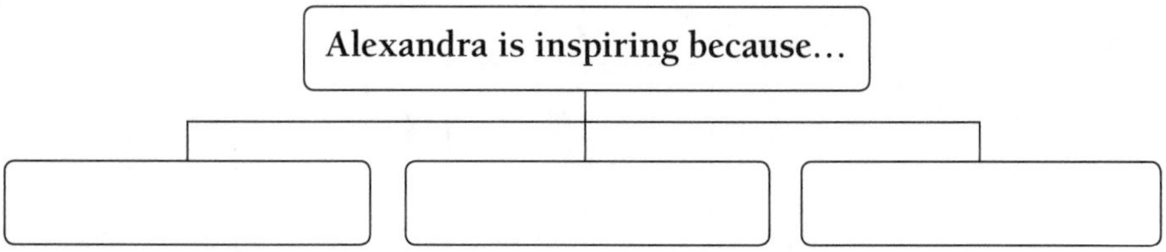

Writing Question:
Now it is time to write. Does ten-year-old artist Alexandra Nechita inspire you? Use the information from your planning page to write an essay explaining how Alexandra uses the ways of using pictures instead of words to inspire. Then tell why Alexandra inspires you personally or why she does not.

Essay Writing Guidelines:
Introduction: Tell what you are going to write about.
Body: Tell how Alexandra uses the ways of using pictures instead of words to inspire.
Reread your writing to make sure the reasons you selected are logically connected.
Conclusion: Tell why or why she does not inspires you personally.
Continue on another page if you need to.

Figure 2.6. Example Planning Page Connecting Two Passages

Complete the chart below in the following two steps:
- Write in the top three boxes three different things that the languages of art can tell us.
- Beneath each response that you wrote in step one, provide a related example of how Alexandra uses art to demonstrate that idea.

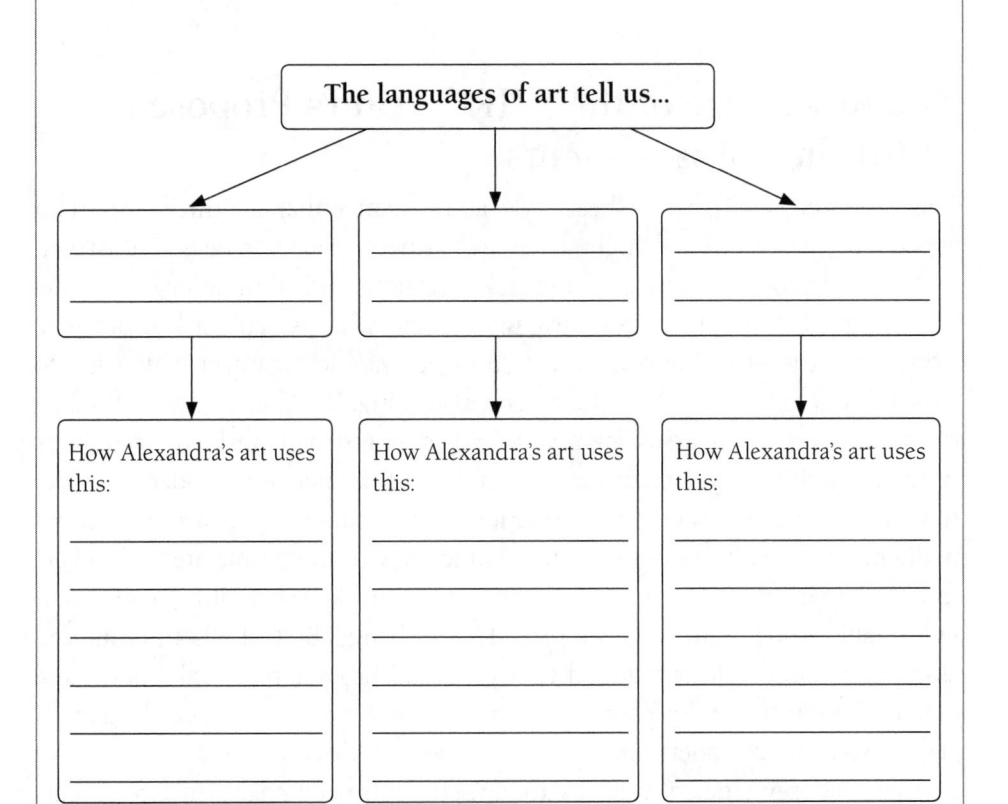

Writing Question on both pieces:

Write a newspaper article encouraging people to attend an art show where Alexandra Nechita is showing her paintings. Use information from BOTH articles that you have read. In your article, be sure to include
- What the languages of art tell you about
- How Alexandra uses the language of art
- How Alexandra uses art to spread her message

Continue on another page if you need to.

level when selecting reading passages for writing assessments. Incorporating two loosely related reading passages is not enough to guide a student to write with clarity and accuracy. Just as improving the legibility of a map would facilitate travel from point A to point B, writing assessments with enhanced interpassage connectivity would enhance student performance outcomes by clarifying the writing tasks.

The Advantage of the WIRC Team's Proposed Thinksheet Assessments

The proposed WIRC thinksheet style assessment enhances three important aspects of the traditional high-stakes assessment: clarity, strategy construct, and student productivity. Clarifying task directions and eliminating distracting illustrations help students to clearly understand what is being asked of them. Converting the planning page into a strategic graphic organizer makes it into a useful tool for constructing the extended writing. By strategically scaffolding the writing tasks, the assessment validity is strengthened: Task connectedness promotes writing connectedness. The end result is increased student productivity and enhanced student performance. By reducing the guesswork, students make more efficient use of their time. Students with more time are more likely to check their work. A strategically enhanced thinksheet writing assessment will enable students to write more and write better. Best of all, an enhanced assessment along with expanded rubrics would provide more valid and more extensive information for planning instruction and would be especially beneficial for struggling readers and writers. Just as today's consumers need to drive high-tech energy-efficient vehicles, today's students need upgraded assessments fine-tuned to measure what they really know and what they can really write.

Self-Assessment

Because they are the ones most affected by instructional decisions, students should be deeply involved in the assessment process. To be active participants, students need to know why they are being assessed and how assessments might affect them. Students should also be guided into self-assessment. Students need to know what the standards or objectives of instruction are (Stiggins, 2004). Students can't work toward a goal if they don't know what it is, what their current capabilities are, or how to take corrective action. As Stiggins (2004) comments,

> We must build classroom environments in which students use assessments to understand what success looks like and how to do better the next time. In effect, we must help students use ongoing classroom assessment to take responsibility for their own academic success. (pp. 25–26)

Standards or objectives tend to be general. The standard should be analyzed into a series of steps that, if followed, will lead to the objective. For instance, the standard "Make predictions, draw conclusions, and make inferences about events and characters" can be broken down into a series of steps. For the prediction portion, steps might include using titles and illustrations to make predictions, using background knowledge combined with information from titles and illustrations to make predictions, using information in the selection to confirm a prediction, altering predictions on the basis of new information, and using information in the section to justify or explain a prediction. For the inference/conclusion component, steps might include using information in the text to make an inference, using details in the article to justify or alter an inference, using information in the text to draw a conclusion, combining information in the article and background knowledge to draw a conclusion, analyzing a conclusion to see if it is logical or likely, and considering several possible conclusions.

As students self-assess, they get to know themselves as learners. They become aware of what things they do well and what things cause them difficulty. They might realize, for instance, that they soak up information as they read, but they don't question its accuracy or fairness. They might then take deliberate steps to slow down and think carefully about what they are reading, or pause after reading and ask critical questions about what they have read.

Feedback

A key element in assessing for learning is to provide feedback (Winters, 2009). The feedback should be timely and specific. The feedback should let the student know what steps he or she might take to reach a specific learning goal. Feedback should not contain information about how the student did in relation to other students, and it should be affirming so that the student feels competent and encouraged. Feedback can be a brief on-the-spot suggestion made as the student is checking a first draft, or it can be lengthier, as when you and the student are conferring about the student's portfolio. The feedback should also help the student self-assess.

Using All Available Resources to Plan Appropriate Instruction

Because comprehension is complex and multifaceted, assessment draws from many sources. No one assessment will provide all the information that is required to plan a program. Assessment can be time consuming, especially if the student has a serious comprehension problem. To make the best use of time, use any information that is available to you. Check the school records for past assessments and any information that might have been provided by previous teachers. In Eduardo's case (the student described at the beginning of this chapter), school records indicated difficulty with retelling in the earliest grades. Retellings were noted as being sketchy, lacking in detail and organization. This suggested difficulty comprehending the textbase and organizing information. Difficulty with listening comprehension was also noted. This indicated that comprehension wasn't just a reading problem. Portfolios can be an especially valuable source of information. The written pieces in Eduardo's portfolios indicated difficulty organizing information and seeing the big picture.

Examine the results of both external and internal tests. External tests are those that are mandated by the school district or state. Eduardo's scores on the Developmental Reading Assessment (DRA) indicated superior decoding but inadequate retelling. Standardized tests typically contain multiple-choice items and provide comparative scores. Knowing how the student compares with other students suggests a level of instruction. If the student's score is significantly below grade level or is below the 40th percentile, then this suggests a more serious problem. Eduardo scored at the average level—52 Normal Curve Equivalent Score—on the Vocabulary subtest of the TerraNova standardized test but below average—36 Normal Curve Equivalent Score—on the comprehension portion of the TerraNova test. (Because they represent equal units, Normal Curve Equivalents are recommended for making comparisons.) Results on the Connecticut Mastery Test (CMT), the state's proficiency test, placed Eduardo in the lowest category. However, his performance was better on the Degrees of Reading Power section of the test, and Eduardo did better on the multiple-choice items than on the items that required constructing responses. Pretests that mirrored the CMT and that were used to plan test preparation activities indicated that Eduardo was having difficulty substantiating and explaining responses. Most of his constructed responses received failing grades. Information from these available sources provides an expanded picture of Eduardo's difficulty with comprehension. By gathering and analyzing a broad spectrum of information, it becomes possible to construct a broad-based plan for instructing Eduardo. That broad-based plan can then be translated into instructional specifics that address the most basic needs.

Identifying the Most Basic Needs

Several pieces of assessment data indicated that Eduardo was experiencing difficulty identifying and deriving main ideas. Noting that a student is having difficulty with main ideas is an important piece of information. However, it is then essential to determine why the student is having difficulty. In a sense, a main idea is a classification statement. It includes all the other sentences in the paragraph. Students who have difficulty determining the main idea typically have difficulty categorizing or seeing similarities and differences. Noting that a student has difficulty with the main idea, the next step is to see how well the student can categorize. You might have the student categorize the following words: *crows*, *robins*, *blue jays*, *eagles* (birds); or tell which of the following sentences includes all the others:

> Buffalo can smell a pool of water that is three miles away.
> Buffalo have sharp senses.
> Buffalo can see moving animals or people that are as far away as a mile.
> Buffalo also have good hearing.

In his first session, it was clear that Eduardo had difficulty categorizing groups of sentences. The next step was to teach Eduardo and see how and under what circumstances he learned. Eduardo had difficulty when the sentences were listed on a sheet of paper. An active hands-on student, Eduardo's performance improved when the sentences were put on cards so that he could manipulate them. The main idea statement was placed at the head of the column and the contributing sentences were placed underneath. Eduardo picked up the concept rapidly and announced at the third session that the sentence exercises were too easy. This indicated that Eduardo had good reasoning ability and was quick to learn. It also indicated that he needed the right level of challenge.

Constructing an Instructional Plan

Testing isn't teaching. The ultimate purpose of assessment is to improve learning. This chapter has explored a variety of formal and informal assessments ranging from observations to constructed responses. Not all of these assessments need to be administered. Select assessments that fit your situation. Don't overtest. Don't administer an assessment if you are not going to use the information it yields, unless, of course, the assessment is mandated. If the assessment is mandated, examine the results to see how you might use the data collected to plan instruction. The ultimate aim of assessment is to improve learning.

ACTION PLAN

- Analyze the demands of the higher level literacy tasks in the curriculum and required tests. Note strategies and skills needed.
- Set a priority of six to eight strategies and skills.
- Determine students' overall reading levels. Use the estimated levels to obtain materials on the appropriate levels.
- Using a variety of measures and informal devices, assess students' comprehension and responding strategies and skills.
- Based on students' needs, set goals.
- Monitor progress and use results to modify the program as needed.

QUESTIONS FOR STUDY AND REFLECTION

1. What comprehension assessments do I currently use? Of all the assessments discussed in this chapter, which ones do I use? Which ones, if any, do I plan to add?

2. As a result of reading this chapter, what changes might I make in the way that I assess higher level reading and writing skills?

3. What are some effective and efficient ways of collecting information on students' higher level literacy skills and strategies?

4. How could I work with an individual student or a small group to use one or more of the assessment measures to obtain additional information on the student's or students' higher level comprehension? How could I then use the information obtained to plan instruction for the student(s)? Observe and reflect on the results and share them with a group.

REFERENCES

Allington, R.L. (2009). *What really matters in response to intervention: Research-based designs.* Boston: Allyn & Bacon.

Applegate, M.D., Quinn, K.B., & Applegate, A.J. (2004). *The critical reading inventory: Assessing students' reading and thinking.* Upper Saddle River, NJ: Pearson Education.

Applegate, M.D., Quinn, K.B., & Applegate, A.J. (2006). Profiles in comprehension. *The Reading Teacher, 60*(1), 48–57. doi:10.1598/RT.60.1.5

Athans, S.K., & Devine, D.A. (2008). *Quality comprehension: A strategic model of reading instruction using read-along guides, grades 3–6.* Newark, DE: International Reading Association.

Beck, I.L., & McKeown, M.G. (2006). *Improving comprehension with questioning the author: A fresh and expanded view of a powerful approach.* New York: Scholastic.

Bond, G.L., Tinker, M.A., Wasson, B.B., & Wasson, J.B. (1994). *Reading difficulties: Their diagnosis and correction* (7th ed.). Boston: Allyn & Bacon.

Calder, L., & Carlson, S.E. (2002). *Using "think alouds" to evaluate deep understanding.* Policy Center on the First Year of College. Retrieved September 23, 2009, from www.uwlax.edu/sotl/tutorial/tutorialstart.htm.

CTB McGraw-Hill. (2004). *New York State Testing Program English Language Arts and Reading Grade 4: 2004.* Monterey, CA: Author.

Diamond, L. & Thorsnes, B.J. (2008). *Assessing reading: Multiple measures: For all educators working to improve reading achievement* (2nd ed.). Novato, CA: Arena Press.

Dewitz, P., & Dewitz, P.K. (2003). They can read the words, but they can't understand: Refining comprehension assessment. *The Reading Teacher, 56*(5), 422–435.

Duffy, G.G., & Roehler, L.R. (1987). Improving reading instruction through the use of responsive elaboration. *The Reading Teacher, 40*(6), 514–519.

Farr, R.C. (2009). *Planning think-along activities.* Retrieved September 23, 2009, from www.rogerfarr.com/mcr/taactivities/taactivities.html

Fiene, J., & McMahon, S. (2007). Assessing comprehension: A classroom-based process. *The Reading Teacher, 60*(5), 406–417. doi:10.1598/RT.60.5.1

Florida Department of Education (2008). *Cognitive complexity classification of FCAT test items.* Tallahassee, FL: Author. Retrieved September 23, 2009, from fcat.fldoe.org./pdf/cog_complexity-fv31.pdf.

Gunning, T.G. (2008). *Developing higher-level literacy in all students: Building reading, reasoning, and responding.* Boston: Allyn & Bacon.

Gunning, T.G. (2010). *Assessing and correcting reading and writing difficulties* (4th ed.). Boston: Allyn & Bacon.

Hampton, S., & Resnick, L.B. (2009). *Reading and writing with understanding: Comprehension in fourth and fifth grades.* Washington, DC: National Center on Education and the Economy; Newark, DE: International Reading Association.

Hirsch, E.D. (2006, Spring). Building knowledge: The case for bringing content into the language arts block and for a knowledge-rich curriculum core for all children. *American Educator, 30*(1) 8–29, 50–51. Available online at www.aft.org/pubs-reports/american_educator/issues/spring06/hirsch.htm

Hosp, M.L., Hosp, J.L., & Howell, K.W. (2007). *The ABCs of CBM: A practical guide to curriculum-based measurement.* New York: Guilford.

Israel, S.E., & Massey, D. (2005). Metacognitive think-alouds: Using the gradual release model with middle school students. In S.E. Israel, C.C. Block, K.L. Bauserman, & K. Kinnucan-Welsch (Eds.), *Metacognition in literacy learning: Theory, assessment, instruction, and professional development* (pp. 183–198). Mahwah, NJ: Erlbaum.

Kintsch, W., & Kintsch, E. (2005). Comprehension. In S.G. Paris & S.A. Stahl (Eds.), *Current issues in reading comprehension and assessment* (pp. 71–92). Mahwah, NJ: Erlbaum.

Klingner, J.K., Vaughn, S., & Boardman, A. (2007). *Teaching reading comprehension to students with learning disabilities.* New York: Guilford.

Leslie, L., & Caldwell, J. (2006). *Qualitative reading inventory-4.* Boston: Allyn & Bacon/Longman.

Lipson, M.Y., & Wixson, K.K. (2008). *Assessment and instruction of reading and writing difficulties* (4th ed.). Boston: Allyn & Bacon.

Loxterman, J.A., Beck, I.L., & McKeown, M.G. (1994). The effects of thinking aloud during reading on students' comprehension of more or less coherent text. *Reading Research Quarterly, 29*(4), 353–367. doi:10.2307/747784

Mokhtari, K., & Reichard, C.A. (2002). Assessing students' metacognitive awareness of reading strategies. *Journal of Educational Psychology, 94*(2), 249–259. doi:10.1037/0022-0663.94.2.249

Mondo Publishing. (2004). *Bookshop.* New York: Author.

Monti, D., & Cicchetti, G. (1996). *TARA: Think-aloud reading assessment.* Austin, TX: Steck-Vaughn Berrent.

National Assessment Governing Board. (2008). *Reading framework for the 2009 National Assessment of Educational Progress.* Washington, DC: Author.

New York State Department of Education. (2000). *New York State testing program scoring guide.* Albany: Author.

Pearson, P.D., & Hamm, D. (2005). The assessment of reading comprehension: A review of practices—past, present, and future. In S.G. Paris & S.A. Stahl (Eds.), *Current issues in reading comprehension and assessment* (pp. 13–69). Mahwah, NJ: Erlbaum.

Pearson, P.D., & Johnson, D.D. (1978). *Teaching reading comprehension.* New York: Holt, Rinehart and Winston.

Phelps, D.R. (2008, December). *WIRC works: Comparative case study final analysis.* Paper presented at the National Reading Conference, Orlando, FL.

Phelps, D.R. & Collins, J.L. (2008). *WIRC think-sheets work: A comparative case study of two fifth grade classrooms.* Buffalo, NY: WIRC, University at Buffalo.

Raphael, T.E. (1984). Teaching learners about sources of information for answering comprehension questions. *Journal of Reading, 27*(4), 303–311.

Raphael, T.E. (1986). Teaching question/answer relationships, revisited. *The Reading Teacher, 39*(6), 516–522.

Schmitt, M.C. (1990). A questionnaire to measure children's awareness of strategic reading processes. *The Reading Teacher, 43*(7), 454–461.

Stiggins, R. (2004). New assessment beliefs for a new school mission. *Phi Delta Kappan, 86*(1), 22–27.

Valencia, S.W. (2001). *Integrated theme tests, Levels 2.1–2.2. Houghton Mifflin Reading.* Boston: Houghton Mifflin.

Wade, S.E. (1990). Using think alouds to assess comprehension. *The Reading Teacher, 43*(7), 442–451.

Webb, N.L., Alt, M., Ely, R., & Vesperman, B. (2005). *Web alignment tool (WAT) training manual draft version 1.1.* Madison: University of Wisconsin, Wisconsin Center for Education

Research. Retrieved August 31, 2009, from wat.wceruw.org/index.aspx

Winters, D. (2009, February). *Multiple pathways to literacy: Using data collected from higher level formative assessments to inform instruction.* Paper presented at the 54th International Reading Association Convention West, Phoenix, AZ.

Yuill, N., & Oakhill, J. (1991). *Children's problems in text comprehension: An experimental investigation.* New York: Cambridge University Press.

LITERATURE CITED

Nodset, J.L. (1963). *Who took the farmer's hat?* New York: Harper.

CHAPTER 3

Using Discussions to Promote Striving Readers' Higher Level Comprehension of Literary Texts

Kristin Bourdage Reninger and Ian A.G. Wilkinson

In this chapter, we describe a classroom-based study that examined the ways striving readers in the fourth and fifth grades used the social interactions of discussions about literary texts to cultivate their literate experiences and higher level comprehension (Reninger, 2007). We also make suggestions about implementing discussions to promote higher level comprehension. We use the term *striving reader* to describe a student who has scored below grade level on state, district, and classroom reading assessments. Although the reading field has other terms to describe these readers, such as *struggling reader*, *low-achieving reader*, or *at-risk reader*, we use striving reader because the term implies these students are working toward acquiring strategic reading skills.

We describe eight striving fourth- and fifth-grade readers in this chapter. They all scored below their grade levels on state, district, and classroom reading assessments but did not score low enough, from the districts' points of view, to qualify for extra reading support. With few exceptions, they were good word callers and fluent readers, yet they struggled to comprehend beyond basic recall and literal renderings of the grade-level texts in their classrooms.

Background of the Study

The aim of this study (Reninger, 2007) was to explore and describe intermediate-level students' participation and talk during text discussions. The first author spent 30 consecutive weeks of the 2005–2006 school year as a participant observer (Spradley, 1980) in one fourth- and one fifth-grade classroom in two different medium-sized school districts in the midwestern United States.

Table 3.1. Study Participants and Data Sources

Characteristics of the Study	Grade 4	Grade 5
Number of students	18	24
Number of striving readers	5	3
Number of teachers	1	1
Number of classroom observations	33	30
Number of recorded discussions	36	26
Number of transcribed discussions	11	11
Number of semistructured interviews	14	14

Each week in the classrooms, she video- or audiorecorded discussions about text, interviewed students and teachers about their discussion practices, and observed the discussion practices and the language arts blocks in which they were conducted. In all, she recorded and analyzed 62 peer- and teacher-led discussions that ranged in length from 15 to 35 minutes. Of the 62 discussions, she transcribed 22 discussions of average length (20–30 minutes) for deeper analyses. The focus of the analyses was on the interaction patterns and utterances of five fourth-grade striving readers and three fifth-grade striving readers and their peers during those discussions. The two teacher participants in the study, Mrs. Ross and Mrs. Pearson (all names are pseudonyms), were experienced teachers who were in their second year of integrating text-based discussions into their classroom practices. Table 3.1 summarizes these data.

Reading Comprehension: A Meaning-Making Process

Reading comprehension is an active and multidimensional process of meaning making (Duke, 2005) that leads to understanding and insight (Hatano & Inagaki, 1991). It has been conceptualized as a result of the interactions between several factors: the reader, the text, the activity (e.g., the purpose and process of reading), and the context (RAND Reading Study Group, 2002). In an ideal reading situation, these factors interact in constructive ways to support the reader's understanding (RAND Reading Study Group, 2002). The following example is a hypothetical classroom-based reading event that portrays the kinds of interactions between the reader, text, activity, and context that promote comprehension.

Imagine a fifth-grade teacher and her class have just finished a unit in social studies about immigration in the United States. To extend student learning about this topic, the teacher designs an independent reading project. The students must choose and read a novel about an "immigrant experience." The novels are historical fiction, a genre that the teacher had introduced earlier in the year, and the vocabulary of the novels is appropriate for fifth graders.

A male student, who describes himself as a good reader, chooses a novel about a 12-year-old Irish boy and recent immigrant to the United States. The student had done well on his immigration project in social studies, so he had acquired background knowledge about the topic. And, as indicated by an informal reading assessment, the student is a strategic reader.

In this example, the background and experience of the reader are a good fit with the text and the activity. The reader has strategic reading skills and adequate background knowledge, both of which would interact well with the content of the novel and with its familiar vocabulary and genre. In addition, the activity or purpose for reading is clear, so the student knows why and how he needs to read the text. Provided the student reads the novel, the reader, text, and activity factors in this scenario would interact in productive ways, likely supporting the student's comprehension.

For many striving readers, the interactions between the reader, text, and activity are not always as productive, which means good comprehension is not always the outcome of a reading event. Sometimes striving readers lack or have yet to acquire the kinds of knowledge, skills, and dispositions that sustain comprehension of grade-level texts (e.g., motivation, metacognitive thinking, strategic reading skills, decoding skills). Likewise, text factors, such as the vocabulary load and text structure, may outweigh the reader factors, overwhelming the striving reader. And if the purpose of reading is unclear, striving readers may not know which strategies they should use to try to make sense of the text.

Now reimagine the fifth-grade scenario with a striving reader who has the motivation to read the novel and is a strong decoder of text, yet she has difficulty integrating her background knowledge with information from the story. She may comprehend the novel at a basic level but would likely struggle to comprehend the text in higher level ways. In other words, the interactions between reader and text are sometimes not sufficient for comprehension and this, along with other conditions such as poor instruction, poor assessment practices, and the increased complexity of reading tasks, can contribute to reading difficulties in the intermediate grades (Allington, 2001; Raphael & Au, 2005).

Higher Level Reading Comprehension

Comprehending at higher levels requires a repertoire of thinking skills such as problem solving, connecting personally to a text, and reflecting on one's reading. We define higher level comprehension as a way of thinking about text that goes beyond a literal understanding or clear-cut interpretation. Literal comprehension comprises an adequate, yet basic, understanding of what the author stated. This is a lower form of comprehension because it requires straightforward thinking about text. On the other hand, Resnick (1987) considers a "higher" form of thinking to be a process that involves "elaborating, adding complexity, and going beyond the given" (p. 42). As such, when readers distill the implicit meanings, check the plausibility of those meanings, and create connections between the text and their prior knowledge and personal experiences, they have gone beyond the given details, comprehending the text at a higher level. Other ways to think of higher level comprehension include, but are not limited to, reasoning about text, interpreting text, and evaluating text.

Our perspective of higher level comprehension is connected to the National Assessment of Educational Progress (NAEP) reading framework for 2009 (National Assessment Governing Board, 2007). The framework identifies three "cognitive targets," which are defined as "mental processes or kinds of thinking that underlie reading comprehension" (National Assessment Governing Board, 2007, p. 35). The first cognitive target is "locate and recall." Readers engaged in this process are able to identify main ideas and major elements of the text, such as the story's problem or the main character. The second cognitive target is "integrate and interpret," which means readers think about the text in ways that include examining relationships, asking questions, making connections, and considering alternatives. The third cognitive target of reading is "critique and evaluate." Within this process, readers consider the text critically and synthesize their views of the text with their experiences as well as with other texts. Together, the three cognitive targets define different levels of comprehension in which a reader may engage. For the purposes of this chapter, the kinds of thinking that go beyond locate and recall signify higher level comprehension.

Higher level comprehension is important for striving readers because intermediate-level educators expect their students to read more challenging texts, to read more often on their own, and to learn from their reading (Chall & Curtis, 2003). If students are to learn from their reading and to read challenging texts more often on their own, they indeed should be equipped to locate and recall main points of the text, but they should also be able to infer implicit meanings and to reason about new ideas that extend their thinking of the text. In short, the goals of intermediate-level reading need to be in line with the expectations we have of all readers. This means even if intermediate-level readers struggle with an aspect of their reading skills (e.g., decoding), they should still practice the thinking skills that undergird higher level comprehension of text (Fisher & Ivey, 2006).

The next several sections illustrate the important role discussions played for a group of striving readers and their classmates. The discussions provided an opportunity for them to engage in and practice forms of higher level thinking about text. For the striving readers in this study, this promoted their higher level comprehension.

What Are Discussions About Text?

Discussions about text are conversations during which participants ask and answer questions of one another and the text to construct meaning and comprehend the text in new and better ways. To do this, participants share ideas, put forth alternatives, and challenge ideas to provoke new ways of thinking and understanding. In general, participants in discussions about text learn about literacy and develop as readers because their social interactions "provide opportunities for the internalization and subsequent utilization of literate modes of thinking and communicating" (Chang-Wells & Wells, 1993, p. 87).

A defining feature of discussions in classroom contexts is the distinct pattern of exchanges between the students and the teacher (Almasi, 1996). If s stands for the student and t stands for the teacher, the pattern of who talks and when in a classroom discussion looks something like this: s-s-s-t-s-s-t-s-s-s-t-s. This kind of pattern is referred to as a *discourse pattern*, and in a genuine discussion, the pattern is open and inclusive, meaning students talk freely to one another without bidding for a turn from the teacher (Chinn, Anderson, & Waggoner, 2001). The teacher is a participant and facilitator during discussions, present and active, yet not the mediator of the students' participation and thinking.

By contrast, a discourse pattern lacking the qualities of discussion looks something like this: t-s-t-s-t-s-t-s-t-s. This interaction pattern is known as recitation (Cazden & Beck, 2003), and its significant feature is the heavy presence of the teacher whose role it is to mediate every student turn. During recitations, the teacher asks almost all the questions and the students usually raise their hands and wait for the teacher to call on them before speaking. This means the teacher controls the topics of conversation and, often, uses the questions to lead the students toward a preconceived interpretation of the text. Because the teacher has a dominant role in recitations, students come to view the goal of the activity as to supply right answers (Dewey, 1916). As a result, students tend to become passive, letting a few classmates raise their hands to speak for the entire group (Nystrand, 1997; Worthy & Beck, 1995).

A genuine discussion encourages students to be active and responsive during the conversation, talking and listening to one another, asking and answering questions, and building upon one another's ideas (Chinn et al., 2001; Mercer, 2000; Nystrand, 1997). Consequently, students become facilitators of their own conversation, drawing on their interests in the text and their prior knowledge and personal experiences to ask questions, to solve problems, and to develop knowledge and understanding together (Almasi, 1996; Bridges, 1979; Langer, 1995; Nystrand, 1997). Because the students share control of the discussion with the teacher, they view the activity as a process in which they have a role in making meaning and learning to comprehend text as a result of their collective efforts (Nystrand, 1997).

The following dialogue is an example of a genuine discussion about text that took place in the fourth-grade classroom during a guided reading lesson. It is an excerpt of a transcript of Mrs. Ross and six students discussing *Weasel* (DeFelice, 1990). Mrs. Ross's instructional goal on that day was to discuss several chapters of the story to promote higher levels of comprehension. *Weasel* is a novel about two children trying to rescue their father from a hunting accident in Ohio in 1839. A theme of the story is the implications of land acquisition by white pioneers for Native American people and culture. In the excerpt, the teacher and the students take up an earlier question about the author's use of the term *savage*.

Mrs. Ross: Let's look on page 42 because the book has a word in there, when we talk about the word *savage*, and on this page, in the second paragraph down, um, let's read that part. Um, Christy, can you read [*reads from text*] "I thought about Weasel cutting out..." as we start that section right there? Can you read that for us?

Christy:	[*reads from text*] "I thought about Weasel cutting out Ezra's tongue and killing Indians and poor settlers and seemed to me has, he has, he was more a savage than anybody I'd ever heard of. Couldn't white folks be savages, too?"
Thomas:	I don't think the Indians were savages in the first place.
Jack:	Uh huh.
Thomas:	[*exclaiming*] What is a savage?
Jack:	Someone who kills somebody.
Brent:	[*simultaneous*] That—
Ashley:	[*simultaneous*] That's, there's different meanings to it because different people have opinions about what it means.
Thomas:	But what about THIS meaning? What does this meaning mean that they're savages?
Ashley:	Um, it says—
Mrs. Ross.:	[*interrupts quietly*] That's a good idea, Thomas.
Ashley:	I think that what it means in here, the savages, in here [*taps book with hand*], it means that someone is just so ruthless to kill someone and they don't even think bad about it. And that, the Indians, they weren't savages at all, even if it says so in this book. 'Cause they use, they only killed what they needed.
Jack:	[*simultaneous*] Yeah, the animals—
Thomas:	[*simultaneous*] They didn't use them over time.
Ashley:	They didn't stock up.
Jasmine:	The Indians didn't kill, they didn't kill all—
Ashley:	[*interrupts*] And if they did kill over what they needed, they used every single bit of it.

The students' conversation is a discussion of the text for several reasons. First, the discourse pattern is open and inclusive (i.e., *t-s-s-s-s-s*). The students talked to one another, controlled their own turn-taking, asked questions of the text, and worked together, exchanging multiple views and interpretations. They created a collective understanding of the word *savage*. Likewise, Mrs. Ross's comments in this episode are purposefully inconspicuous. Her comments positioned her as a facilitator who encourages looking back to the text for information. These qualities illustrate how students work together in a discussion, constructing new understanding and improving their comprehension.

Characteristics of Productive Talk During Discussions

In this section, we review evidence-based features of talk that appear to be reliable indicators of students' higher level thinking and that might contribute to their higher level comprehension. Drawing from a large-scale research project on text-based discussion practices, Soter et al. (2008) identify several elements of productive talk during discussions about literary texts. When students and the teacher discuss text, there are features or elements of their talk that demonstrate that students are thinking in higher level ways about the text. And if they are thinking in higher level ways about text, the students are engaging in the kinds of thinking that we believe undergird their higher level comprehension of text.

Soter et al. (2008) argue that particular elements of talk could serve as proximal indices of student learning and higher level thinking because there is good theoretical warrant for believing the features are linked to higher level comprehension, and there is empirical research demonstrating such connections. According to Soter et al., the following elements of talk during discussions about text serve as indicators of student higher level thinking and comprehension: authentic questions and uptake (Nystrand, 1997); higher level thinking questions that elicit generalization, analysis, and speculation (Nystrand, 1997); elaborated explanations (Webb, 1992); reasoning words (Wegerif & Mercer, 1997); exploratory talk (Mercer, 2000); and questions that elicit extratextual connections (affective responses, intertextual connections, and references to previously shared knowledge). The first author added references to text (Anderson et al., 2001) as an additional connection during the study. In effect, these elements of talk characterize productive discussions about text in terms of what might need to be asked and said during discussions to facilitate higher level comprehension. Table 3.2 portrays these elements within two broad categories, questions teachers and students ask and what the questions elicit from students.

Table 3.3 shows an excerpt from a transcript of a peer-led, small-group discussion with coded indicators of higher level thinking. The excerpt is from a discussion by a group of four fifth graders (Erica is a striving reader) about "Victor" by James Howe (1995). "Victor" is a short story about Cody, a boy who

Table 3.2. Elements of Productive Talk During Discussion About Text

Elements of Productive Talk	Examples
Questions (from teachers or students)	
Authentic question	Is there something about the character that pulls your thinking in a certain direction?
Uptake (follow-up question)	Why do you think that?
Higher level thinking question	How do we know that Victor could be an angel?
Responses and Comments (from students)	
Higher level thinking (e.g., generalization, analysis, speculation)	Victor could be an angel because only Cody sees him.
Affective response	I remember when something like that [event from the story] happened to me at my friend's house.
Intertextual response	I saw something like this on the Discovery Channel. They said dreams were a "portal to another realm."
Shared knowledge response	This is like what we were talking about in social studies.
Reference to text	No, I don't think so because it said on page 6 that she didn't want to go to the picnic.
Elaborated explanation	I think that what it means in here, the savages, in here [*taps book with hand*], it means that someone is just so ruthless to kill someone and they don't even think bad about it. And that, the Indians, they weren't savages at all, even if it says so in this book. 'Cause they use, they only killed what they needed.
Exploratory talk	**Jack:** He would have said something. **Thomas:** Yeah, and Rye would probably say, "You know what, Poppy? Did you know Ragweed is my brother and he did die from Ocax and gotten eaten" and all that, and he'd probably be that important. He'd be that sad but he would tell Poppy about it. **Ben:** Yeah, but if my brother would have died, I would never have speaked about him ever again. **Trevor:** But maybe— **Thomas:** [*interrupts*] Yeah, but there's no crying in here [the book].

(continued)

Table 3.2. Elements of Productive Talk During Discussion About Text
(*continued*)

Elements of Productive Talk	Examples
Exploratory talk	**Jack**: If my sister died, I would have said something if nobody knew I was her brother. **Trevor:** Maybe he was his little brother and because usually little brother and little sisters get all the attention, so he didn't care about him. **Thomas:** Didn't what? **Jack:** Or maybe Ragweed and Rye never seen each other for a long time and they forgot about each other. **Ben:** What if they were best friends? **Jack:** But don't you think he might have still said something?
Reasoning words (e.g., because, maybe, if, so, could, would, agree/disagree, I think, how)	I agree. Maybe he was his little brother and because usually little brother and little sisters get all the attention, so he didn't care about him.

Adapted from Soter et al., 2008.

is in the hospital and unconscious on his 13th birthday. Cody, inspired by the ceiling tiles above his bed, creates a world he refers to as "The Land Above." However, the real story is about Victor, a mysterious person who visits Cody and gives him courage to pull through his illness.

The excerpt illustrates students' talk in terms of the elements that indicate higher level thinking about the story. In addition, the excerpt shows how students might learn about higher level comprehension from one another in the context of a discussion. For example, Nicole's responses in turns 7 and 9 reveal to the others how she made inferences about Victor's identity, connecting details across the story. And in turn 10, Evan built on Nicole's proposal, which characterizes the typical way the social interactions of discussions mediated the students' thinking and extended their understanding of the stories. Likewise, the excerpt characterizes the cooperative efforts that emerge when the norms of productive talk are in place. There is a real sense in the excerpt that the students were working together, listening and responding to one another to coconstruct an understanding of the story.

Table 3.3. Excerpt of a Coded Transcript

Turns From the Transcript	Indicators of Higher Level Thinking Coded in the Turn
1. Nicole: Okay. Alright, first question...uhm. Who is Victor?	Authentic question; higher level thinking question
2. Erica: Uhm...	
3. Nicole: Go ahead.	
4. Erica: Okay, I think Victor is a thing from the ceiling, I forget what that was called.	Generalization/analysis
5. Alex: The Land Above.	Generalization/analysis; Speculation
6. Erica: Uhm.... He used...yeah...he used his imagination for the ceiling people so maybe... he made up Victor...and it could be the old man who died and told him the stories...his spirit could change his name like...yeah... that's pretty much it.	Generalization/analysis; Reference-to-text; Elaborated explanation
7. Nicole: Uhm...I thought Victor was God, and the Land Above was Heaven, because uhm... Victor...because...uhm...in the text it says he was old which you know, God...two thousand years...so the last time he visited Earth was 2006 years ago—	Generalization/analysis Generalization/analysis; Reference-to-text
8. Alex: [interrupts] Yeah, but even then he only partly visited Earth.	
9. Nicole: And um and so he's very old and he was strong but he didn't say...but it said he wasn't strong like "bodybuilding strong" he was strong like a strong man like he was...he was like—	Authentic question; higher level thinking question; generalization/analysis
10. Evan: You mean like in the heart and soul?	

Striving Readers' Higher Level Thinking During Discussions

To identify striving readers' talk that indicated their higher level thinking, the first author used a coding scheme adapted from the work of Soter et al. (2008) on 22 transcripts of discussions in the research study (Reninger, 2007) described at the beginning of the chapter. The coding work confirmed that all of the striving readers thought in higher level ways about the texts during the discussions. For instance, Colin, a fourth-grade student reading at a second-grade level, made an important and thoughtful affective connection (a connection between the text and his personal experiences) in relation to the main character of *Weasel* (DeFelice, 1990). He said,

> Yeah, I did that once when I was putting this big earring in my ear once. And it all started to go black.

In another example of higher level thinking, Elena, a strong word caller but poor comprehender, made an inference in the *Ruby Holler* (Creech, 2002) discussion that showed generalization and analysis. She said,

> I think that Z is Dallas's and Florida's father because he was married to their mom and he might know 'cause he hasn't told them [*unclear*].

These examples are representative of the kinds of comments that all of the striving readers made during the discussions. This suggests striving readers can and do think in higher level ways about text, and they indeed participate in discussions in ways that demonstrate their higher level thinking about text. But to what extent did the striving readers ask questions or make comments that were indicative of higher level thinking during the discussions? In a sample of eight typical discussions in each of the two classrooms, the first author calculated the frequency with which striving readers participated, asked questions, and made comments indicative of higher level thinking. Table 3.4 displays the number of turns (i.e., number of times students participated in the discussion), the number of authentic questions they asked during the discussions, and the incidence of the elements of their talk that indicated higher level thinking.

The data shown in the table suggest that discussions about text might provide meaningful instructional activities for striving readers because they provide students the opportunities to practice and engage in the kinds of thinking that undergird higher level comprehension. In two different classrooms, all of the striving readers asked genuine questions or made numerous comments that reflected higher level thinking about text (e.g., analyses, speculations, references to text) during these discussions. This is important because higher level thinking about text is necessary for enabling readers to move beyond a literal interpretation of text and to generate higher level comprehension. We do not yet know what is optimal in terms of the number of indicators of higher level thinking a student ought to make in a discussion. Likewise, we do not yet know which indicators of higher level thinking matter more for comprehension. These are areas for future research.

Table 3.4. Frequency Counts for Striving Readers' Total Number of Turns, Authentic Questions, and Indicators of Higher Level Thinking in Eight Typical Discussions

Student Name	Fourth-Grade Students					Fifth-Grade Students		
	Colin	Elena	Jack	Lucas	Matthew	Erica	Derek	Mia
Total turns	180	65	350	250	108	273	53	248
Authentic questions	9	9	9	14	0	11	2	12
Indicators of Higher Level Thinking								
Generalization/analysis	50	27	105	46	42	83	9	67
Speculation	27	15	75	10	16	23	4	25
Affective connection	4	0	13	5	1	5	0	5
Intertextual connection	1	0	0	1	0	5	0	1
Shared knowledge connection	0	0	3	0	0	0	0	0
Reference to text	4	4	11	5	4	13	1	10
Elaborated explanation	0	1	12	0	7	8	0	2

The Mediating Potential of Talk for Higher Level Comprehension

The frequency counts of higher level thinking comments demonstrate that striving readers can and do engage in higher level thinking during discussions about text. A more significant finding from the study, however, was the way the discussions transformed the striving readers' initial levels of comprehension. In discussions in both classrooms, the striving readers used the dialogue during discussions as a tool to improve their initial levels of understanding and to generate interpretations of the texts. A typical example of this phenomenon occurred in a fourth-grade discussion about the novel *A Lion to Guard Us* (Bulla, 1981).

A Lion to Guard Us is a story set in England during colonial times. A servant of a wealthy and unlikable homeowner dies and leaves her three children in the custody of the homeowner, Mistress Trippett. Amanda, the oldest child, devises a plan to use what little money her mother had to sail to Virginia. In the excerpt below, Mrs. Ross and the students in a guided reading group discuss a part of the story where Amanda asks Mistress Trippett for the money but gets thrown out of the house for her daring request. Lucas, Elena, and Matthew are striving readers in the group.

During the discussion, Lucas used the dialogue to move beyond a literal understanding of the story. He built upon other students' responses and used the teacher's authentic question to construct a plausible interpretation of the story. Lucas's comments demonstrate the way the dialogue served as a vehicle for mediating his thinking and fostering his higher level comprehension:

1. Mrs. Ross: Who asked who for money?

2. Matthew: Amanda.

3. Elena: Amanda asked Mrs. Trippet for the money.

4. Lucas: Amanda asked Mrs. Trippet for the money to get on the ship, but—

5. Matthew: And her son, um, kicked her out.

6. Lucas: But she, but she stole all the money from her purse.

7. Ben: Yeah, didn't the big fat chubby dude—

8. Lucas: Randall!

9. Ben: Randall, yeah, kick them out?

10. Matthew: Yeah.

11. Lucas: Yeah, he picked them up and threw them out.

12. Mrs. Ross: But why?

13. Matthew: And then he—

14. Lucas: Because he's, he's because he said [*paraphrasing the text*], "How dare you make blah, blah," [*indistinct*] and then she fainted.

15. Ben: Yeah, didn't he say to NEVER show your face in here again?

16. Matthew: Yeah. [*reads from text*] "*Get out, and don't ever show your face here again!*"

17. Lucas: There! That's the problem. Randall has a very bad temper issue.

This excerpt shows the potential of discussions for striving readers' higher level comprehension. Lucas seemed to use the dialogue as a tool for his own thinking, allowing his classmates' comments to inform his emerging interpretation of the story. For example, Lucas and the other students in the group recalled the literal details of the story (turns 1–5) and then started to build an interpretation when Mrs. Ross asked an authentic follow-up question, "But why?" (turn 12). This question led to further problem-solving (turns 14–16) and then to Lucas's comment about Randall's "bad temper issue."

The proposition about Randall's temper issue is a plausible and creative interpretation, likely based on this character's angry and violent outbursts in the story, some of which Ben and Matthew reported in lines 15 and 16. It is Lucas's reaction in line 17, when he said, "There!," that implies Ben's and Matthew's comments had shaped his thinking. In other words, Lucas may have constructed his own, original interpretation of the story because of what the others had said during the discussion. This kind of evidence of the mediating potential of talk occurred often in the discussions in the study, supporting our argument that the talk contributed to striving readers' higher level thinking and comprehension.

Many striving readers reported in interviews after discussions that the discussions helped them think better about the text, confirming what we noticed in the transcripts. For example, in small-group interviews with all the students toward the end of the school year, the first author asked students to reflect on their year spent discussing texts. In one of the group interviews, Derek, a striving reader, recalled a particular discussion event that helped him construct an understanding of James Howe's (1995) "Victor":

Kristin: Can you think of a time a discussion helped you understand something in school?

Derek: Yeah. Uh. The "Victor" thing.

Alex: It helped me understand that story a lot better.

Derek: It helped me understand who Victor was. Someone said the 80-year-old man in our group and someone said, uh, Cody. I don't know why, but...um...I said that, I think I said that... [*pause*]. Well, at first I said Victor was the 80-year-old man but then they talked and they made me change my mind like just about the other question, like one opinion, then I had one, then they talked and they said it was Cody, and I agreed. Cody had this box and it was from Victor so it had to be him since he had a box already....

Kristin: So, you changed your mind?

Derek: Yeah. Big time...big, big, big, big time.

Derek's words suggest the dialogue during the "Victor" discussion became a tool for improving his understanding of the story. When Derek said, "and then they talked," he is recounting exactly how the dialogue transformed his thinking. Almost all of the striving readers reported similar experiences of their participation in discussions, suggesting that the discussions indeed became a tool for understanding the stories. In many cases, thinking manifested in the talk included interpretations and evaluations of the text, which is the kind of thinking that generates higher level comprehension.

Getting Started With Discussions

The model of discussion employed in the study and presented in this chapter is known as Quality Talk (Wilkinson, Soter, & Murphy, 2010). Quality Talk comprises elements of discourse (discussed earlier in the chapter as productive features of talk), an instructional framework, a set of pedagogical principles, and suggestions for teacher modeling and scaffolding that promote productive talk about text (see www.quality-talk.org). Drawing on Mrs. Ross's and Mrs. Pearson's own implementations and interpretations of Quality Talk, we discuss three broad instructional techniques that will help you get discussions up and running in your classrooms:

1. Use ground rules to establish the norms of productive talk.
2. Use authentic questions and follow-up, uptake questions to give students opportunities to engage in productive talk.
3. Use informal assessment strategies during discussions, listening for evidence of the elements of talk that indicate higher level thinking.

Establishing the Norms of Productive Discussions

Students are more likely to talk productively about text and to engage actively in conversation if they understand the norms for productive discussions. One way to foster these norms is to explain, model, and practice a set of ground rules for discussion. The original ground rules described here come from the research of Mercer and his colleagues (e.g., Mercer, 1995, 2000; Wegerif, Mercer, & Dawes, 1999) and their efforts to motivate and improve classroom talk in British schools. Table 3.5 shows Mercer's (1995) ground rules for exploratory talk juxtaposed with Mrs. Ross's reframing of those ground rules in student-friendly language.

The ground rules are important because they become a set of "handles" that the students can reach for during discussions (Reninger & Rehark, 2009). For

**Table 3.5. Two Versions of Ground Rules for Discussions
and Examples of Students Using the Ground Rules**

Mercer's (1995) Ground Rules of Exploratory Talk	
Proposals are stated. Evaluate proposals. Challenge ideas. Consider each other's views.	Provide reasons to back up claims and opinions. Give alternative opinions and ideas. If appropriate, participants ask each other for reasons. Seek agreement.

Mrs. Ross's Ground Rules of Exploratory Talk	
How to Talk and Listen Share your thinking (use words such as "I think," "because," "maybe," "what if," "I agree"). Backup your opinions with reasons and/or evidence from the text. It's okay to challenge ideas or to disagree with an idea.	It's okay to change your mind. Ask each other questions. Listen to each other so you can build on others' ideas. Look at the people in the group. "Jump in" the conversation, if there is a space. Invite others into the conversation.

Examples of Students Using the Ground Rules

Erica: <u>I do disagree with her</u> [Share your thinking]<u>'cause like, um 'cause like</u> he said that he kind of didn't want him there but then he did and then <u>I think</u> [Share your thinking] Victor would have mentioned something and wouldn't come if he [Cody] said he didn't want him there but then he did."

Nicole: Um...I thought Victor was God, and the Land Above was Heaven, because um... Victor...because...um...<u>in the text it says he was old which you know,</u> [Backup your opinions with reasons and evidence from the text] God...two thousand years...so the last time he visited Earth was 2006 years ago

Christy: And he got in jail for playing it. [*indistinct*] and then they were putting cuffs on him, but then he knocked one of the police officers down, so he had to go to jail.

Lucas: <u>Yeah, he knocked one of the cops down...with his guitar.</u> [Listen to each other so you can build on others' ideas]

Matthew: <u>Yeah, I sort of disagree with myself.</u> [It's okay to change your mind]

Teacher: You do?

Matthew: [*overlapping*] Yeah, 'cause it—

Teacher: [*overlapping*] Okay, you're changing your mind, huh?

Matthew: Yeah, because if it [she] was their mom—

Ashley: That's, there's different meanings to it because different people have opinions—

Thomas: <u>But what about THIS meaning? What does this meaning mean that they're savages?</u> [Ask each other questions]

Jack: <u>I also agree with Thomas and I disagree with Trevor. Because if Rye probably would have said something if</u>—[It's okay to challenge ideas or to disagree with an idea]

example, by knowing that "share your thinking" and "ask questions" are ground rules for discussions, students are equipped and inclined to reach for phrases in their talk such as *I think* and *I agree*, or to ask questions such as *Why do you think that?* Also, knowing general conversation rules, such as "jump in when there's a space" or "look at the person who is talking," reminds students to wait for a turn to speak and to listen to their classmates.

Mrs. Ross and Mrs. Pearson both coached their students in these ground rules, modeling them in minilessons and reinforcing them during discussions. After some practice with the ground rules in the fall of the school year, the discussions in both classrooms resembled high-quality, thought-provoking conversations. The discussions were generally on topic, focused on the text, and adult-like in that the students often listened to and built upon one another's comments. We believe that when students understand the ground rules and come to see them as part of their goals for talking, the discussions become instructive and supportive of collective and individual efforts to understand the text. As the norms and ground rules become routine, teachers can begin to focus on listening for the elements of productive talk that indicate higher level thinking and comprehension of the text.

Asking Questions to Promote Higher Level Thinking During Discussions

Teachers can get conversations going and begin to promote higher level thinking during discussions by asking certain kinds of questions (Nystrand, 1997; Soter et al., 2008). According to Nystrand (1997), by asking authentic questions and follow-up questions that incorporate students' responses—a practice referred to as *uptake*—teachers convey to students that they have an important role to play as meaning makers. Authentic questions are questions that have multiple right ways to answer. As such, authentic questions create an open floor where students can jump in with their own thinking. For example, in the "Victor" discussion, "*Who is Victor?*" was an authentic question because the author made Victor's character ambiguous. So the phrasing of the question presupposed lots of ways to respond. By contrast, a nonauthentic or test question (Nystrand, 1997) is asked or phrased in such a way as to suggest to students that there is one prespecified answer. For example, in the "Victor" discussion, if the teacher had asked, "Is Victor a mysterious person?" there would have been only one answer—"Yes."

According to Nystrand (1997), authentic questions draw out and sustain multiple student responses because they send a signal that what is valued in the discussion is good thinking, original thoughts, and personal interpretations. As a result of this perceived purpose, the students see themselves as meaning makers and interpreters of text. On this point, Nystrand wrote, "When teachers ask authentic questions—encouraging individual interpretation—they open the floor to student ideas for examination, elaboration, and revision" (p. 38). At the heart of these student ideas is the higher level thinking that includes generalizations, analyses, speculations, connections to other texts and personal experiences, and so on. In short, authentic questions have the potential to promote higher level thinking and to engage students in higher level comprehension of text.

How teachers reply to student responses is as important as asking authentic questions to promote good thinking. Nystrand (1997) identified uptake as a kind of follow-up question that builds on students' responses. It is an intentional move in that the teacher is trying to validate students' thinking or to extend their ideas. For instance, in the following excerpt from a discussion about *A Lion to Guard Us* (Bulla, 1981), notice the way Mrs. Ross, in turn 5, builds on the students' responses with uptake and the way the uptake seems to push their thinking:

1. Lucas: Randall!
2. Ben: Randall, yeah, kick them out?
3. Matthew: Yeah.
4. Lucas: Yeah, he picked them up and threw them out.
5. Mrs. Ross: But why?
6. Matthew: And then he—
7. Lucas: Because he's, he's because he said [*paraphrasing the text*], "How dare you make blah, blah," [*indistinct*] and then she fainted.
8. Ben: Yeah, didn't he say to NEVER show your face in here again?

The question "But why?" is an instance of uptake because it builds on a previous response (turn 4), pushing the students' thinking further than if it had not been asked. In the dialogue after the teacher's use of uptake, the students continued to probe the meaning of the story (turns 6–8). We can only speculate that if the follow-up question had not been asked, the students probably would not have continued to analyze Randall's character traits. Uptake is a move a teacher (or a student) makes to "stir" the conversation, and it likely improves the quality of the dialogue by prompting more extended responses (Nystrand, 1997).

Using Informal Assessments to Improve the Quality of Discussions

After students are equipped to carry on productive discussions about text (i.e., they use the ground rules of discussion consistently), and they have an understanding that what they have to say is important and that using talk to think together is the goal, teachers can begin to fine-tune the discussions, coaching the elements of productive talk to ensure higher level thinking and comprehension. Mrs. Ross and Mrs. Pearson used informal, ongoing assessments of discussions to inform their instruction about and to improve the quality of the talk. For example, Mrs. Ross was able to listen for the use of the ground rules (see Table 3.5) and the elements of productive talk (see Table 3.2) as the students were talking. She made notes about what students were using and not using in their dialogues. Based on these observations and her analyses, she planned short minilessons for future discussions.

These minilessons were about a particular ground rule or an element of talk Mrs. Ross wanted to encourage the students to incorporate in their dialogue. For instance, after listening to a discussion that lacked a lot of reasoning, Mrs. Ross decided to make explicit the idea of elaborated explanations, one of the elements of productive talk. An elaborated explanation is an extended response that incorporates reasons or evidence to support a claim (e.g., I think Victor is an angel because nobody saw him in the story except Cody and he tried to help Cody pull through his illness). To coach in this way of talking and thinking, Mrs. Ross began the reading groups with a short minilesson about elaborated explanations. She drew a picture of a chain on the board and asked the students what they thought a chain of reasons was. They discussed this idea for several minutes, and, as a class, they decided to define a *chain of reasons* as "linking ideas together so you show the people in your group your reasons and evidence." In essence, Mrs. Ross introduced the idea of an elaborated explanation by scaffolding students' understanding through a guided discussion of a relevant metaphor for giving an extended, reasoned response. During the discussions that day, she reinforced students giving chains of reasons and encouraged them to build on and link ideas together.

Discussions Are Tools to Support Striving Readers

As teachers, we look for many ways to support striving readers in the classroom. One of those ways is by using discussions that give striving readers a rich, sophisticated context for talking and thinking about texts. Striving readers sometimes have difficulty with comprehension because what they bring to the text (e.g., their background knowledge and reading strategies) might not be enough to support their higher level comprehension. Through the dialogue of the discussions described in this chapter, however, the striving readers talked and thought in higher level ways about text, and they developed interpretations of text that promoted higher level comprehension. Could these students have done this on their own, reading independently at their seats? Maybe or maybe not, but by giving them an opportunity to engage in discussions with their peers, we were able to provide authentic, collaborative contexts that seemed to motivate their higher level thinking about text.

At the end of the study, the first author asked Mrs. Ross and Mrs. Pearson if their views about discussions "had changed at all during the year." Mrs. Pearson replied, "A lot!.... I can now stand up at a faculty meeting and be an advocate for discussions. I could not have done that at the beginning of the year." At this, the first author asked, "What do you mean *advocate*?" Mrs. Pearson replied, "I mean tell other teachers in our building that they need to have discussions to let students become better thinkers." To the same question, Mrs. Ross responded, "I don't think I could have reading instruction without discussions anymore—discussions let students practice comprehension." In response to the first author's follow-up question, "Is there anything you would tell a new teacher about discussion?" Mrs. Ross replied, "I would tell every teacher to do discussion. It's too important. It's wrong *not* to allow kids to talk about ideas they have."

It is important to remember that many students have not had many opportunities to use their talk to collaborate and to "think together" about text in highly productive ways. Their notions of discussion about text are often related to raising hands and answering the teacher's questions about the story. This means you must practice genuine discussions about text with your students and then reflect with your students on the outcomes of those discussions. Before a practice session, it is important to choose a good text and to think of several authentic questions. When you practice, you should take time to model the ground rules of productive talk and to let students know the goals of their discussion; that is, use their talk to make meaning and to understand the story better. Also, let students know you will talk little and contribute only when you have something important to ask or to add, and remind the students that the discussion is theirs to create. This action plan assumes you and your students will be discussing texts in a new(er) way than you have done in the past, so you are learning the ground rules and using some of the elements of productive talk for the first time.

Planning the Practice Discussion

- Choose an interesting short story, such as "Victor" by James Howe (1995). Read the story at least twice. Knowing the story well will make thinking of authentic questions as well as facilitating the discussion easier.

- Anticipate areas of interest your students may have about the story and write three to four authentic questions; alternatively, have the students read the story and talk or write about what was interesting to them, and then plan your authentic questions. (Tip: To test the quality of a question, ask yourself if you would like personally to talk about the question. If you answer yes, then it is indeed a good question. If you answer no, rephrase the question or throw it out and start again with a new one.)

- Plan to ask follow-up questions (uptake) too, such as Why do you think that? What makes you say that? Is there evidence from the story to back up what you're saying? Use uptake when students make claims or judgments about the story without giving reasons or evidence. (Tip: Think of your role in the discussion as that of a facilitator who sits back and waits until it is time to stir the conversation. Use uptake as a way to do the stirring.)

- Have the students read or listen to the story in any way that makes sense for the story and your students (e.g., independent reading, shared reading, paired reading, read-aloud).

- Consider planning a short prediscussion activity, such as writing a short journal entry or having students write their comments and questions about the story on sticky notes and adhering them to the story itself while they read.

Modeling the Practice Discussion

- Organize a fishbowl modeling activity. Rearrange your room so there is a small group of desks or a table in the middle of a large circle made up of the rest of the desks. Inform the class that you and a small group of students (four or five students) will model a kind of discussion that you will use in your reading groups in order to talk about the texts they read. (Tip: When choosing the small group to model the discussion inside the circle, select students who seem willing to talk in front of others and who cooperate with you.)

- Introduce and review the ground rules with the whole class. You could do a couple of things here. You could coconstruct several ground rules with your students and discuss them, or you could write several ground rules (from this chapter) on the board and discuss them with the class, explaining them and emphasizing their significance for having really good conversations about the students' reading. (Tip: Begin with an explanation of four or five ground rules, and, in your subsequent practice sessions, add the other ground rules until the class is comfortable with and using all of them regularly).

- Give directions for the fishbowl activity. The group in the middle (with the teacher) will have a discussion about the story. The group on the outside of the circle will observe, listening for the ground rules that you just reviewed. You could have students on the outside of the circle make notes of the ground rules and other things they observe that they think are positive and productive. Tell the group on the outside of the circle that their comments will be used to talk about the discussion.

- Conduct a short 7- to 10-minute discussion with the small group in the middle of the fishbowl. Reiterate the goals of the discussion and the ground rules that they should try to practice, and remind students that if there is silence in the discussion, it is okay. Pose the best authentic question you thought of from the planning phase. (Tips: Sit back and let the students talk without interruption from you. If you have to, avert your eyes down a little, so students talk to each other. Find a place in the discussion to practice uptake.)

Practicing and Reflecting on the Outcomes of the Practice Discussions

- Stop the discussion after several minutes and begin a reflective discussion with the whole class on the outcomes related to the ground rules. Ask the group on the outside of the fishbowl to share their observations of the discussion. Use what students say to reinforce, encourage, coach, and explain the goals and ground rules. (Tips: Try to keep the practice discussion to fewer than 10 minutes. After 10 minutes or so, the group on the outside will begin to lose focus on their task. Once the discussions get going in your classroom, a more typical length will be roughly 20 minutes.)

- Break the class into small groups of four or five students and have them practice discussing the story using their new ground rules. Circulate during the discussions and listen for what students are doing or not doing. Ask yourself the following: Which ground rules are being used? Which ones are not being used and need more practice? Are students giving reasons? Do they refer to the text when talking? Use this information to form the explanations you use in your next practice session. (Tip: If there is time, give students a chance to reflect on the outcomes of their discussions.)

- Repeat this action plan a few times, each time encouraging and focusing on the ground rules for productive talk. After students know and enact the ground rules, you can begin to model and to practice elements of productive talk such as referring to the text or making chains of reasons and evidence to support a claim.

QUESTIONS FOR STUDY AND REFLECTION

1. How would you characterize higher level comprehension in your own words?

2. Is there anything about the study described here that pulled your thinking in a certain direction?

3. Review Table 3.2. Which element of productive talk would you like to begin coaching in your students' talk right away, and why?

4. How would you compare the discussions about text in your classroom to the ones described here? Is there something you read that you want to try when facilitating discussions in your class?

REFERENCES

Allington, R.L. (2001). *What really matters for struggling readers: Designing research-based programs.* New York: Longman.

Almasi, J.F. (1996). A new view of discussion. In L.B. Gambrell & J.F. Almasi (Eds.), *Lively discussions! Fostering engaged reading* (pp. 2–24). Newark, DE: International Reading Association.

Anderson, R.C., Nguyen-Jahiel, K., McNurlen, B., Archodidou, A., Kim, S.-Y., Reznitskaya, A., et al. (2001). The snowball phenomenon: Spread of ways of talking and ways of thinking across groups of children. *Cognition and Instruction, 19*(1), 1–46. doi:10.1207/S1532690XCI1901_1

Bridges, D. (1979). *Education, democracy, and discussion.* London: University Press.

Cazden, C.B., & Beck, S.W. (2003). Classroom discourse. In A.C. Graesser, M.A. Gernsbacher, & S.R. Goldman (Eds.), *Handbook of discourse processes* (pp. 165–197). Mahwah, NJ: Erlbaum.

Chall, J.S., & Curtis, M. (2003). Children with reading difficulties. In J. Flood, D. Lapp, J.R. Squire, & J.M. Jensen (Eds.), *Handbook of research on teaching the English language arts* (pp. 413–420). Mahwah, NJ: Erlbaum.

Chang-Wells, G.L., & Wells, G. (1993). Dynamics of discourse: Literacy and the construction of knowledge. In E.A. Forman, N. Minisk, & C.A. Stone (Eds.), *Contexts for learning: Sociocultural dynamics in children's development* (pp. 58–90). New York: Oxford University Press.

Chinn, C.A., Anderson, R.C., & Waggoner, M.A. (2001). Patterns of discourse in two kinds of literature discussion. *Reading Research Quarterly, 36*(4), 378–411. doi:10.1598/RRQ.36.4.3

Dewey, J. (1916). *Democracy and education.* New York: Macmillan.

Duke, N.K. (2005). Comprehension of what for what: Comprehension as a nonunitary construct. In S.G. Paris & S.A. Stahl (Eds.), *Children's reading comprehension and assessment* (pp. 93–106). Mahwah, NJ: Erlbaum.

Fisher, D., & Ivey, G. (2006). Evaluating the interventions for struggling adolescent readers. *Journal of Adolescent & Adult Literacy, 50*(3), 180–189. doi:10.1598/JAAL.50.3.2

Hatano, L., & Inagaki, M. (1991). Sharing cognition through collective comprehension activity. In L.B. Resnick, J.M. Levine, & S.D. Teasley (Eds.), *Perspectives on socially shared cognition* (pp. 48–69). Washington, DC: American Psychological Association.

Langer, J.A. (1995). *Envisioning literature: Literary understanding and literature instruction.* New York: Teachers College Press.

Mercer, N. (1995). *The guided construction of knowledge: Talk amongst teachers and learners.* Clevedon, England: Multilingual Matters.

Mercer, N. (2000). *Words and minds: How we use language to think together.* London: Routledge.

National Assessment Governing Board. (2008). *Reading framework for the 2009 National Assessment of Educational Progress.* Washington, DC: Author.

Nystrand, M. (1997). *Opening dialogue: Understanding the dynamics of language and learning in the English classroom.* New York: Teachers College Press.

RAND Reading Study Group. (2002). *Reading for understanding: Toward an R&D program in reading comprehension.* Santa Monica, CA: RAND.

Raphael, T.E., & Au, K.H. (2005). QAR: Enhancing comprehension and test taking across grades and content areas. *The Reading Teacher, 59*(3), 206–221. doi:10.1598/RT.59.3.1

Reninger, K.B. (2007). *Intermediate-level, lower-achieving readers' participation and high-level thinking in group discussions about literary texts.* Unpublished doctoral dissertation, The Ohio State University, Columbus.

Reninger, K.B., & Rehark, L. (2009). Discussions in a fourth-grade classroom: Using exploratory talk to promote children's dialogic identities. *Language Arts, 86*(4), 268–279.

Resnick, L.B. (1987). *Education and learning to think.* Washington, DC: National Academy Press.

Soter, A.O., Wilkinson, I.A., Murphy, P.K., Rudge, L., Reninger, K., & Edwards, M. (2008). What the discourse tells us: Talk and indicators of high-level comprehension. *International Journal of Educational Research, 47*(6), 372–391. doi:10.1016/j.ijer.2009.01.001

Spradley, J.P. (1980). *Participant observation.* Orlando, FL: Harcourt Brace Jovanovich College Publishers.

Webb, N.M. (1992). Testing a theoretical model of student interaction and learning in small groups. In R. Hertz-Lazarowitz & N. Miller (Eds.), *Interaction in cooperative groups: The theoretical anatomy of group learning* (pp. 102–119). New York: Cambridge University Press.

Wegerif, R., & Mercer, N. (1997). A dialogical framework for researching peer talk. In R. Wegerif & P. Scrimshaw (Eds.), *Computers and talk in the primary classroom* (pp. 49–65). Clevedon, England: Multilingual Matters.

Wegerif, R., Mercer, N., & Dawes, L. (1999). From social interaction to individual reasoning: An empirical investigation of a possible socio-cultural model of cognitive development. *Learning and Instruction, 9*(6), 493–516.

Wilkinson, I.A.G., Soter, A.O., & Murphy, P.K. (2010). Developing a model of quality talk about literary text. In M.G. McKeown & L. Kucan (Eds.), *Bringing reading research to life: Essays in honor of Isabel L. Beck.* New York: Guilford.

Worthy, J., & Beck, I.L. (1995). On the road from recitation to discussion in large-group dialogue about literature. In K. Hinchman & C. Kinz (Eds.), *Perspectives on literacy research and practice* (44th yearbook of the National Reading Conference, pp. 312–324). Chicago: The National Reading Conference.

LITERATURE CITED

Bulla, C.R. (1981). *A lion to guard us*. New York: Harper.

Creech, S. (2002). *Ruby Holler*. New York: Scholastic.

DeFelice, C. (1990). *Weasel*. New York: Avon.

Howe, J. (1995). Victor. In J. Hurwitz (Ed.), *Birthday surprises: Ten great stories to unwrap* (pp. 74–86). New York: Beech Tree.

CHAPTER 4

Shifting Talk About Text: Developing Struggling Readers' Comprehension Processes During Talk About Text

Kathleen F. Clark

Teachers typically have two general foci when reading texts with students. One is to foster students' meaning construction of a specific text at hand, the other to develop students' ability to construct meaning from texts generally—that is, to develop their comprehension processes (van den Broek & Kremer, 2000). The latter focus is what enables students to be able to understand, enjoy, and learn from texts across contexts and time. Recent research that has investigated effective reading instruction has documented that teachers who explicitly teach students how to engage in the *thinking* involved in making sense of text as they read are more successful in increasing students' reading ability than those who do not (Taylor, Pearson, Clark, & Walpole, 2000; Taylor, Peterson, Pearson, & Rodriguez, 2002). Such instruction is important for all readers (Trabasso & Bouchard, 2002) and is particularly important for struggling readers, for these students most often need teachers to make explicit for them what may be implicit to others (Pearson & Dole, 1987).

Following Durkin's (1979) landmark study documenting a paucity of comprehension instruction in classrooms, researchers and educators allocated considerable attention to approaches to teaching students comprehension processes. These approaches are more commonly referred to as comprehension strategies instruction. Trabasso and Bouchard (2002) provide a comprehensive yet succinct description of these processes and related instruction: "Comprehension strategies are specific learned procedures that foster active, competent, self-regulated, and intentional reading. Classroom teachers implement comprehension strategy

instruction by demonstrating, modeling, or guiding their use during the reading of a text" (p. 177). Many articulations of such instruction exist. For comprehensive reviews of these articulations and their effectiveness, I direct interested
readers to Pressley (2000), the RAND Reading Study Group (2002), the
National Reading Panel report (National Institute of Child Health and Human
Development, 2000), and Trabasso and Bouchard (2002).

Learning to engage students in comprehension strategy instruction is challenging. It involves learning how to make cognitive processes visible to students, finding texts that are appropriate for the task and within students' zones
of proximal development, learning to release increasing control to students as
they gain proficiency, and learning to coordinate the employment of strategies
across reading contexts (El-Dinary, 2002). With so many challenges, it is no
wonder that Hilden and Pressley (2007) report that teachers often feel overwhelmed by the complexity of strategy instruction.

What I share in this chapter is an approach to strategy instruction that can
serve as a toehold of sorts for those who are interested in beginning the process of learning how to teach students to comprehend while they are reading
or listening to text. It is an approach that is focused upon a shift in a teacher's
instructional language from one that fosters students' comprehension but does
not make the processes involved in comprehension explicit for students, to one
that does make those processes explicit. One third-grade teacher, Ms. Adams
(a pseudonym), and I recently used this approach in a 12-week preexperimen-
tal study in her classroom. We used the approach with all the students in the
classroom, during small-group reading lessons and whole-class read-alouds. To
assess any change in students' comprehension ability or metacognitive knowledge, we administered to students alternate forms of the informal reading inventory that came with the reading series used in the class and the Metacognitive
Strategy Index (Schmitt, 1990) before and after the study. We anticipated that all
students would benefit from the instruction; however, the results revealed that
only the struggling readers made statistically significant gains in comprehension and metacognitive knowledge across the 12 weeks. Although the study was
small and of fairly limited duration, we found the apparent impact that the shift
in instructional language had on struggling readers' comprehension progress
quite compelling. Moreover, the shift in instructional language was manageable
for Ms. Adams as a place to start learning to teach comprehension processes.
In the teacher–student exchanges below, I represent the kinds of language that
characterized Ms. Adams's and the students' talk before and after the shift.

Prior to the study, Ms. Adams's instructional language was representative of language that teachers often use while reading with or to students. Consider the following excerpt from a prestudy small-group reading lesson. The students in the group are of somewhat mixed comprehension abilities. All are able to read the text with sufficient accuracy and fluency. They are in their second day of reading a biography of Helen Keller.

Ms. Adams: Let's share what we learned about Helen yesterday, at the beginning of the book. What did we learn?

S1: She was like a kid.

Ms. Adams: She was a kid. What happened to her when she was very young?

S3: She got really sick. She got deaf and blind.

S2: Because of the kind of sick she got.

Ms. Adams: Yes, probably scarlet fever. The doctors couldn't cure scarlet fever back then. Does Helen get along with the other students?

All: No!

Ms. Adams: Why not, do you think?

S3: Because she hits...um...because she can't find her way around and she bumps into stuff. And the kids, they're scared 'cause she might hit 'em or run into 'em.

Ms. Adams: So she doesn't have the best of manners, does she? She's probably not very pleasant to be around. Let's look at Chapter 2. What's the title of this chapter?

S4: "The Stranger"

Ms. Adams: Who do you think the stranger is going to be?

S3: Well in my book, it's this girl, and she comes and helps Helen.

Ms. Adams: You're reading the other book on Helen Keller, aren't you. Okay, so a girl comes to help her. Why would they call this chapter "The Stranger" then?

S5: Maybe she doesn't know the girl who comes to help.

Ms. Adams: That makes sense. It could be. Let's read to find out who the stranger is and how she'll help Helen.

In these exchanges, Ms. Adams uses questions to prompt students' summarization of the previous day's reading—what they learned about Helen Keller as a young child. In the course of the summary, she prompts students' inferential thinking with a question. Following that, she has students make an inference about the upcoming chapter from the title. Finally, she sets the purpose for reading. There is nothing wrong, per se, with Ms. Adams's instructional language. It fosters students' meaning construction. However, it does not make the processes involved in that construction explicit for students. Therefore, the language primarily benefits students' understanding of that specific text. It has more limited utility for helping students to develop their own comprehension processes.

The Shift in Instructional Language

To shift the instructional language that Ms. Adams used when working with students, she and I applied two concepts inherent in comprehension strategy instruction—direct explanation and scaffolding. We drew heavily upon the work of Duffy (2003). Duffy shares that direct explanation involves providing students with explicit, verbal representations of the thinking involved in engaging in cognitive processes. The purpose of explaining, he emphasizes, is to help students become aware of how to construct meaning when reading. Scaffolding is supportive assistance in the form of questions or prompts that enable students to engage in a complex process while their abilities are still developing (Clark & Graves, 2005).

To shift her instructional language from that which engendered but did not make comprehension processes explicit to that which did, Ms. Adams and I first identified the possibilities the texts she selected for instruction presented for comprehension strategy employment. We then prepared language that directly explained and scaffolded their use. Following this work, Ms. Adams used that language when reading with the students. Below I share an excerpt from Ms. Adams's small-group instruction following the shift. It's approximately eight weeks into our study. The same group of students is beginning a new book, *Caught by the Sea* (Keating, 1999), a leveled chapter book—a thriller of sorts—for developing readers. It recounts a scuba diver's struggles when she is swept out to sea.

Ms. Adams:	We have a new book today. One thing we know skillful read-ers do before, during, and after they read is use thinking strat-egies. So before we read, let's share some thinking strategies we can use to get ourselves ready to understand our book.
S1:	We should read the title.
Ms. Adams:	Good idea. What else should we do?
S2:	Look at the pictures.
S3:	Read the Table of Contents.
S4:	Read the back of the book.
Ms. Adams:	Wonderful ideas. What information do these things give us about the book? How do they set us up to understand?
S3:	We get clues.
Others:	Yeah, clues, hints.
Ms. Adams:	Excellent thinking. Now, what other knowledge can we use to help us get ready to understand? Remember, we all have another important source of knowledge we can use [*points to her head*].
S4:	What we know.
Ms. Adams:	You've got it. We can use what we already know to help us understand what might happen in a story. Let's use the clues the author gives us, and what we already know, to make an inference about the story—what it will be about. What clues did you notice?
S2:	There's a scuba diver.
S5:	Stuck in the water.
S1:	The weather is getting bad.
Ms. Adams:	Now, what do we already know about what could happen if you're a scuba diver in the water and the weather is getting bad?
S4:	You could get struck by lightning.
S1:	If it's thundering....
S2:	And you have metal on, like your tank....
S3:	You could get sucked out to sea.

S4:	And get drowned….
S5:	Or eaten by sharks….
Ms. Adams:	Lots of unpleasant possibilities. Let's make our inference. The story is going to be about….
S2:	A guy who is a scuba diver.
S1:	He's in the water with a friend and a storm comes up.
S5:	He might get sucked out to sea and sharks might get him.
Ms. Adams:	We'll have to see. Now, let's identify our purpose for reading. There are four chapters, so we probably won't find out if the diver survives. We'll just get a start on the book. So, what do we want to find out today?
S4:	How he got stuck in the sea. Like what happened exactly.
Ms. Adams:	Do we agree?
Students:	Yeah, yeah.
Ms. Adams:	Well then, let's read to find out how exactly the diver became stuck in the sea.

In the above exchange, Ms. Adams begins by reminding students that skillful readers use thinking strategies. She prompts them to make an inference about the upcoming story. The students identify the more concrete tasks inherent in making the inference, that is, looking for information the author provides (i.e., "clues"). Ms. Adams prompts the students to identify how the activities they name help them get ready to understand. Then, she prompts the other source of knowledge upon which students will draw to make the inference, that is, their own prior knowledge. Her point to her head serves as a physical mnemonic to cue students' thinking. Following that, she has the students connect the information from the two knowledge sources to make the inference. Finally, Ms. Adams has the group set a purpose for reading. She makes this step in their prereading process explicit for students as well.

In both the biography of Helen Keller and the *Caught by the Sea* (Keating, 1999) excerpts, Ms. Adams fosters students' understanding of the specific texts at hand. However, only in the *Caught by the Sea* (Keating, 1999) excerpt does her instructional language make the cognitive processes in which they should engage visible for students. Through her use of direct explanation and supportive questions and prompts, Ms. Adams helps students to become aware of the processes involved in constructing meaning.

In the remainder of this chapter, I share a set of procedures for making the shift in instructional language and present examples of how such language might look. The procedures begin with text selection and go on to generating the instructional language.

Procedures for Shifting Instructional Language

Selecting Text

Students should be able to read the texts for teacher-guided reading instruction focused on comprehension strategy practice with at least 97% word recognition accuracy and between 70% and 89% comprehension, regardless of the lesson framework a teacher uses. As is highlighted elsewhere in this volume, we don't want word recognition challenges to impede students' ability to focus upon comprehension. Texts for teacher-guided instruction can be leveled books or literary texts. In contrast, good read-aloud texts typically are literary in nature and reflect students' age and interests. Texts for both reading purposes should be challenging enough so that students have something to think about and practice, but not so difficult that they are unable to be successful with teacher support (El-Dinary, 2002). Further, they must present clear opportunities to employ comprehension strategies, for, although comprehension necessarily involves the employment of multiple thinking processes, some texts present more definitive opportunities than others for making these processes explicit for students.

Identifying Opportunities for Comprehension Strategy Employment

Following text selection, the next step, clearly, is to read the text. Read it several times. As you read, use sticky notes, durable tabs or flags of some sort, or some other kind of text marker to identify places in the text that lend themselves to particular strategies—for example, inferring, questioning, imaging, or summarizing. If a text has illustrations, which those for young students often do, as you read, also consider whether the illustrations lend themselves to comprehension strategy development. The text *Peter's Chair* by Ezra Jack Keats (1998) comes to mind. The illustrations in this text provide rich sources of information for making inferences about characters' feelings, motivations, and actions.

Preparing Instructional Language

When you've identified places in the text that lend themselves to strategy employment, create explanations, think-alouds, questions, and prompts to accompany the salient text. The level of explicitness you employ in your instructional language will depend upon how much experience and facility students have with the strategies. When students are new to the strategies, identify, explain, and think aloud to model them for students. Then question and prompt to scaffold their employment. When students have been introduced to the strategies and have some experience using them, you may only need to identify, prompt, and support their use. When students have more experience, you may only need to prompt students to think of strategies that would be appropriate and provide a question or prompt or two.

Next, I present examples of instructional language that I've prepared to show what teaching inferring in this manner might look like. I focus upon inferring because it is a comprehension process with which struggling comprehenders have particular difficulty (Oakhill, Cain, & Yuill, 1998). In the first set of examples, I show three articulations of language. Each articulation shows what language might look like, for the same piece of text, if it were intended for students who a) were just learning the strategy, b) had some experience with the strategy, or c) had more experience with the strategy. I do this to illustrate the different levels of explicitness and support that are possible. Then I provide a set of examples that illustrate language that reflects the gradual release of responsibility (Pearson & Gallagher, 1983) for engaging in the strategy, from teacher to students, across successive examples in a lesson. I do this to show how a lesson may proceed. In this second set of examples, I share language for an early-primary-grade text and then language for an intermediate-grade text.

Models of Instructional Language: Three Articulations

For this first set of examples, I draw upon Patricia McKissack's (2003) wonderfully engaging chapter book for second-grade readers, *Tippy Lemmey*. *Tippy Lemmey*, to quote a child who attends the university reading center I direct, is a "great dog story." I have to agree. Tippy Lemmey is a rambunctious Chow puppy who, in his youth and exuberance, unwittingly terrorizes a group of friends. In the course of the book, threatening circumstances arise in which the friends must save Tippy Lemmey and Tippy Lemmey must save the friends. The story is told from the perspective of one of the friends, a girl named Leandra. The story takes place at the time of the Korean War. Leandra recounts that the friends are engaged in their own war of sorts at home, with Tippy Lemmey, the new dog in town.

Language for Students Just Learning the Strategy

For an initial experience with a strategy, the instructional language should identify, explain, and model the thinking involved in the strategy. Language for an initial experience with making inferences would look something like this:

> When I read this, I wondered what kind of dog Leandra thinks Tippy Lemmey is. To figure this out, I'm going to make an inference. An inference is like a thoughtful guess we make from using clues that the author gives us and our own knowledge. Let me show you how I do this. When I read, I noticed that Leandra described Tippy Lemmey as *the enemy*. That's a good clue. Now I use what I already know about an enemy. I know an enemy is someone who wants to harm you or cause you trouble. So I put those ideas together. My inference is that Leandra thinks Tippy Lemmey is a mean dog, a dog who wants to harm her and her friends. Making inferences lets us figure out what is happening in a story even if the words aren't written on the page.

Language for Students With Some Experience

When students have had some experience with a strategy, the language can be a little less supportive. The teacher probably still will need to identify the strategy and support its use, however. Language used when students have had some experience might look something like this:

> What kind of dog does Leandra, the little girl telling the story, think Tippy Lemmey is? Let's make an inference to figure out what she thinks. What two kinds of information do we connect to make an inference about what Leandra thinks? [*Students may respond with, for example, clues on the page, what you already know.*] Find the on-the-page word that is a good clue about Tippy Lemmey. [*Enemy.*] Now ask yourself, What do I already know about enemies? Let's share what we know. [*Responses may include someone/something that will hurt you/harm you/get you in trouble.*] Now connect the two. If Leandra says Tippy Lemmey is an enemy, and an enemy is someone or something

that wants to hurt you, what kind of dog does she think Tippy Lemmey is? [*A mean dog who wants to harm her and her friends.*]

Language for Students With More Experience

When students have had more experience with the strategy, the language would look something like this:

> What strategy can we use to help us figure out what kind of dog Leandra thinks Tippy Lemmey is? [*Inferring.*] What inference did you make about the kind of dog Tippy Lemmey is? What clues on the page made you think that? What information from your own knowledge did you use?

Models of Instructional Language: Successive Examples Within a Single Lesson

For this second set of examples, I draw upon two texts. The first, for early-primary-grade readers, is Darleen Bailey Beard's (1999) *Twister.* The second, for intermediate-grade readers—approximately fifth grade—is Karen Levine's (2003) moving informational text *Hana's Suitcase.*

Twister

I heard a second-grade teacher in Minnesota read this appealing, evocative text aloud to her students during tornado preparedness week some years ago. The story inspired much good thinking on the part of the students as they reviewed their learning across the week and considered their own experiences with tornados. Below, I provide four examples with *Twister* to show how a teacher's support would vary across the lesson as students gain experience.

Beginning the Explanation. A story synopsis and introduction to the target strategy would look something like this:

> We're going to read *Twister* by the author Darleen Bailey Beard today. The story is told from the point of view of a little girl, Lucille. Lucille lives with her mother and her little brother Natt. They live in tornado country, like we do. In the story, a tornado strikes. I chose this book because it's tornado safety week at our school and because I want to teach you a new reading strategy. That strategy is making inferences. Authors don't tell us exactly what they mean all the time. We have to figure it out on our own.

When readers make inferences, they use clues the author gives them and their own knowledge to figure out what an author means. As we read together today, we're going to practice how to do this. I'll do an example for you, and then we'll do some together.

Thinking Aloud. In the first part of the story, Lucille shares how the day is hot and sultry. She and her brother are playing outside while their mother works in the yard. A little farther along, Lucille relates how the sky is turning green, the air feels thick, and it is starting to rain. At this point in the story, to model making an inference, a teacher would think aloud in something like the following manner:

> Let me show you how I can use the clues the author gives me and my own knowledge to figure out what is happening. I say to myself, 'Well, in the story Lucille says the sky looks green and the air feels thick. I live in the Midwest, so I know that when the air is sticky and still, and the sky turns green, a tornado may be coming. Since the title of the story is *Twister*, and I know that's another word for tornado, my inference is that a tornado is probably on the way.' This is how, boys and girls, I use the clues in the story along with my own knowledge to figure out what is happening.

Scaffolding Students With Considerable Support. In the next part of the story, Lucille shares that they go inside and her mother lights a candle and turns on the radio. The children watch the storm from a window. Lucille describes how a cloud in the distance looks like a lion with its tail dropping down to the ground. Their mother shouts that it's a twister. At this point in the story, to support inference making, a teacher might talk with students in the following manner:

> Things are looking pretty scary for the family. We know from an illustration that they live in a mobile home, and we know that mobile homes are not safe places to be in a tornado. As a reader, I'm wondering what they're going to do to be safe. Let's make an inference together about what the family is going to do. The clue in the book is their home, a *mobile home*. To make our inference, we're going to have to use what we already know about tornado safety. So let's call to mind what we know. When the tornado siren goes off, what do we do? [*Students might give the following responses: Go to the basement; go to the lowest level of the house; if you're in a car or a mobile home, leave it and find other shelter; lie flat in a ditch if you're caught outside.*] Now since we know Mama, Lucille, and Natt live in a mobile home, which of these things makes sense for them to do? [*Students might give the following responses: Leave and seek other shelter—in the neighbor's house, which is in an illustration, or maybe in a ditch.*] So our inference is that they

will leave their mobile home and seek shelter somewhere—in the house next door or maybe there is a ditch they can get into. Let's read on to find out what they do.

Scaffolding Students With Less Support. In the next part of the story, the mother and children run to the storm cellar in their yard. The mother puts Lucille and Natt in the cellar. She tells them to stay there while she gets their elderly neighbor. The children are frightened in the cellar by themselves, Natt more demonstrably so than Lucille. Lucille describes Natt's face as being *white* and shares that his voice is *tiny* and *quivery*. To provide a little less support to students as they make an inference about how Natt feels, a teacher would say something like this:

> Now I'd like you to try to make an inference without as much help from me. I'm going to ask you questions to help you think, but I want you to do most of the thinking. Remember, you need to do two things to make an inference. Think about the clues on the page the author has given you—the words on the page—and what you already know those words mean about someone's feelings. So, what are the clues—the words on the page—the author gives us? [*Students may respond with white face, voice tiny and quivery.*] Now, use your own knowledge. What are *you* feeling when your face gets white and your own voice is tiny and quivery? [*Responses may include afraid, scared, nervous.*] So, how do we think Natt is feeling down in the cellar without his mother? What's our inference? [*Natt is scared.*]

Hana's Suitcase

The author begins this text by sharing that in the book she recounts two stories. One story is that of the director of the Japanese Holocaust Center and a group of children who pursue information about Hana Brady, the little girl whose suitcase is on display in the center's museum. The other is Hana's story. She and her family are Czechoslovakian Jews who become victims of the Nazi regime during World War II.

Beginning the Explanation. To introduce the day's reading and target strategy, a teacher would use language similar to this:

> Today we're reading the chapter entitled "Nove Mestro, 1939." Remember, Nove Mestro is the name of the town in which Hana and her brother George live. In 1939, the Nazis have decided that Jews cannot do the same things as other people. They have placed what we call restrictions on Jews. They can't go certain places, and they can only be out in the town during certain times of the day. At other times of the day,

they must stay in their homes. We're going to read about some of the experiences Hana and George have with the restrictions, and we're going to learn a new strategy. The strategy is making inferences. When authors write, they don't say all that they mean directly on the page. They rely on readers to use clues that they give us, together with our own knowledge, to figure out—or conclude—what they mean. So, when readers make inferences about an author's meaning they use clues the author gives them and their own knowledge to conclude what the author means. As we read together today, we're going to practice how to do this. I'll do an example for you, and then we'll do some together.

Thinking Aloud. In the first paragraph, the author describes how Hana and George go to see *Snow White and the Seven Dwarfs*. However, when they get to the cinema, they are not allowed to enter because they are Jewish. When the children are turned away, the author writes that their faces are red and their eyes burn. Language for an initial exposure to the strategy of inferring would look something like this:

> When Hana and her brother go to the theater and see the "No Jews Allowed" sign, I am wondering how they feel. The author doesn't directly tell me. So, I need to make an inference. I'm going to use the clues the author gives me and my own knowledge to make the inference. I see that the author describes the children's faces as *red* and says their *eyes were burning*. These are good clues about the children's feelings. Now, I'm going to think about my own experiences with these clues. When my face gets red I'm usually embarrassed, upset, or angry. And when my eyes burn it's usually because I'm trying not to cry. I can use my experiences with these words to conclude—make an inference—about what Hana and George are feeling. I think they're feeling really angry and upset.

Scaffolding Students With Considerable Support. On the next page, the author relates how, as time goes by, Hana's friends stop coming over to play. Her friends' parents had told them not to go near Hana. The parents were concerned that the Nazis would punish their families if their children played with Jewish children. To guide students in making an inference, a teacher would use language similar to this:

> Hana's life has really changed since the Nazis took over the town. As a reader, I'm again wondering how Hana feels. Let's make an inference together. Let's infer how Hana feels by using the clues the author gives us together with our own knowledge of what these clues suggest. The clues about the changes in Hana's life are that her playmates and her best friend have stopped coming over to play. Now, put yourself in Hana's shoes. Given your own experiences, how do you feel when no one will come

over to play with you? [*Responses may include sad, unhappy.*] How might you come to feel if this happened for a long time? [*Lonely.*] Now what inference do you make about how Hana feels since she's lost all her friends? [*Students may respond with sad, lonely.*]

Scaffolding Students With Less Support. Shortly thereafter, the author describes how the Nazis arrest Hana's mother and send her away. The night before she is sent away, Hana's mother sings a lullaby from Hana's earliest years over and over to Hana while she falls asleep. The lullaby had been Hana's favorite. While singing, Hana's mother stokes her hair. To provide a little less support to students as they make an inference about how Hana's mother feels at this time, a teacher would say something like this:

> I'd like you to make an inference about how Hana's mother feels as she tucks Hana into bed the night before she must leave. I'm going to have you make this inference without as much help from me. To make the inference, do the two things we've practiced—use the clues the author gives you and your own knowledge of how people feel. What clues does the author give us that let us know how Hana's mother feels about her? From your own knowledge, how might a mother feel if she wasn't going to see her child again for a very long time or perhaps ever? This is the situation that Hana's mother was facing that night. Given the author's clues and what you know, what inference do you make about how Hana's mother was feeling when she was tucking Hana into bed?

Teaching Strategies: Worth the Effort

The approach to comprehension strategy instruction shared here is one that can serve as a beginning for teachers. It draws upon the essential principles of any strategy instruction: direct explanation, modeling, and scaffolding. Teachers can layer this approach on to their existing small-group reading lessons or classroom read-aloud experiences. It does not require additional resources or materials. Rather, it is grounded in teacher and student talk about text.

Students in a classroom who do not experience comprehension difficulties with grade-level materials perhaps do not need the explicitness of this approach. However, students who struggle with comprehending grade-level (or below-grade-level) materials surely do. As such, the approach can serve as one way of differentiating reading instruction for students of varying comprehension abilities.

Learning to shift one's instructional language away from that which engenders comprehension but does not explicitly teach it takes effort. One must think through the strategic processes and learn to articulate them in ways that students can understand. The reading specialists with whom I work often reflect with me, as we work with preservice and inservice teachers, upon how challenging it is to plan language that is to the instructional point, clear, and student appropriate. Invariably, though, we conclude that the benefits to students make it worth the considerable effort.

ACTION PLAN

To try the technique described in this chapter, plan, implement, and reflect upon a small-group reading lesson. Teach the lesson to a reading group in which one of your struggling students participates. Use your usual lesson framework (e.g., Directed Reading Activity) to create the lesson. Layer upon this lesson plan the explicit, strategic talk you wish to try. To accomplish this, engage in the steps below.

- Select a text that is appropriate for the planned reading experience (e.g., small-group instruction, whole-class read-aloud).

- Identify opportunities in the text for explicit, strategic talk. Choose no more than three to five places to stop. You want to focus upon using comprehension strategies as students read or listen, but you don't want to overwhelm them.

- Prepare the strategic language associated with each place in the text that you want to stop and instruct students. Use the language shared in this chapter to help you.

- Build your strategic talk into the appropriate places in your lesson plan (i.e., prereading, during reading, postreading). If you can, make a recording of your lesson.

- After the lesson, listen to your audio recording if you made one, or talk with a reading coach or other colleague about the lesson. Share what went well and the challenges the lesson presented. Talk about how you will refine your practice in your next strategic reading lesson.

QUESTIONS FOR STUDY AND REFLECTION

1. Think about the kinds of reading opportunities in which your students currently engage in the classroom. Which of these reading opportunities lend themselves to the kind of explicit, strategic instructional language described in this chapter? Which do not? For reading opportunities that do, how might you incorporate this more explicit, strategic language?

2. Think about your students and their varying comprehension abilities. On a sheet of lined paper, create a grid in this manner: List the names of a few students who you know struggle with understanding when they read. Skip three to four lines between students' names. Across the top of the page, list a couple of strategies that you feel are important for the students to develop facility with at this point in their schooling. Consider which level of support the specific students will require for each strategy you identified across the top of the grid. In the boxes of the grid that correspond to each student per strategy, note the level of support your instructional language will likely need to provide this student.

3. If you can, get together with other teachers at your school who share your interest in comprehension instruction. As a group, think about which strategies may best be focused upon at different grade levels. Are there some that you think students should develop proficiency in during the primary grades? Are there some that should be introduced during the primary grades but really focused upon in later grades? How might teachers work together across grades to help students to develop a level of proficiency in a set of strategies across time?

REFERENCES

Clark, K.F., & Graves, M.F. (2005). Scaffolding students' comprehension of text. *The Reading Teacher, 58*(6), 570–580. doi:10.1598/RT.58.6.6

Duffy, G.G. (2003). *Explaining reading: A resource for teaching concepts, skills, and strategies.* New York: Guilford.

Durkin, D. (1979). What classroom observations reveal about reading comprehension instruction. *Reading Research Quarterly, 14*(4), 481–538. doi:10.1598/RRQ.14.4.2

El-Dinary, P.B. (2002). Challenges of implementing transactional strategies instruction for reading comprehension. In C.C. Block & M. Pressley (Eds.), *Comprehension instruction: Research-based best practices* (pp. 201–218). New York: Guilford.

Hilden, K.R., & Pressley, M. (2007). Self-regulation through transactional strategies instruction. *Reading & Writing Quarterly, 23*(1), 51–75. doi:10.1080/10573560600837651

National Institute of Child Health and Human Development. (2000). *Report of the National Reading Panel. Teaching children to read: An evidence-based assessment of the scientific research literature on reading and its implications for reading instruction* (NIH Publication No. 00-4769). Washington, DC: U.S. Government Printing Office.

Oakhill, J., Cain, K., & Yuill, N. (1998). Individual differences in children's comprehension skill: Towards an integrated model. In C. Hulme & R.M. Joshi (Eds.), *Reading and spelling: Development and disorders* (pp. 343–367). London: Erlbaum.

Pearson, P.D., & Dole, J.A. (1987). Explicit comprehension instruction: A review of research and a new conceptualization of instruction. *The Elementary School Journal, 88*(2), 151–165. doi:10.1086/461530

Pearson, P.D., & Gallagher, M.C. (1983). The instruction of reading comprehension. *Contemporary Educational Psychology, 8*(3), 317–344. doi:10.1016/0361-476X(83)90019-X

Pressley, M. (2000). What should comprehension instruction be the instruction of? In M.L. Kamil, P.B. Mosenthal, P.D. Pearson, & R. Barr (Eds.), *Handbook of reading research* (Vol. 3, pp. 545–561). Mahwah, NJ: Erlbaum.

RAND Reading Study Group. (2002). *Reading for understanding: Toward an R&D program in reading comprehension*. Santa Monica, CA: RAND.

Schmitt, M.C. (1990). A questionnaire to measure children's awareness of strategic reading processes. *The Reading Teacher, 43*(7), 454–461.

Taylor, B.M., Pearson, P.D., Clark, K.F., & Walpole, S. (2000). Effective schools and accomplished teachers: Lessons about primary-grade reading instruction in high-poverty schools. *The Elementary School Journal, 101*(2), 121–165. doi:10.1086/499662

Taylor, B.M., Peterson, D.S., Pearson, P.D., & Rodriguez, M.C. (2002). Looking inside classrooms: Reflecting on the "how" as well as the "what" in effective reading instruction. *The Reading Teacher, 56*(3), 270–279. doi:10.1598/RT.56.3.5

Trabasso, T., & Bouchard, E. (2002). Teaching readers how to comprehend text strategically. In C.C. Block & M. Pressley (Eds.), *Comprehension instruction: Research-based best practices* (pp. 176–200). New York: Guilford.

van den Broek, P., & Kremer, K.E. (2000). The mind in action: What it means to comprehend during reading. In B.M. Taylor, M.F. Graves, & P. van den Broek (Eds.), *Reading for meaning: Fostering comprehension in the middle grades* (pp. 1–31). New York: Teachers College Press.

LITERATURE CITED

Beard, D.B. (1999). *Twister*. New York: Farrar, Straus and Giroux.

Keating, R. (1999). *Caught by the sea*. Wellington, New Zealand: Learning Media Limited.

Keats, E.J. (1998). *Peter's chair*. New York: Viking.

Levine, K. (2003). *Hana's suitcase*. Morton Grove, IL: Albert Whitman & Company.

McKissack, P.C. (2003). *Tippy Lemmey*. New York: Aladdin.

CHAPTER 5

Using Writing to Develop Struggling Learners' Higher Level Reading Comprehension

James L. Collins and Timothy P. Madigan

For the past three years we have been conducting a major research study to determine if writing can be used to improve reading comprehension in low-performing schools. The answer, we are delighted to report, is a resounding *Yes*. Writing does indeed improve reading comprehension, even for students who struggle with reading and writing. We realize this claim must seem preposterous—how can students who cannot read very well possibly write about their reading? And how can the one or two broken sentences they might independently write possibly improve their reading comprehension? In this chapter we answer these questions by describing how assisted writing in the form of interactive thinksheets can be used to develop reading comprehension. A thinksheet consists of several pages of questions and answer spaces that help students write about the reading they are doing, and an interactive thinksheet is one that the writer uses in collaboration with teachers and peers. In what follows, we make the case that interactive thinksheets scaffold higher level thinking by helping struggling learners write about their reading, and we offer guidelines for teachers who want to develop thinksheets to use with their own students.

The official title of our research study is "Writing Intensive Reading Comprehension (WIRC): Effects of Comprehension Instruction With and Without Integrated Writing Instruction on Fourth- and Fifth-Grade Students' Reading Comprehension and Writing Performance." We conducted the study in low-performing urban elementary schools, and as its title suggests, the WIRC research investigated the hypothesis that bringing together reading and writing will improve reading comprehension and writing performance. The research brought reading and writing together by developing a curriculum innovation that uses assisted reading and writing supported by thinksheets.

As we have said, a thinksheet is a guide to writing about reading that teachers use interactively with students. Thinksheets have been shown in previous research to be effective tools for guiding the writing processes of struggling students (Collins, 1998; Collins & Collins, 1996; Collins & Godinho, 1996; Englert, 1995; Englert & Mariage, 1990; Raphael, Kirschner, & Englert, 1986, 1988; Tierney & Readence, 2000). By developing interactive thinksheets and testing their effectiveness through experimental research, the WIRC study challenged the conventional assumption that low-achieving students cannot use writing to make sense of their reading. It also challenged traditional ways of teaching reading and writing, such as teaching them separately, teaching them with reading coming first, and teaching them with extended writing about reading being little used or withheld entirely until reading skills and background knowledge are sufficiently in place. We reasoned instead that it makes sense to use scaffolded writing about reading with struggling readers because writing during reading can contribute to comprehension and help build background knowledge.

The results of the two year-long experiments at the heart of the WIRC research support our argument. Integrating reading and writing through the use of thinksheets in the WIRC experimental group produced levels of reading comprehension achievement and writing performance superior to the traditional instruction in the control group. Hierarchical linear modeling analyses of multiple-choice answers and constructed-response writing on pretests and posttests from 1,062 fourth- and fifth-grade students in 50 classrooms in 10 low-performing urban schools (four 2-year experimental, three 1-year experimental, and three control schools) also reveal greater effects for special education and low-income students in the experimental group. WIRC-related classroom activities with interactive use of thinksheets as scaffolding tools contributed to the greater gains in reading and writing. In summary, the WIRC study found the following:

- Students using thinksheets to write about their reading improved more than students receiving traditional instruction.
- Fourth-grade students in the experimental group showed statistically significant gains on multiple-choice items but not on constructed-response items. Once we controlled for teacher fidelity of implementation, fourth-grade experimental students showed greater gains than controls for both multiple-choice and constructed-response items.

- Fifth-grade students in the experimental group outperformed controls on both multiple-choice and constructed-response items even before controlling for teacher fidelity of implementation; gains became larger once we controlled for fidelity.

- Students using thinksheets in the experimental condition for two years (that is, in both fourth and fifth grades) outperformed all other groups.

Bringing Together Reading and Writing

The main theoretical assumption we brought to the WIRC study is that writing about text not only benefits from development of reading ability but contributes to it as well. We also believe something is seriously wrong in schooling in the United States: Writing about reading is one of the most frequently occurring activities in educational settings, yet large proportions of elementary students fail to meet proficiency standards on tasks requiring them to write to demonstrate understanding of reading. Results are even grimmer for students who are economically disadvantaged. Our conclusion is that serious deficits in the ability to use writing to make sense of reading contribute to the achievement gap so visible in schools.

Writing about reading deficits also helps account for differences between low-scoring responses and high-scoring ones in tests of reading comprehension that ask students to write about text. For example, a recent New York State assessment of fourth-grade English language arts (CTB McGraw-Hill, 2004) asked students to write after reading an essay and a poem about whales, and the prompt clearly specified that students should use information from the texts they had read in their responses:

Test Question:
Do you think that fishing boats should be allowed in waters where whales swim? Why or why not? Use details from BOTH the article and the poem to support your answer. In your answer, be sure to
  - State your opinion.
  - Explain your reasons for this opinion.
  - Support your opinion using information from BOTH the article and the poem.
Low-Scoring Response:
They should not be a loud where whale are. Because whale need to siw or they will die.

High-Scoring Response:
I think fishing boats should not be allowed where whales are because the people might hurt the whale or get it in the fishing net and the whale might eat the fish in the fishing net and the people might throw a spear at it. They might even go and kill the whale for no reason what so ever. They might even hurt the whale with the boat and it might get killed that way. That is why I think that fishing boats and not allowed where whales are.

Where the second writer presents a relatively full, organized, and interesting answer, the first writer uses information minimally, far from the extent necessary to form a skilled argument. Conventional wisdom suggests that the second writer is a talented reader and writer and is therefore successful at using writing to express an understanding of the reading. Notice that the test prompt makes this same assumption, that writing is to be used to *express understanding achieved prior to the act of writing* by asking students to state an opinion, explain it, and use details from the reading to support it. The first writer in this conventional view is talented neither at understanding the reading nor at writing to communicate this understanding.

Instead of seeing reading to comprehend and writing to communicate as separate activities, the WIRC research argues that both students are using writing to make sense of their reading. The general theory here is that comprehension and expression happen together and coconstructively—comprehension contributes to expression, and expression contributes to comprehension. This is true of all language activities; talking and writing and even thinking in words help to construct meaning by capturing ideas and images in language. In this manner, comprehension and communication of meaning happen together because meaning is actively constructed as we use words to understand ideas and images.

What, then, accounts for the differences in the two samples of writing we just presented? The second writer shows higher achievement with writing about reading because she uses writing not only to repeat ideas from the reading but to connect and develop them as well; in the process of doing so, she constructs and transforms her knowledge of the reading. The first writer appears to be stuck at the stage of listing isolated ideas from the reading; he uses writing to tell what he knows by simply copying from the text. This suggests that he needs more assistance and practice with using writing to construct an understanding of reading. It is this view that reading and writing are reciprocally related, each serving the other by contributing to the representation and processing of knowledge, that allowed us to design thinksheets to scaffold writing about reading activities for struggling learners.

Using Thinksheets to Improve Higher Level Literacy

Thinksheets assist students with identifying information from literature to construct new meaning as they write about their reading. This is a reading strategy we call *Targeted Reading*, and its function is to help readers build a textbase for understanding the selection by writing down key ideas from their reading. Maintaining a consistent three-part structure (ideas, organization, extended writing), our thinksheets also assist students in choosing content and structuring it as they use a graphic organizer to plan and write their essays. This is a writing strategy we call *Select and Connect*, and its function is to construct a mental model of the reading, first graphically and then verbally.

A thinksheet for the story *The Gardener* (Stewart, 1997), shown in Figure 5.1, illustrates the three-part structure of the WIRC thinksheets. The thinksheet opens with a main question, in this case, straight out of the "Think and Respond" section at the end of the story in the fourth-grade textbook used in our study: "How does Lydia Grace show strength during her year away?" The first five pages of the thinksheet provide probes and inquiries, such as "How do we know that Lydia Grace and Emma are good friends?" which target information relevant to answering the main question from the story being read. On the sixth page, the graphic organizer, a diagram that asks students to list setting and plot details as they relate to the characters, assists students in selecting from the ideas they have identified on the first five pages, and it also assists them in connecting the ideas to plan the extended writing. Finally, the last two pages of the thinksheet provide the main question again and space for writing an elaborated response to it based on the idea identification and organization the writer has already done.

We want to say a little more about Targeted Reading and will do so by distinguishing it from cover-to-cover reading. Cover-to-cover reading refers to reading a selection from beginning to end, usually for pleasure rather than information; it is the style of reading children and adults often enjoy doing for its aesthetic rewards—think of a winter evening, a fireplace, an easy chair, a piece of homemade fudge, and a good book. Targeted Reading refers to efferent reading aimed at achieving a focused purpose, such as getting specific bits of information from a

Figure 5.1. Example Thinksheet

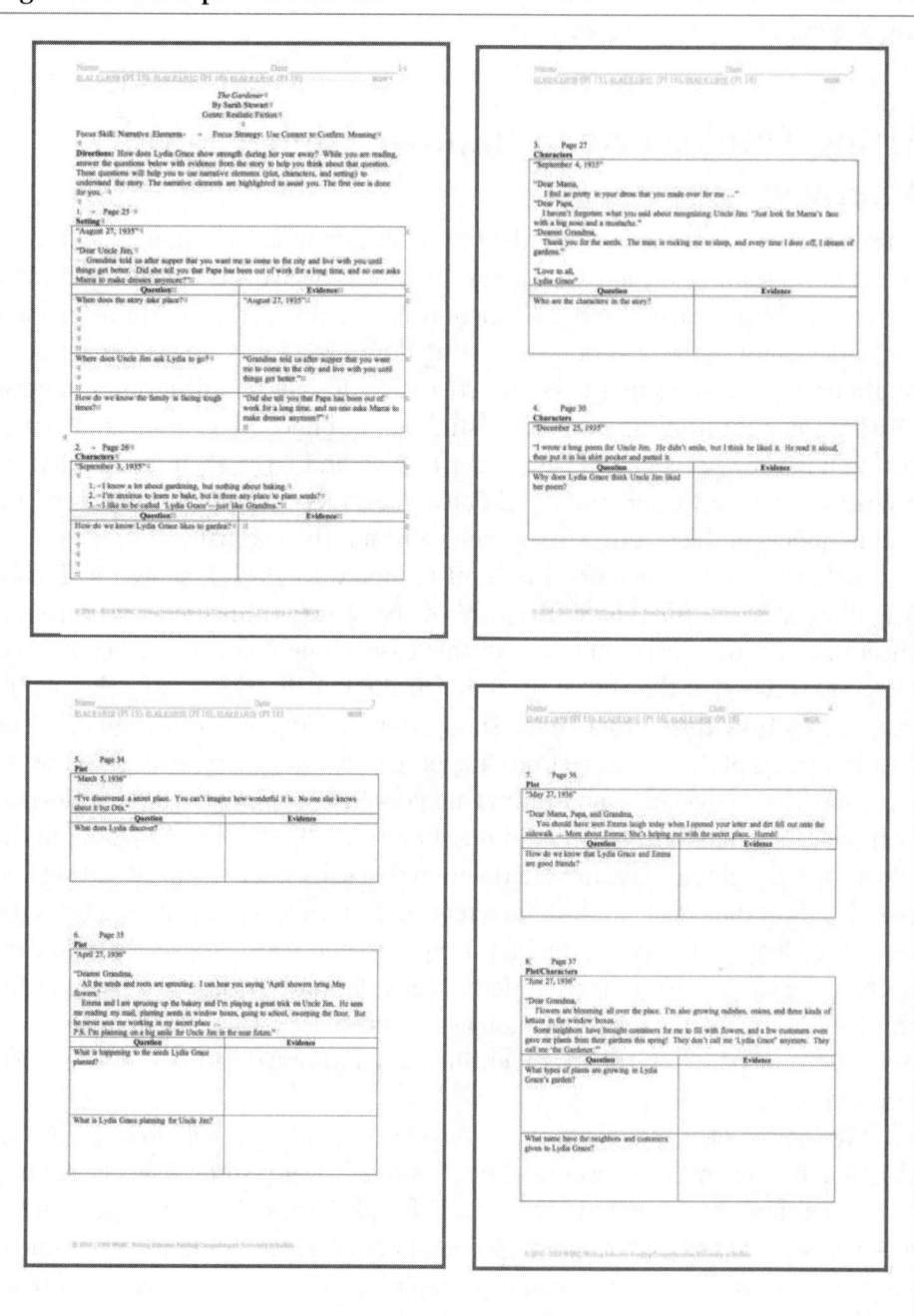

(continued)

Figure 5.1. Example Thinksheet (*continued*)

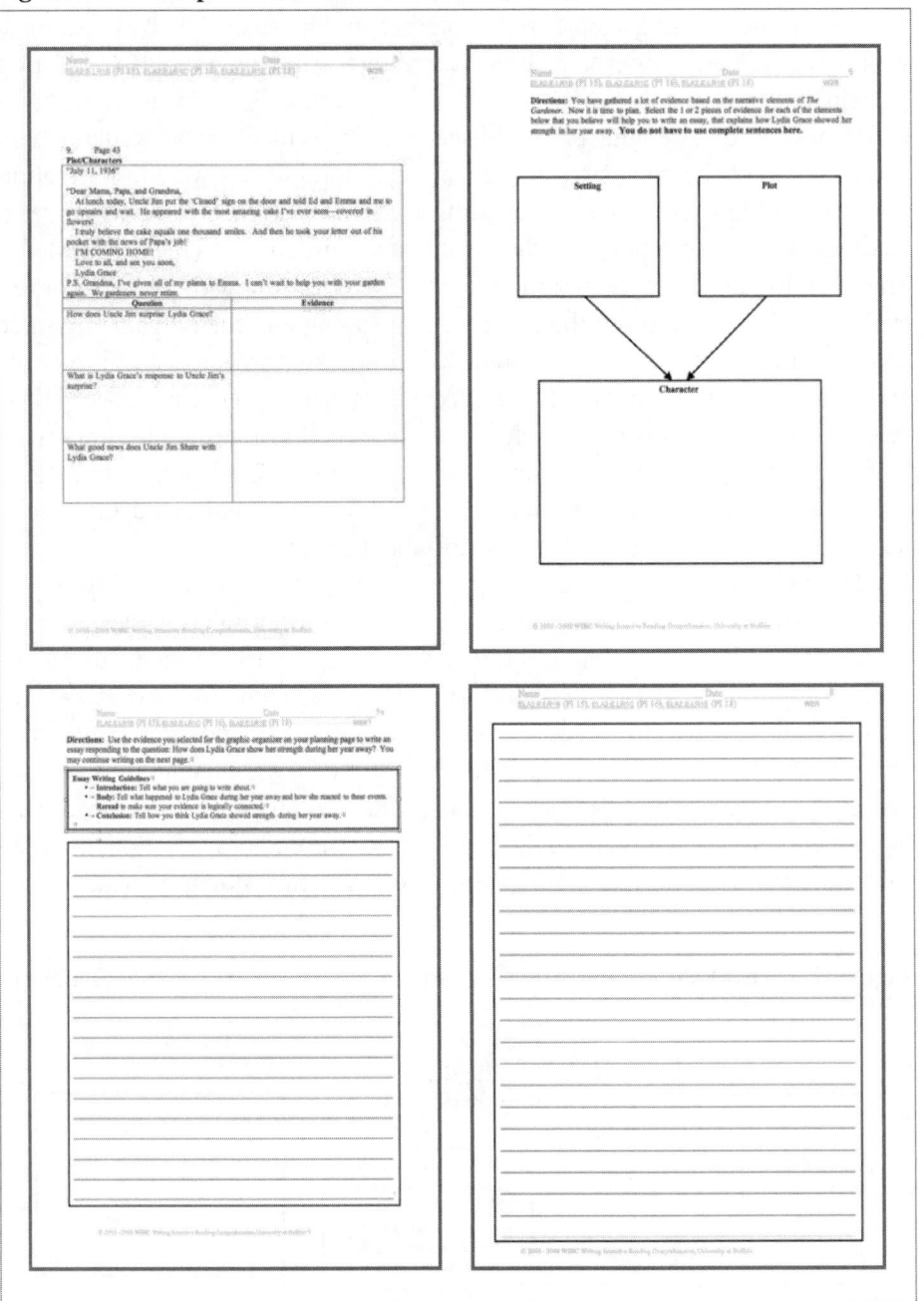

Excerpts from THE GARDENER by Sarah Stewart, pictures by David Small. Text copyright © 1997 by Sarah Stewart. Reprinted by permission of Farrar, Straus and Giroux, LLC

specific text; it is the style of reading adults do when reading the newspaper, using an index, or researching a topic on the Internet, and it usually involves reading to get information and doing something as a result—studying a problem, ordering an item, fixing a flat tire, playing a video game, printing directions to a new destination, writing an academic piece. Targeted reading is focusing one's attention on specific areas of text to answer a question or respond to a writing task. In addition to identifying ideas to use in building a textbase and mental model, targeted reading offers a good foundation for Bereiter and Scardamalia's (1987) Knowledge Transforming model of the writing process. By beginning with a search for relevant bits of information in the text they are reading and then organizing these related but discrete bits into a coherent whole, students are encouraged to create and structure meaning and thus construct and transform their knowledge of their reading. We believe this is precisely where the benefits of writing for improving higher level reading comprehension are derived. Figure 5.2, adapted from Bereiter and Scardamalia, illustrates our theory of how thinksheets assist students in solving cognitive problems involved in writing about reading.

Throughout our WIRC research, we observed that students using one of our thinksheets begin writing only after rereading portions of the selection they are writing about, rather than right after receiving the task. Students using our thinksheets and the knowledge transforming approach tend to do what we have come to call "two-handed reading." They write with one hand on the book they are writing about and one hand on the thinksheet they are using. In this manner, even students who "can't read" (those who can't independently read with high fluency and retention from the beginning to the end of a selection; i.e., they can't do cover-to-cover reading by themselves) can track down information we

Figure 5.2. Thinksheets and Cognitive Processes in Writing About Reading

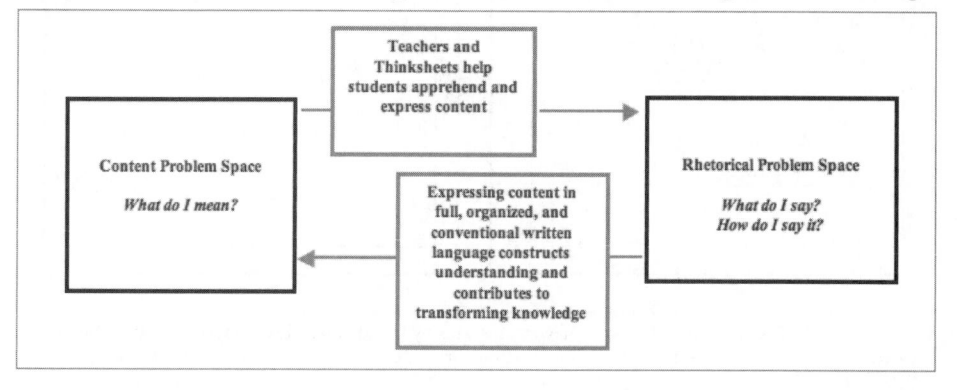

have targeted and write down the information so that it connects with other ideas and thus constructs and communicates understanding. Certainly this is a valuable skill, one that adults use for important purposes, and one that students should learn and practice in school.

Thinksheets Are Not Worksheets

Thinksheets are step-by-step guides to writing about reading, but they are not meant to be stand-alone worksheets. Throughout our work in developing thinksheets for the WIRC intervention, we have been careful not to allow educators to view the use of thinksheets as a solution in itself, without devoting the instructional resources needed to use the thinksheets wisely. We did not want teachers to hand thinksheets to students and then walk away, and we certainly did not want thinksheets to be seen as reductive or formulaic busywork. From the beginning of our work, we envisioned teachers using thinksheets interactively and discursively with students in focused reading-writing workshops where discussions, individual conferences, and teacher modeling guide the use of thinksheets for students, including students who struggle with literacy.

Researchers and educators have argued for decades that collaborative instruction, active learning, explicit modeling of cognitive strategies by teachers, and repeated, increasingly independent practice by students enhance the reading comprehension of struggling readers and writers (see, for example, Beers, 2003). To this mix of collaborative instruction, active learning, and strategic modeling the WIRC research added the necessity of bringing reading and writing together at the point of transaction with text. We did this by developing thinksheets that engage students with reading and writing simultaneously by helping them think through, with teacher assistance, the problems they encounter while writing about reading. Thinksheets, thus, are meant to activate higher level thinking while students are writing during reading.

The earliest thinksheets were developed by Carol Sue Englert, Taffy Raphael, and Becky Kirschner in the mid-1980s, and their thinksheets were initially designed as part of a study to examine the metacognitive abilities of students during the writing process. Expanding on this work, Englert and Raphael (1988) developed a writing program called Cognitive Strategy Instruction in Writing (CSIW), which focused on teaching writing strategies to special education students. Englert and Raphael (1989) provide a clear definition of *thinksheet*, and at the same time explicitly provide the difference between a thinksheet and a traditional worksheet:

The term, think-sheet, was selected to underscore their differences from traditional worksheets. Worksheets are typically used in elementary classrooms to promote students' independent practice of learned skills…. In contrast, think-sheets were developed as a tool for use during modeling and peer interactions. Their purpose is to provide support for teachers during modeling of writing component subprocesses, and later, to serve as reminders to students of appropriate strategy use during the subprocess in which they are engaged. (p. 125)

For the CSIW program, thinksheets were packaged in a series to guide students through the writing process and to scaffold writing by presenting a series of prompts to help writers to remember the self-questions and strategies for each writing subprocess (Englert & Raphael, 1988).

An example of the thinksheets developed by Englert and Raphael is presented in Figure 5.3. This *Plan* thinksheet was developed to help learning disabled

Figure 5.3. The Plan Thinksheet

Name: _____ Date: _____
TOPIC: _____

WHO: Who am I writing for?
_____
_____

WHY: Why am I writing this?
_____
_____

WHAT: What do I know? (Brainstorm)
1. _____
2. _____
3. _____
4. _____
5. _____
6. _____
7. _____
8. _____

students overcome their struggles with activating their background knowledge and organizing that knowledge prior to and during writing. It was followed by an *Organize* thinksheet to guide students as they consider text structure and then a *Self-Edit* thinksheet that helps students focus on both the content and organization of their work. The process of evaluation is then repeated with a peer editor who completes an editor thinksheet. The peer editor and the author then talk about their respective evaluations and brainstorm ways to improve the paper. The final step is for the writer to make revisions and prepare a final draft for publication.

Since the early 1990s, there had been little progress in the development of thinksheets until the beginning of our WIRC study. A sign of this appears in Tierney and Readence (2000) as their citations of thinksheet design note only the work of Englert, Raphael, and Kirschner from the 1980s. We find scattered references to thinksheets (or *think sheet*, *think-sheet*) in the literature, but much of the work since Englert and Raphael unfortunately simply uses the term *think-sheet* in place of the traditional term *worksheet*. One telltale sign of this is that articles and books that reference the use of thinksheets provide no theoretical support and no mention of Raphael, Englert, and their colleagues (for example, see Bloodgood & Pacifici, 2004).

Thinksheets at WIRC

Thinksheets in our view are interactive instruments that help students learn to write about their reading. We design thinksheets to provide scaffolded problem-solving strategies for thinking, reading, and writing. We have used thinksheets as short as one page and as long as a dozen pages, but typically they are five to seven pages and are completed over a period of several days as students study a literary selection. As noted earlier, our thinksheets have a three-part structure:

- Targeting information to identify and explore ideas
- Organizing by selecting and connecting ideas using a graphic organizer
- Extended writing to build understanding of reading

Thinksheets scaffold the process of using writing to make sense of reading by helping students become active and reflective readers. They do this by breaking large tasks into component pieces and by providing support for completing the component tasks. The questions we ask on thinksheets are not test questions, but rather the kinds of questions teachers ask in writing conferences with students to encourage them to think and say more about their topics. We also intend our thinksheets to be both transactional and interactive. By this we mean students transact with their reading as they complete the thinksheet and, at the same time, interact with the teacher and with peers while working on thinksheets. As we said earlier, thinksheets support students through the process of writing about reading by bringing together two cognitive problem spaces for students: the rhetorical and the content spaces (see Bereiter & Scardamalia, 1987). Often these cognitive problem spaces are viewed as disconnected, such as when teachers work separately on course content and then on rhetorical principles and devices, but our view is that teachers and students using thinksheets are operating in a third problem-solving space, one that stands midway between content and expression and that works to unite them. We see thinksheets as bringing together content and expression by easing the cognitive burden of matching content from reading with rhetorical expression while writing.

A thinksheet records on paper the result of reading, writing, and conversing; it presents anticipated problems in writing about reading while assisting students in working toward solutions. Having students write their way through reading comprehension problems may be better than only talking them through the same problems because a thinksheet records the effects of the dialogue students have with teacher, peers, and text. Thinksheets, furthermore, ensure that every student contributes to the work of building an understanding of the selection; this is often not the case with class discussion.

How to Design Thinksheets

Throughout the WIRC research, we used formative experiments (Reinking & Bradley, 2004) to design and test our thinksheets. As a result, the WIRC thinksheets evolved throughout the project. We want to describe the key turning points in this evolution because doing so will highlight the major principles to keep in mind while designing and using thinksheets. Our WIRC thinksheets are matched with selections in the Harcourt Trophies Series (e.g., Beck, Farr, & Strickland, 2003) of textbooks for grades 4 and 5, but in graduate courses we have had teachers use the same principles to design thinksheets for other literary selections and for other content areas, including science, social studies, math, art, music, and even physical education.

The first key component of the WIRC thinksheets has already been mentioned several times: the three-part structure of Ideas, Organization, and Extended Writing. All WIRC thinksheets have this structure, and we strongly recommend it to anyone designing thinksheets to help students comprehend their reading by writing about it. The Ideas section asks students to go back into the reading to find and appropriate specific information; this is the targeted reading strategy at work. The Organization section provides a graphic organizer, or a choice of graphic organizers, to guide students in choosing which ideas to include and how to establish relationships among these ideas as they are spelled out completely in the Extended Writing section; together these comprise the select-and-connect writing strategy.

All WIRC thinksheets have the Extended Writing section at the end, and the first step in designing a thinksheet is to write (or borrow from the textbook) the question students will answer in this extended writing section. Once the question is identified, it is written on the extended writing page and the first pages of the other two sections. We repeat the question in this manner to keep students focused on the task at hand and to help ensure that the work students do on the Ideas and Organization sections of the thinksheet builds toward and scaffolds their writing in the Extended Writing section.

In the Ideas section of *The Gardener* (Stewart, 1997) thinksheet, we provide page numbers from the textbook as well as blocks of selected text excerpts to assist students with targeting specific information to respond to questions in the Ideas section. This is a thinksheet from early in the year, and in later thinksheets we provide only the page number. Also in the early thinksheets, we ask students to not only respond to a question but also to provide the specific textual evidence from the reading selection that supports their answers. For example, on the thinksheet for *The Gardener*, the thinksheet asks, "How do we know that Lydia Grace and Emma are good friends?" Students respond to the question, and in the adjacent space, they provide the specific evidence from the text that led them to their answer. In a formative experiment, our effort to assist students with their thinking as well as guide them to support their responses led us to include the textual evidence requirement. This is how we learned that students benefit from providing their answers and showing the evidence to support their thinking. This also assists students with targeting their reading as they have to return to the selection to respond.

The most notable alteration to the Extended Writing section in one of our formative experiments came as a result of teachers in focus group sessions or our experimental-group teacher training sessions asking us to revise the extended writing section to appear more like the fourth grade New York State English Language Arts (ELA) Assessment (CTB McGraw-Hill, 2004) that is given each year in January. Teachers and students spend a lot of time preparing for this standardized assessment, and it was right of the teachers to ask if we could assist them and their students with that preparation. By setting up the extended writing page to appear similar to an extended writing ELA task, students could become familiar with the formatting of the prompt and develop a metacognitive awareness that the generation of ideas from a reading selection and the organization of selected ideas for how to respond to a writing prompt are connected.

Similarly, we altered wording in the directions of the Extended Writing section to more closely mirror that of the ELA assessment. Rather than refer to the graphic organizer in the extended writing prompt, the directions asked students to use the information on the planning page, just as the ELA assessment refers to the blank page prior to their extended writing task as a planning page for students to organize their thoughts prior to writing.

In another formative experiment we switched from providing a specific graphic organizer on each thinksheet to providing a page with our six most frequently used graphic organizers, such as a T-Chart, a Compare–Contrast Venn Diagram, a Cause and Effect Table, a Web of Related Ideas, a Story Structure Guide, and an Essay Structure Guide. Along with this, we included a blank planning page for students to draw the graphic organizer they selected from the choices, the one they felt best assisted with organizing their thoughts for the specific writing task. The WIRC team also developed a classroom poster with the same six graphic organizers for teachers to post in their classrooms. The idea here was that students would always have a selection of graphic organizers to assist with planning their writing, whether or not it was related to ELA reading or thinksheets. The formative experiment that introduced a choice of graphic organizers resulted in the graphic organizer being taken much more seriously, both on the subsequent thinksheets and on the posttest for the main experiment in our study. We highly recommend that once students are familiar with a variety of graphic organizers, they be given a choice of which to use and that they be required to draw the one they choose to fit their plans for writing.

How to Teach With Thinksheets

Before addressing the central concern of this section, we begin with an example of how *not* to teach with thinksheets from a lesson observed in a fifth-grade classroom by the principal investigator and three other WIRC researchers. As students worked through each item on the thinksheet, they followed the teacher's instruction and underlined or highlighted main ideas and details within the paragraphs presented on the thinksheets. However, the teacher's instruction did not stop there. Students were provided some time to complete pieces of the thinksheet on their own as the teacher circulated around the room—mostly, we observed, for classroom management purposes rather than to provide guidance with the writing. The teacher led so much of the work that students were told to have on their desks only the thinksheet and a pen or pencil. They were not required to have their textbooks in front of them. The final extended writing piece was also teacher led and constructed. This instruction resulted in 18 students having identical responses that began, "Waves moving across the ocean carry energy." Three students had different responses; two of them wrote about tsunamis and a third about the size of waves. The two tsunami responses, however, wrote the same details about wave energy on their thinksheets leading to the writing task. Much of the thinksheets in this example, in short, had been completed by having students record directly ideas and sentences presented by the teacher. From our perspective, the teacher focused on the product— the extended writing outcome—rather than on scaffolding students' cognitive processes, which should lead to the product. This approach, of course, is not uncommon during writing instruction, especially for low-performing students and especially when preparing them for high-stakes assessment.

In composition instruction the practice of extended periods of teacher-dominated discussion is referred to by George Hillocks (1984, 1986) as the Presentational Mode of instruction. This manner of instruction is teacher directed and provides little opportunity for students to interact and engage in the processes through which they make meaning. Teachers in this mode facilitate instruction through a series of Initiation, Response, Evaluation (IRE) sequences (Cazden, 1986) as they ask questions that necessitate single-word or similar, easily evaluated responses from students. As a result, the teacher in the lesson we are describing led the students through each section of the thinksheet, interpreting each question on the thinksheet as an IRE sequence, often going so far as to put the question on the board and ask students to respond. When students could not respond quickly enough, the teacher filled in the answer for the students and instructed them to fill in their blanks with her answer. Again, although a common practice, this did not give students the opportunity to revisit and think about the reading they had done.

Instead of the presentational mode of teaching dominated by teacher talk, we recommend a workshop-style approach to instruction in which the teacher leads brief (3 to 5 minutes) minilessons followed by 5 to 10 minutes of work, or writing time, for the students. Several of these throughout a block of time devoted to literacy instruction would help students to stay on task and focused. The specific method of alternating periods of instruction with periods of writing that eventually evolved from this understanding of the reading-writing workshop is illustrated in Figure 5.4. As the figure indicates, we expect a 30- or 40-minute lesson to have several blocks combining minilessons with workshop-style reading and writing focused on thinksheets. Also, our intervention design indicated the minilessons were to get shorter at the same time the workshop blocks get longer. This style of instruction reflects the "Gradual Release of Responsibility" model of reading comprehension (see, for example, Pearson, 2009).

Another lesson we observed used a thinksheet from the selection *William Shakespeare & the Globe* by Aliki (2000), and this lesson can be used to illustrate the teaching methods we are recommending. The teacher began the lesson by reminding the students that he and the students' peers were allowed to help with the thinksheet, as he said, "Everyone will work together for a few minutes. I'm allowed to help you on the thinksheets." The students laid their thinksheets out with page one on top of their desks and their anthologies opened to the two pages referred to on the thinksheet. The teacher led them through the first question, which was completed as a group, aloud. The next question was completed the same way. Then the students went to work on their own or with a partner if needed. The teacher circulated around the room, conferring with individual students

Figure 5.4. The WIRC Method of Teaching in the Reading–Writing Workshop

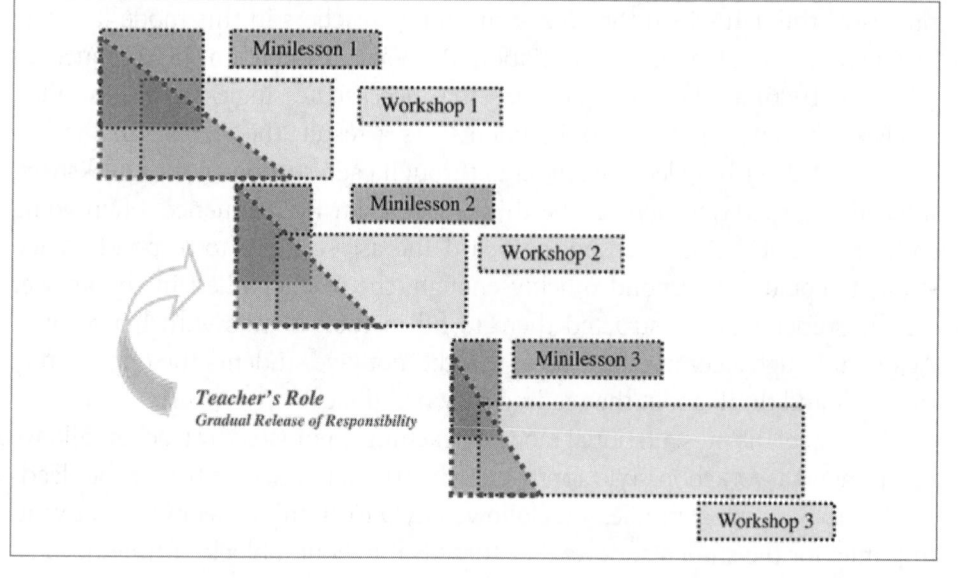

and clarifying and responding to student questions. After about five minutes the teacher led a discussion in which the completed questions were reviewed by the group. Another question from the thinksheet was then answered as a group, and the teacher emphasized the need for the students to refer to the text directly when responding to the questions. Completing these pieces and referring directly to the text constituted what we referred to as Targeted Reading earlier. Targeted Reading is focusing one's attention on specific areas of text to extract information and think about it to answer a question or respond to a writing task.

Throughout the completion of the Ideas section, students wrote in roughly five-minute chunks of time. The break time between writing sessions was used to review answers and to allow students to maintain their focus on the task without overwhelming them with too much extended writing.

When it came time for the Organization section, several students hesitated. One said, "I am not good at putting things into a paragraph." The teacher responded,

> Make a list, then I'll come by and show you how to put it into a paragraph. Do the best you can. Use information from the Ideas section. If you put it down, we can help. That's the thing about writing; you have to put it down before we can help you.

The students then wrote their paragraphs for about 10 minutes before the lesson ended.

Telling students to "put it down [in writing]" was key to the lesson. Likewise, circulating around the room and focusing on students who needed assistance is a central method in the lesson. These writing conferences can also take place at the teacher's desk or another location. We recommend keeping the conferences short and focused on the thinksheet tasks; this is the best way to help students with the higher level thinking, reading, and writing the thinksheet requires.

We want to add a note about some students' tendencies toward verbatim, unreflective copying when responding to questions on thinksheets. We recommend that teachers be extremely tolerant of copying verbatim from the text in the Ideas section of the thinksheets. Students are often told to put their responses in their own words. More often than not, students who struggle with reading may not have their own words and background knowledge ready to use in place of the words in the text they are reading. As a result they copy directly, and sometimes seemingly mindlessly, from a text. This, according to Collins (1998), is a default strategy. Struggling writers do not have a better way to put information on the page. The result often is copying, not in the malicious, deceitful sense but rather as a means to an end.

On the other hand, successful student writers reappropriate the words (language) of a text to construct their own meaning in their responses. Some of the words of successful writers are the same as those in the passage, but they are combined with the students' own newly developed ideas about the text based on the construction of new knowledge that took place during the reading and writing processes—as in the knowledge transformation model by Bereiter and Scardamalia (1987) that we discussed earlier.

Part of the WIRC approach is that students can develop this reappropriation of words from a text as they get to the Organization and Extended Writing sections of the thinksheets. Over time, through the use of additional thinksheets, they interact with the teacher and have meaningful transactions as they return to the text they are reading (or rereading). Through this process students will get better at paraphrasing text and transforming ideas. We noted three stages in this manner of development that provided evidence for students' moving forward from knowledge telling to knowledge transforming:

1. **Direct copying**. This stage consists primarily of responding to questions with large blocks of text borrowed directly from a selection in the hope that the text copied provides an answer to a question. This demonstrates low-level skill and involves little or no knowledge transforming. Still, it is a valuable starting place for struggling readers and writers because using direct copying in the Ideas section of the thinksheets helps them appropriate the language and knowledge for the Organization and Extended Writing sections.

2. **Less copying and more overlap**. Here *overlap* means stating an idea from the text partly in words borrowed from the text and partly in one's own words. Students may use strings of words directly from the text mixed with their own words in response to a question. This demonstrates a step toward knowledge transformation, a move toward higher level thinking in terms of knowing how to use text to respond to questions.

3. **High overlap/strategic copying**. This stage involves the students' reappropriating strings of words from a given text as a way to make new meaning to respond to a question logically and completely. This demonstrates higher levels of thinking as well as the ability to go into a text and target only those words or strings of words that specifically serve to respond appropriately to the question. This represents the students' strategic use of words from a given text to construct new knowledge as they write. Over time, these ideas have become increasingly important

in the analysis of student writing in the WIRC project (see Brutt-Griffler, Collins, & Lee, 2006; Collins & Lee, 2005).

One more note on this matter of copying. The WIRC research measured connections between a student's written text and the original literary passage in categories of copying, quoting, paraphrasing, overlapping, and transforming. We studied how students appropriate material from literary selections in their writing about the selections by using an automated analysis tool to report the total number of words and strings of words at least three words in length that have been copied from texts and the percentage of words copied out of the total number of words written. Automated analysis in all the categories showed no significant differences between experimental and control sections. Because students in both experimental and control groups showed significant gains between pre- and posttest, with the WIRC students outperforming the others, we conclude that thinksheets help students get better at higher level literacy. We also found that the WIRC instructional materials and methods, which elicit a great deal of appropriation of language from reading being written about, do not contribute to an increase in copying when students are assessed using tasks that ask them to write about their reading. Used judiciously, copying is a way of getting smarter, both about comprehending texts and about outgrowing copying.

The True Value of Thinksheets

We've said several times that the value of thinksheets is that they bring reading and writing together. Students progress through gathering and developing ideas from their reading to accomplish their writing task by generating ideas, organizing those ideas on their thinksheets, and finally writing about them in an extended piece. Doing so fosters higher level reading comprehension as students learn to use the text they are reading to write their thoughts. Doing this repeatedly guides them to deeper comprehension and meaning making.

The typical writing process as it is known in school follows the traditional linear model of prewriting, drafting, editing, revising, and publishing. Dean (2006) writes of this process:

> Despite the original intent that process be recursive, in the classroom, process began to look a lot like the old black-and-white movie, only with more detail: Monday was prewriting, Tuesday was drafting, Wednesday was revision, Thursday was editing, and Friday was publishing.... What happens to the individual writing process when it goes to school? It generally gets put into a pattern that fits school more than the individual. (p. 3)

According to Dean, the process approach to writing instruction follows a series of distinctive stages or steps that, as Flower and Hayes (1981) note, "reflect the growth of a written product, and these stages are organized in a *linear* (emphasis in original) sequence or structure" (p. 365).

Thinksheets, while they can fit into such a model, are not intended to focus on such a linear structure. Rather, thinksheets are intended to assist students with the cognitive processes that proficient writers use. Thinksheets also provide a social component to foster development of these cognitive processes because they enable students and teachers to literally be on the same page during reading and writing. Thinksheets provide the structure through which struggling writers can return to their reading to access ideas relevant to the extended writing task. It is important to remember that thinksheets are designed to assist with problem-solving activities during writing. Struggling writers have difficulty coming up with relevant or appropriate ideas about which to write. Assistance with generating ideas for writing not only provides struggling writers with content for their writing, it also provides an avenue through which they can internalize how to approach writing about reading problems. The eventual goal is higher level literacy, meaning that students will be able to generate, organize, and write about their ideas independent of thinksheet and teacher assistance.

ACTION PLAN

To try the thinksheet design and implementation methods described in this chapter, select a literary selection and plan a thinksheet to assist students in writing about the selection. You might want to discuss the plan and answers to the questions below with one or more other teachers. Use your plan to design a thinksheet with the three-part structure discussed in the chapter. Finally, try the thinksheet with students using the interactive teaching methods recommended in the chapter. Reflect on the Questions for Study and Reflection as you design and try out your thinksheet.

QUESTIONS FOR STUDY AND REFLECTION

1. How are thinksheets different from worksheets?
2. How do the authors theorize reading and writing as involving the transformation of knowledge?
3. What differences do you see between targeted reading and cover-to-cover reading?
4. How do thinksheets assist writers with problems they might encounter while writing about reading?
5. How does copying and appropriating knowledge fit into the WIRC perspective on teaching higher level literacy?
6. How might I make use of thinksheets to help my struggling readers and writers?

NOTES

The research reported here was supported by the Institute of Education Sciences, U.S. Department of Education, through Grant #R305G040153 to the University at Buffalo, The State University of New York. The opinions expressed are those of the authors and do not represent views of the Institute or the U.S. Department of Education. A full report of the experimental results of the WIRC study may be obtained from the first author of this chapter: jcollins@buffalo.edu

REFERENCES

Beck, I.L., Farr, R.C., & Strickland D.S. (Eds.). (2003). *Distant voyages*. Boston: Harcourt.

Beers, K. (2003). *When kids can't read: What teachers can do. A guide for teachers 6–12*. Norwood, MA: Christopher-Gordon.

Bereiter, C., & Scardamalia, M. (1987). *The psychology of written composition*. Hillsdale, NJ: Erlbaum.

Bloodgood, J.W., & Pacifici, L.C. (2004). Bringing word study to intermediate classrooms. *The Reading Teacher*, 58(3), 250–263. doi:10.1598/RT.58.3.3

Brutt-Griffler, J., Collins, J., & Lee, J. (2006, December). *A model and method for analyzing reading-writing connections*. Paper presented at the annual meeting of the National Reading Conference, Los Angeles, CA.

Cazden, C.B. (1986). Classroom discourse. In M.C. Wittrock (Ed.), *Handbook of research on teaching* (3rd ed., pp. 432–463). New York: Macmillan.

Collins, J.L. (1998). *Strategies for struggling writers*. New York: Guilford.

Collins, J.L., & Lee, J. (2005, December). *Bringing together reading and writing to enhance comprehension*. Paper presented at the annual meeting of the National Reading Conference, Miami, FL.

Collins, J.L., & Godinho, G.V. (1996). Help for struggling writers: Strategic instruction and social identity formation in high school. *Learning Disabilities Research & Practice, 11*(3), 177–182.

Collins, K.M., & Collins, J.L. (1996). Strategic instruction for struggling writers. *English Journal, 85*(6), 54–61. doi:10.2307/819828

CTB McGraw-Hill. (2004). *New York State Testing Program English Language Arts and Reading Grade 4: 2004.* Monterey, CA: Author.

Dean, D. (2006). *Strategic writing: The writing process and beyond in the secondary English classroom.* Urbana, IL: National Council of Teachers of English.

Englert, C.S. (1995). Teaching written language skills. In P.T. Cegelka & W.H. Berdine (Eds.), *Effective instruction for students with learning difficulties* (pp. 304–343). Boston: Allyn & Bacon.

Englert, C.S., & Mariage, T.V. (1990). Send for the POSSE: Structuring the comprehension dialogue. *Intervention in School and Clinic, 25*(4), 473–487.

Englert, C.S., & Raphael, T.E. (1988). Constructing well-formed prose: Process, structure, and metacognitive knowledge. *Exceptional Children, 54*(6), 513–520.

Englert, C.S., & Raphael, T.E. (1989). Developing successful writers through cognitive strategy instruction. In J.E. Brophy (Ed.), *Advances in research on teaching* (Vol. 1, pp. 105–151). Greenwich, CT: JAI Press.

Flower, L., & Hayes, J. (1981). A cognitive process theory of writing. *College Composition and Communication, 32*(4), 365–387. doi:10.2307/356600

Hillocks, G., Jr. (1984). What works in teaching composition: A meta-analysis of experimental treatment studies. *American Journal of Education, 93*(1), 133–170. doi:10.1086/443789

Hillocks, G., Jr. (1986). *Research on written composition: New directions for teaching.* Urbana, IL: National Council of Teachers of English.

Pearson, P.D. (2009). The roots of reading comprehension instruction. In S.E. Israel & G.G. Duffy (Eds.), *Handbook of research on reading comprehension* (pp. 3–31). New York: Routledge.

Raphael, T.E., Kirschner, B.W., & Englert, C.S. (1986). *Students' metacognitive knowledge about writing.* East Lansing: Michigan State University, Institute for Research on Teaching.

Raphael, T.E., Kirschner, B.W., & Englert, C.S. (1988). Expository writing program: Making connections between reading and writing. *The Reading Teacher, 41*(8), 790–795.

Reinking, D., & Bradley, B.A. (2004). Connecting research and practice using formative and design experiments. In N.K. Duke & M.H. Mallette (Eds.), *Literacy research methodologies* (pp. 149–169). New York: Guilford.

Tierney, R.J., & Readence, J.E. (2000). Expository reading-writing think-sheets. In R.J. Tierney & J.E. Readence (Eds.), *Reading strategies and practices* (5th ed., pp. 278–284). Boston, MA: Allyn & Bacon.

LITERATURE CITED

Aliki. (2000). *William Shakespeare & the Globe.* New York: HarperCollins.

Stewart, S. (1997). *The gardener.* New York: Farrar, Straus and Giroux.

CHAPTER 6

Teaching Struggling Readers to Respond in Writing to Open-Ended Questions: Making the Writing *and* Reading Strategic

Nancy N. Boyles

I t's a scene that has played itself out for me countless times as I visit classrooms. I meet with intermediate-grade struggling students to discuss a piece of literature or informational text. "Who can connect with the main character here and the problem she faces?" I ask. "What do you think the author of this text valued? Why do you think she wrote this book?" The conversation is animated, and I am impressed by the depth of thinking expressed by many of the students in the group who offer thoughtful, insightful oral responses to my higher level open-ended questions.

Then those same students return to their seats to write answers to the questions we just discussed. Later as I peruse the sparse, superficial responses they have scribbled onto their papers, I wonder to myself, could these be the same kids who performed so brilliantly in our discussion? Working alongside struggling readers in the classroom, I realized that while some struggling students may have the thought in their head and can articulate an answer to an open-ended question orally, they are somehow unable to transform that thought into a coherent written response.

The implications of this are grave. It is a sign of the times that students' capacity to read is measured by their capacity to write. High-stakes literacy assessments in nearly every state require students to respond to open-ended questions to evaluate their comprehension of text. While this potentially affects *all* students, it can be especially devastating to low-performing students who are often plagued both by low reading and low writing skills. Hence, those scores published in local newspapers heralding the percentage of students who meet the state's annual reading goal reflect much about their writing as well as their reading.

Open-Ended Questions and Higher Level Thinking

By their very nature, open-ended questions require higher level thinking. Open-ended questions focus on more than students' basic capacity to construct meaning; they rely on the ability to reason and to apply knowledge. Open-ended questions are not as clear-cut as multiple-choice questions; they are not questions that demand a single correct response. Nor are they questions where any response is acceptable. Rather, open-ended questions address essential concepts, processes, and skills. In general, they require complex thinking and yield multiple solutions. Open-ended questions require teachers or evaluators to interpret and use multiple criteria in evaluating responses. Such questions also require more from students than simply memorizing facts (Badger & Thomas, 1992). It is no wonder that open-ended questions are especially difficult for struggling readers when the answers require a written response.

This chapter describes instructional strategies that lead struggling readers to greater success in writing responses to open-ended comprehension questions. It is based on extensive work in classrooms from grade 2 through middle school over more than a decade. These strategies have been implemented in urban and suburban districts not just by me, an outside consultant and university faculty member, but by hundreds of classroom teachers, reading specialists, special education teachers, and teachers of English-language learners. The strategies are easy to apply and have been credited with raising the level of student performance on high-stakes assessments as well as on day-to-day classroom literacy tasks.

When I first identified this problem, the solution seemed fairly simple: Just show teachers how to teach written response as a writing genre, gradually releasing responsibility until students could respond to a question independently. Hence, this chapter begins with an explanation of the principles and procedures behind that concept of gradually releasing responsibility to students as they learn to produce high-quality answers to open-ended comprehension questions. It provides specific guidelines to help those students who have the thought in their head but can't quite seem to get it down on paper.

While this notion of teaching written response, governed by the systematic release of responsibility, remains central to students' success as they respond to literature, my school visits showed me once again that nothing in the classroom is ever as straightforward as it might appear in theory. The complication this time is that some students who struggled with written response didn't have "the thought in their head." They couldn't write good answers not because they didn't understand *how* to write their response but because they had no idea *what* to write. (These are typically the quiet ones who are not actively engaged in discussions about text; it's hard to gauge how much they know before they pick up their pencil.) The difficulty for these students, I concluded, was not with the strategy for writing but with the strategy for reading. What these students needed to know was how to retrieve the evidence necessary for answering a particular question as they read the text. So the second part of this chapter explains what teachers need to do to make the reading strategic and explicit.

The final part of this chapter targets a basic consideration that many teachers overlook when addressing open-ended questions with struggling students: Teachers ask very sophisticated questions before determining whether students have a solid grasp of prerequisite skills. This leads to frustration for both teachers and students. While there is no lock-step scope and sequence for introducing open-ended questions related to specific comprehension objectives, it is evident that some questions presume an understanding of foundational knowledge, which must be clearly established before moving to questions that build upon that foundation. We can end this struggle by outlining the questions and objectives that should come first and those that ought to follow.

In a nutshell, this chapter will explore what it takes to help struggling readers achieve success and independence in responding to open-ended comprehension questions by examining the following:

- How to make *writing* strategic
- How to make *reading* strategic
- How to build a logical hierarchy of thinking skills

Making the Writing Strategic

Those low test scores that pronounce many of our students "below proficiency" in their capacity to comprehend text are really a symptom of a problem that reaches way beyond testing into all corners of academic life, from the primary

grades through college graduation, from literacy to the content areas, from afflu-
ent suburbs to impoverished urban centers: Many struggling students find it
difficult to respond in writing to open-ended questions. Throughout their entire
academic career, students will be asked to write answers to open-ended comprehension questions. What kind of support would struggling students need to
demonstrate higher level thinking about text not just on "the test" but on open-
ended questions in the classroom? The four-stage approach to teaching written
response strategies that I will describe became my first step in helping teachers
help their students to resolve this crucial problem.

In my mind I see the word *teach* in a bigger, bolder font. The National
Reading Panel (National Institute of Child Health and Human Development,
2000) suggested that instruction that is "explicit" and "systematic" bodes well
for student success, not just in terms of comprehension but for many dimensions of reading. Exactly what is "explicit" instruction? One researcher has said,
"Explicit teaching is about making the hidden obvious; exposing and explaining what is taken for granted; demystifying mental processes; letting children in
on the information and strategies which will enable them to become powerful
literacy users" (Wilkinson, 1999, p. 7).

To make explicit instruction "systematic" there needs to be a logical
sequence of mental processes that progresses in an organized manner. Pearson
and Gallagher (1983) identified the following systematic processes that lead
students to independence in addressing a literacy task:

- **Modeling.** Teachers model learning behaviors such as building criteria,
  self-assessing, seeking feedback, making adjustments, goal setting, and
  reflecting.
- **Sharing.** Teachers share exemplars of quality work and teach students to
  identify quality samples of their own work.
- **Guiding.** Students and teachers assume joint responsibility through guided practice.
- **Reaching independence.** Students practice, demonstrate, and apply
  learning behaviors that help them become self-directed learners.

My challenge then became one of designing an explicit, systematic model for instructing students in written response to open-ended comprehension
questions. I responded to that challenge with a sequence of question–response
scaffolds for many generic comprehension questions at different thinking levels

(Boyles, 2002). For example, an inferential question that students could be asked at any grade level, for any literature selection might be, "Choose a word that best describes [a particular character/person] and provide evidence from the text to support your choice." Although the content of the response would vary by text (are you describing Clifford the big red dog or Rosa Parks?) the components to be included in a quality answer to that question would remain constant. I have reworked the Pearson and Gallagher model just a bit to better reflect an order that I believe is best suited to elementary and middle school learners with regard to written response, as follows:

- **Explain** the criteria.
- **Model** the process.
- Provide **guided practice** with the support of an Answer Organizer or Answer Frame.
- Move to **independent application** without graphic support.

Explain the Criteria

The first thing students need in order to write a good response to a question is a clear set of expectations. Exactly *what* do you want this answer to contain? For the question about describing a character, I would want a paragraph response that includes the following:

- A topic sentence with the name of the character or person and his or her important trait.
- Two or three specific examples of things that happened in the text where the character showed this trait.
- A quote from the text that proves the trait with the author's own words.

Clarifying the criteria helps both teachers and students. Students feel safe knowing exactly what the teacher wants as they craft their response. Likewise, the teacher knows what to look for and can assess students' products more fairly. Without supplying the criteria up front, students, especially struggling students, are left guessing, "What does my teacher want here?" And even the teacher can be a bit vague about what constitutes a worthy response—until one sort of "pops up" as he sifts through a set of papers.

Notice a few elements of this list that make it manageable for struggling students. First, there are only three criteria. This wouldn't be as effective with eight or nine elements to synthesize into an answer because you ultimately want students to remember the criteria without looking at the chart on the wall so they can write their answer independently. It is unlikely that struggling students could remember many steps, but they can remember a few. Also note that this is a "no frills" list that only includes the basics. As with any initial instruction, the goal is to give students just enough guidance to get them started. Struggling students become easily overwhelmed when the task seems too complex. Save the fine points for later when students feel good about what they've accomplished so far.

Another critical piece related to explaining the criteria to struggling students is that they benefit from both oral and visual presentation of a modeled response that meets the criteria. I write the criteria on a chart and display the chart prominently for all to see. I also review the criteria out loud many times, giving several students the opportunity to identify the components so that I am sure that there is at least some metacognitive awareness of what the task entails. Such repeated practice is invaluable to struggling students (Marzano, Pickering, & Pollock, 2001) who often don't expect to be held accountable to their learning and who, without teacher monitoring, may opt to tune out early on in the lesson.

Model the Process

In this second phase of the instructional sequence, we need to show students *how* they will reach their goal. What does a good answer to this question look like? Modeling means that the teacher engages in whatever is involved in the learning task exactly as students are expected to perform it, in a manner that is clear and learnable. This instructional component is especially critical to students who have processing problems and memory retrieval problems because it provides a learning map.

Literacy experts have recognized for a long while the value of modeling (Pressley & Harris, 1990), but for the concept to be "clear and learnable," in addition to breaking the task into bite-size chunks and introducing them through multisensory techniques, the teacher must engage students by demonstrating enthusiasm, maintaining a lively pace, and frequently checking for understanding. A common misconception about modeling is that the teacher is the performer and the students are the audience. Good modeling is very interactive and is definitely not a spectator sport.

Another modeling misconception is that it gives too much away. Sometimes teachers ask, "If students are writing about a specific character, and I model that response for them, won't they just copy mine?" Remember that what is being modeled here is the process of responding, not information about this one character, so any text may serve as the basis of the model. Here is a model I might produce regarding the Big Bad Wolf in "Little Red Riding Hood":

One word that really describes the Big Bad Wolf is clever. He showed this many times in the story. First, he was clever when he met Little Red Riding Hood in the forest and used his charming manners to get her to talk to him. Then he was clever when he pretended he actually *was* Little Red Riding Hood to get Granny to unlock her door. The wolf was also clever when he explained to Little Red Riding Hood why his eyes were so big. He said, "The better to see you with, my dear." As you can see, the wolf was certainly one clever fellow!

What I really want students to do is transfer their understanding of the response criteria to the description of the character about whom they are writing: What words would they use to describe Grace in *Amazing Grace* (Hoffman, 1991), Little Willy in *Stone Fox* (Gardiner, 1980), or Jonas in *The Giver* (Lowry, 1993)? Regardless of the level of text sophistication, the criteria are essentially the same.

For struggling students, modeling is generally most effective when the teacher constructs the model in front of them rather than distributes a completed response and expects them to deconstruct it for themselves. I think aloud about the criteria as I go along, for example, by saying, "Okay, now in this first sentence I want to make sure I include the character's name and the trait I've chosen.... Let's see, did I do that?" This is a good place to pause for some student input. Get a student to verify that you've met the criteria for the response. Then go a step further and invite someone to underline the character's name in blue marker and the character trait in red to incorporate additional visual cues as well as a tactile element. The best modeling gradually transitions to guided practice as the teacher recognizes that students are getting it. Evidence for drawing this conclusion might include not-so-scientific, but nonetheless quite reliable, measures, such as smiles of recognition, a sparkle in the eye, and an increase in the number of hands waving in the air, signaling students who are eager to participate.

Provide Guided Practice With the Support of an Answer Organizer or Answer Frame

One of my favorite lines regarding the role of practice in explicit instruction is "Practice doesn't make perfect. Practice makes permanent" (Jones, 1987, p. 14). I wish I'd thought of that! It describes perfectly what really happens when kids perform a learning task over and over. It becomes embedded in their memory exactly as they practice it. That's why it is important to make sure that the practice is well matched to the desired outcome and that it helps students perform the task successfully.

Guided practice affords students the opportunity to practice a task not just until they master it but also until it becomes automatic. Guided practice serves teachers by helping them monitor and assess students' progress, analyze errors, provide individual feedback, and determine a remediation plan if necessary.

Guided practice is *not* a worksheet or workbook page that takes the place of instruction. However, the Report of the National Reading Panel (NICHD, 2000) offered strong evidence that the use of graphic organizers is one of the seven most powerful research-based practices in developing students' comprehension. With this in mind, I propose two forms of graphic support (Boyles, 2002): the Answer Organizer (see Figure 6.1) and the Answer Frame (see Figure 6.2).

The Answer Organizer offers less support than the Answer Frame and usually provides sufficient guidance for most learners in a regular classroom setting at grades four and above. Take another look at the criteria provided during the first phase of instruction (explanation of the response criteria). Note that the Answer Organizer simply takes these criteria and breaks them into bite-size chunks. This assists struggling readers in staying focused and helps them see that this seemingly complex question is really made up of smaller pieces that can be addressed in a logical, step-by-step fashion. Additionally, this organizer serves the teacher's needs as she assesses students' responses. Either the topic sentence contains the required information or it doesn't. It's easy to sort through details in a designated location to determine whether they contain sufficient connection to the specific content of the text. And finally, it's easy to use this information diagnostically to figure out the needs of students and to map out the next instructional step.

Does almost everyone get the notion of a topic sentence? Then the teacher can confer individually with the one or two students who are still having difficulty with this concept. Are there five or six students who do not seem to make the distinction between general or specific details? It would be appropriate for

Figure 6.1. Answer Organizer

> **Choose one word that best describes [name of character/person] (kind, friendly, lazy, responsible, etc.) and provide evidence from the text to support your choice.**
>
> **ANSWER ORGANIZER**
> Write a topic sentence that includes the name of the character or person and his/her important trait.
>
> _____
>
> Write one or two sentences about one event in the text that shows this trait.
>
> _____
>
> Write one or two sentences about a second event that shows this trait.
>
> _____
>
> Write one or two sentences about a third event that shows this trait. (You can skip this part if you can't find another example.)
>
> _____
>
> Write a sentence with a quote from the text that proves this trait in the author's own words.
>
> _____

Reprinted from Boyles, N.N. (2002). *Teaching written response to text: Constructing quality answers to open-ended comprehension questions*. Gainesville, FL: Maupin House. Used with permission.

the teacher to meet with these students for a few sessions in a small, skill-based group. Is almost everyone still deficient in, for example, finding a quote from the text to support an opinion? Maybe this could be addressed in a whole-class, shared lesson.

Some students, especially those in the primary grades, and those who struggle with reading even in later grades, benefit from more guidance than that afforded by the Answer Organizer. For these students, there is the Answer Frame. The frame offers even more concrete assistance by providing sentence starters and the written language structures that some students just can't figure out on their own—at least initially. Giving students an Answer Frame to begin the response process makes success attainable for even our lowest performing students.

Moving Toward Independence

It is critical to remember that organizers and frames are a good place to begin, but the instructional sequence is not complete until students are "off

Figure 6.2. Answer Frame

> **Choose one word that best describes [name of character/person] (e.g., kind, friendly, lazy, responsible) and provide evidence from the text to support your choice.**
>
> **ANSWER FRAME**
>
> One word that really describes _____
>
> is _____ . One time s/he showed this was when
>
> _____
>
> _____ .
>
> Another time s/he showed this was when _____
>
> _____ .
>
> A third time s/he showed this was when _____
>
> _____ .
>
> Here's a quote from the author that proves that this character/person was very _____
>
> _____ :
>
> " _____
>
> _____
>
> _____ . "

Reprinted from Boyles, N.N. (2002). *Teaching written response to text: Constructing quality answers to open-ended comprehension questions.* Gainesville, FL: Maupin House. Used with permission.

the organizer." When I make this statement to teachers it feels like I'm telling them to remove kids from life support. And in a sense, I suppose that *is* what I'm saying. Teachers sometimes lull themselves into a sense of complacency when they see what a great job students are doing filling in those lines on the Answer Organizer or Answer Frame. Wonderful, they conclude: mastery! But real mastery means performing the task without any help at all—without referring to a list of steps or a teacher model, and especially without the aid of graphic support.

This means we need to work backward. If students require the Answer Frame today, we should provide them with that until they are competent and confident in its use. Then we should take away the Answer Frame and offer the Answer Organizer. Let them work with that until that, too, becomes nearly automatic. Henceforth, just a quick review of a modeled response should suffice before eventually handing them a blank piece of paper on which to respond.

Next, a quick glance at the list of steps before boldly putting pen to paper should be all the support that is needed. And finally, they'll read that question, whether on a high-stakes test or on a classroom comprehension assessment, and write a perfectly accurate and wonderfully organized and elaborated response with no scaffolding whatsoever. Figure 6.3 provides an at-a-glance visual representation of this model.

What the Field Testing Has Shown

In case all of this sounds like one of those ideas in education that is too good to be true and that could never actually work with real students in real classrooms, my experiences in many schools over the past decade, and additional reports from hundreds of teachers, offer evidence to the contrary: Following this explicit, gradual release model has helped many, many intermediate grade students—especially struggling students—understand the process of written

Figure 6.3. Gradual Release of Responsibility: Moving Students Toward Independent Writing

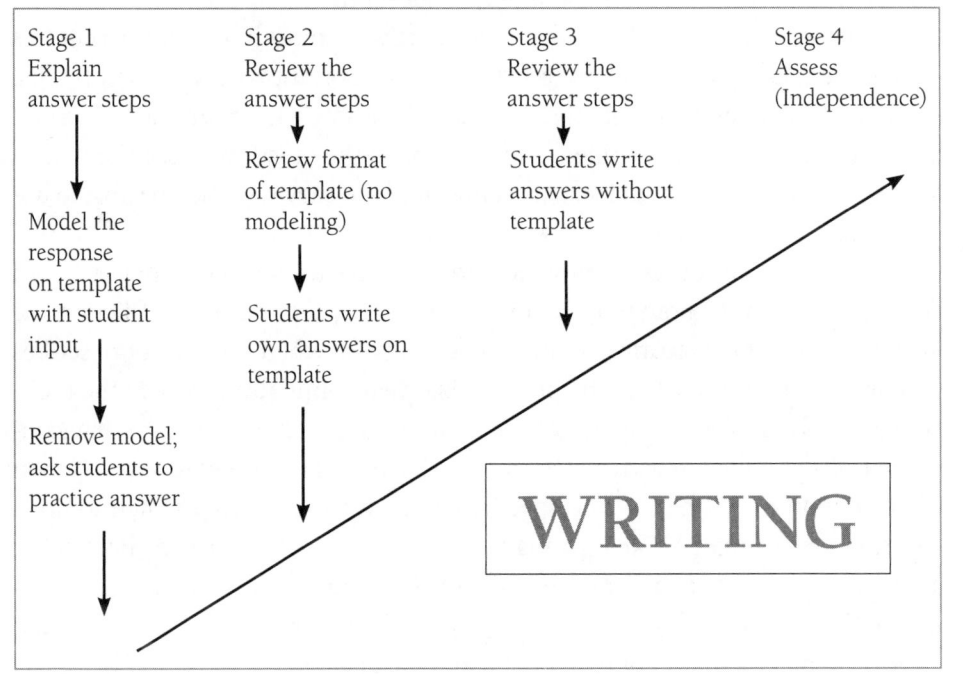

response. For many children, their answers to open-ended questions about literature showed better organization and elaboration with regard to both their classroom work and on high-stakes assessments.

But as I and other teachers field-tested this response model in classrooms, we saw that not all students improved as dramatically as we would have liked. Why not? we wondered. What else could we do for these struggling students whose answers to open-ended questions were still below standard despite explicit instruction in the art of written response?

What I saw as I analyzed students' responses was that the students who weren't getting it were missing the mark not because they didn't know how to write a response but because they didn't know what to write. Here is a too-typical scenario: Destinee (pseudonym) eagerly handed me her written response about "the most important part" of the picture book *The Other Side* (Woodson, 2001), which said, "I think it wasn't fair when Annie wouldn't play with Clover." This was way off the mark! This didn't even address the question, and it definitely didn't supply specific textual evidence. This signaled an entirely different problem. It was a problem that had to do with reading, not writing. What Destinee (and so many other students) needed was the reading strategy to locate the essential evidence for responding to a question.

When the question asks students to identify the most important part of this text and explain why you think it is the most important part, who will be able to answer that question? Only the students who know what counts as important in a text will know what evidence to look for as they read. Because they know how to read strategically to locate this information, they will then be able to use the evidence they find to write their responses.

As a proficient reader, I know how to strategize to find the evidence I need for this question. I know that the most important part of a piece of fiction, for instance, could be its turning point. It could also be where the author describes a character's motives, where the problem is revealed initially, or where the problem gets solved. There may be other possibilities, too, but even these few considerations provide me with a focus as I read. Now, as I respond to that question about importance, I have some specific places in the text from which to draw information. I might be able to make a case for any one of them. Remember that these are open-ended questions, so there is not necessarily just one correct answer; we can all be correct if we can defend our thinking. Locating that defense demands that I approach the text strategically.

Making the Reading Strategic

We hear so much these days about the value of comprehension strategy instruction. The research tells us that if we provide direct, explicit instruction in comprehension strategies and give students opportunities to transact with strategies in meaningful ways, this will have a positive impact on their performance as readers (Pressley et al., 1992). We can identify essential metacognitive processes and instructional practices in the classroom that help students use these strategies efficiently and effectively (Harvey & Goudvis, 2000; Keene & Zimmermann, 1997; Miller, 2002). But these classroom applications often don't go far enough: What do these strategies do for us as readers? In other words, how does that personal connection enhance our understanding of this text? How do those questions we ask about a text lead us to a deeper understanding of the main character's feelings or the theme of the story? What is the point of all that inferring and synthesizing anyway?

Students need to understand from the start that they are learning these metacognitive strategies not just to get good at using strategies but to get good at comprehending. How can these strategies lead to deeper thinking about characters, plot, theme, author's craft, and the features of nonfiction? I addressed this in *Constructing Meaning Through Kid-Friendly Comprehension Strategy Instruction* (Boyles, 2004) but recognized through students' responses to literature that for the purpose of answering open-ended questions in writing, we needed to take comprehension strategy instruction to the next level; we needed to help students become strategic about how they retrieve evidence for meeting individual comprehension objectives.

It's not as much about having a strategy as it is about being strategic. It is one thing to know what a strategy is and quite a different thing to be inclined to modify it as the task changes (Paris & Winograd, 1990). The concept of a strategy as a means of retrieving evidence to support a response became central as I considered the next step to take in improving struggling students' responses to literature. What if I could provide students with guidance for how to approach a text to summarize it, find the main idea, or respond to a host of questions that frequently follow the reading of a text? Would making the actual *reading* strategic improve students' written responses? What would be included in a reading lesson that could offer that kind of support? My work in classrooms during the past half-decade has helped to answer that question (now also fully described in Boyles, 2007, and Boyles, 2009).

But how do I teach students *how* to approach a text? Teachers ask me this question a lot. It is perplexing to me that so many years after Durkin (1978) suggested that something big was missing in the teaching of comprehension that there have not been more substantial changes in teachers' understanding of what goes into a good comprehension lesson. It is for the purpose of answering this *how* question that I spend several days each week visiting classrooms. I model literacy lessons showing teachers how to help students think strategically about a text.

After the lesson is finished, the teachers who observed the lesson, the reading consultant or coach, and I (sometimes joined by the school principal) all sit together to talk about the lesson I taught. To analyze the lesson meaningfully we need first of all to recognize the components of a reading comprehension lesson that make it powerful, that move students a little closer to independence in responding to text to meet a specific comprehension objective.

A worthy reading comprehension lesson scaffolds students before, during, and after reading, incorporating the following components:

Before Reading

Activate prior knowledge, make predictions, set a purpose.

Introduce essential vocabulary.

Explain how to retrieve evidence for meeting the objective.

During Reading

Teacher models where, how, and when to retrieve the best evidence to meet the objective.

Students practice finding evidence for the objective.

Students apply comprehension monitoring strategies as appropriate.

After Reading

Oral discussion that includes response to a question directly related to the objective, as well as other comprehension questions.

Written response to a question directly related to the objective.

While a rich comprehension lesson will include more than the elements in the planning template (as noted in the list of lesson components), these are the elements that will most directly apply to making the reading strategic. Figure 6.4 provides an example of a planning template filled in for the objective, What part of this text do you think was the most important?

Figure 6.4. Sample Completed Planner for Literature Response

PLANNER FOR LITERATURE RESPONSE

Choose an objective:
(Identify an objective that is important for students at this developmental level.)

> **CE2-a:** Which part of the story/article do you think was most important? Use information from the story to explain why you chose that part.

> Which part of *The Other Side* do you think was most important? Use information from the story to explain why you chose that part.

Choose your text:
(Identify a text that is well suited to this objective.)

> *The Other Side* by Jacqueline Woodson

How will you make the reading strategic?
(What tips or hints can you offer to students so they will know what evidence to look for in the text?)

> The turning point of a story is often considered the most important part. In some books, like this one, lots of parts could be considered the turning point—when something important changes. As we read this book, decide which part you think is really when things begin to change in the biggest way. Think about the evidence from the text and be able to explain why you think this is the most important part.

Where can the strategy be applied in the text?
(Some of these applications should be <u>modeled by the teachers</u> and some should be <u>practiced by the students</u>.)

Modeling

> p. 16: Annie and Clover met at the fence, introduced themselves, and Annie smiled.
>
> p. 17: Clover smiled back at Annie; Annie talked about how nice it was up on the fence.
>
> p. 20: Annie helps Clover climb onto the fence.

Practicing

> p. 22: Clover ignored her friends' disapproval of her friendship with Annie.
>
> p. 24: Clover's mom seemed to approve of her friendship with Annie.
>
> p. 25: All of the girls played jump rope together.
>
> p. 28: The girls all sat on the fence and became friends.
>
> p. 29: They talked about taking the fence down.

(continued)

Figure 6.4. Sample Completed Planner for Literature Response (*continued*)

How will you make the writing (or oral response) strategic?
(Can you give students a format to follow in order to write a well-organized response?)

Provide students with a template such as:
I think the most important part of the story was when _____

_____
_____

I think this was the most important part of the story because it showed_____

_____
_____

Here is some proof from the story: _____
_____

Model the response using the template.
Remove your template and ask students to write their own response based on the incident you chose or another incident in the story.

Begin With an Objective

Note that the lesson is organized around an objective rather than a text. This alone represents a significant change of perspective from the way many teachers decide what they will teach. Holding a book close to their heart, teachers declare, "I love this book! What can I teach with this book?" Although this approach may afford much personal satisfaction, it does not necessarily address students' most urgent literacy needs.

Students' needs are identified by the data we have, both formative and summative. To best meet students' needs, it is important to begin by looking at what the data says: What is it, specifically, that students are struggling with? It's the level of specificity that makes an objective useful—and measurable. What is the main problem in the story? This is a good objective because it is clear exactly what students are expected to know and be able to do; hence, it is easy to measure their degree of success.

By contrast, the objective to identify or infer important characters, settings, problems, events, relationships, and details within a written work (incorporating all story elements) is too global. It may satisfy the criteria for a state standard, but it is too broad to be taught—or measured—in a single lesson. (A hierarchy of possible comprehension objectives is delineated in the section on Developing a Logical Sequence of Objectives.)

Choose a Text

After choosing an objective that students need, select a short text that is a good match for it. A matching text is one that offers multiple opportunities for modeling and practicing the identified objective at a developmentally appropriate level. For short text, I frequently use picture books (my favorite form of short text), though poetry, nonfiction articles, and other brief selections can also be used effectively. I introduce the objective in a shared, whole-class lesson where I do the reading. This allows struggling readers to participate in the lesson based on their thinking, without worrying about word-level skills that frequently get in the way of their ability to access meaning in their own reading.

Beyond the objective and the text, the remainder of the lesson contains the components that are part of any lesson that gradually releases responsibility to students to help them achieve independence. In the first part of this chapter, I outlined how to apply the gradual release model to teach struggling students to produce a well-organized, fluent written response. Here I apply this model to help students find the evidence to make their response accurate and suitably elaborated.

Explain the Criteria

As proficient readers ourselves, we don't think very much about our own reading process. We've summarized a story or found the main idea in a nonfiction text so many times that we're basically on automatic pilot as we read a text to respond to those (or other) end-of-chapter questions. Not so with struggling students. They do not have the wisdom of our years or for some, the natural inclination to analyze a reading task and break it into its component parts. But we can help them do this. We can examine a task and decide, How do I approach this? What do I do first? What do I do next? How do I know when I've achieved my goal? That's what we mean by explaining a strategy. If we can make this strategic thinking visible to students, they, too, will be able to find the evidence in their reading.

For example, think about what you need to know and be able to do when you summarize a narrative text. You need first of all to be familiar with the narrative elements because a good summary accounts for all of these: character, setting, problem, attempts to solve the problem, resolution, ending. It is also helpful for the teacher to explain (or review) where in a story to look for these elements: As a proficient reader you know to look for the characters, the setting, and the problem near the beginning of the story. You know that sometimes the author doesn't lay out the problem right away but first describes what life was like before the advent of the problem or conflict. You know that the bulk of the story will describe several attempts to resolve the problem. You know to look for the resolution at the end of the story, and you know that the actual solution may be followed by some sort of closure (happily ever after or some other wrap-up). Just knowing where to retrieve what you're looking for helps students to be strategic because if you've read too much of the story and still don't have a sense of these basic story parts, you realize you probably missed something along the way; you should go back and reread to fix up your comprehension.

To make sure that a summary is truly a summary, I tell students that they need to sift through all the stuff that happens in the middle of the story and choose no more than three (or whatever number seems appropriate for a given text) examples of what happens on the way to resolving the problem. They will have to select the attempts that they think are the most important. This avoids those summaries that go on and on, morphing into a retelling.

Note that students will get much more from the modeling if a clear explanation precedes it. Here's an example that relates to nonfiction: finding the main idea, a concept that frustrates struggling readers (and their teachers) from the early elementary grades onward. I once watched a very good teacher model finding the main idea. She had a nonfiction passage on the overhead projector. "Watch me as I read this article and underline the main idea," she told her group of remedial students. She proceeded to read the passage orally and then think aloud: "OK, I'm noticing right here that this sentence is the main idea of the whole text." She then carefully underlined the main idea statement with a purple marker so students could plainly see exactly where the main idea was located within the article.

What students could not see so plainly, however, was *how* their teacher had figured out that this particular sentence was the main idea. It's this *how* part that is always the essence of strategic thinking: How could we make that thinking process visible so students could understand and apply that main idea strategy themselves?

I've found that to help students think strategically, it helps to think like a student. As adults capable of abstract reasoning, we read a nonfiction passage, synthesize the salient points, and convert them into a general statement that describes the intent of the entire piece. But it's different for young students and struggling older students who are more concrete than abstract in their reasoning. After many years of bungling my way through the teaching of main idea, it finally occurred to me that I was approaching the task in the wrong order: Rather than asking students to determine the main idea and then support it with relevant details, a better strategy would be to ask them first to identify the details and then step back to see what all of those details had in common. That common thread is the main idea.

That one simple turnabout makes all the difference! When you ask students to first find the main idea and then prove it with supporting details, you are asking them to think *deductively*, moving from the general to the specific. When you ask them to note the details first and then describe the main idea, students use *inductive* reasoning, moving from specific instances to a general theory. It is much easier for struggling readers to think inductively in order to draw a conclusion because they are typically very concrete in their thinking. We need to honor this logic. That's just one hot tip we can share with our struggling students that will help them solve this prickly main idea problem.

Whether you call it a *hot tip* or a *hint* or a *strategy*, what you are doing is explaining to students *how*—how to go about reading a text so that in the end they can summarize the story, or find the main idea of a news article, or attack whatever the comprehension task is. "But isn't that cheating?" a teacher once asked me. "Shouldn't students figure this out for themselves?" "No," I assured her, "this is not cheating. In this game we want everyone to win." Furthermore, getting all students to the goal (in this case, high-quality responses to comprehension questions) is the responsibility, first of all, of the classroom teacher —not the special education teacher, not the reading consultant. Response to Intervention (RTI) mandates appropriate "first teaching" by the classroom teacher (Tier I) before prescribing other interventions (Shanahan, 2008). So, if explaining the criteria to struggling students is the path to that goal, then that is what teachers need to do.

It would be impossible to provide a complete list of how to explain every comprehension objective here because there are way too many objectives, and the explanation must, to some extent, match students' developmental level. The good news is there is no wrong way to explain how to find the evidence for meeting a particular objective; any insight that a teacher can provide to make the reading more strategic is one more hint than students knew before the lesson. You can always add another strategy tomorrow, or anytime. The bad news is that most teachers are not even aware that they should explain the how. This feels awkward at first, and it is not always so easy to describe your thinking process in language that a struggling reader can understand. But it is absolutely worth the effort. Offering an explanation of how to find the evidence for meeting an objective is what makes the modeling meaningful.

Model the Process

If teachers don't explain how they will look for and recognize evidence, their modeling will appear entirely random to students. For example, maybe today's objective is to figure out a character's motives. The teacher pauses as she reads aloud a traditional version of "Cinderella": "I notice right here, where Cinderella's stepmother is handing her a mop, that she is trying to keep Cinderella from going to the ball." This would have made more sense to students if the teacher had told them first that a character's motives are often revealed through his or her words, actions, and thoughts. That would have helped students connect the dots during the think-aloud: "Remember when we said that you can often figure out a character's motives just by her actions? Well, right here is an action we should notice: Cinderella's stepmother is making her mop the floor. I'm figuring out that she might be doing that so Cinderella won't have time to go to the ball."

A good explanation provides a context for good modeling. Beyond that, what does good modeling of a reading strategy entail? I'm beginning to think that literacy instruction is suffering from what I call "modeling gone wild." Not so long ago, teachers didn't do much modeling at all. Then research demonstrated the power of teacher modeling, which brought the practice into the classroom full force. The result, in some cases, is that teachers go on and on, thinking aloud about their metacognitive processes—seemingly unaware that their students tuned them out back on the first page.

As teachers show their own thinking, less is often more. Teachers need to model just long enough to show students a few good examples of how they are finding evidence to meet a particular objective. Sooner rather than later, the goal is to transition to a place where students are finding some of the evidence themselves. This initiates that gradual release of responsibility so critical to the ultimate goal of student independence.

Provide Guided Practice—Prompted and Unprompted

Sometimes the transition from teacher modeling to student practice is so subtle that you can't say for sure where one stops and the other starts. As in modeling for written response, indicators of students' readiness to move forward are largely unscientific. Before beginning the lesson I tell students, "I will be stopping as I read to show you how *I* find the best evidence. Then after a while I will stop when I notice something useful on a page and ask if *you* can identify the evidence. But what I'm really hoping will happen, what will really show me that you get it, is if *you* stop *me* to tell me about evidence you have found even before I pause to remind you to look for something important."

Unprompted finding of evidence for a particular objective does not always happen in an introductory whole-class lesson, and illustrates the need for gradual release not just within a single lesson but within a sequence of lessons. And that's especially true for meeting the needs of struggling readers. It is appropriate for teachers to initially present a few (two or three) whole-class shared lessons to introduce and reinforce an objective. But beyond that, the work needs to move to the small-group level (or to individual application in a reader's workshop) so that students can practice the objective with text they can read themselves. Figure 6.5 depicts the gradual release of responsibility for readers as they move from much scaffolding toward independence on a given objective.

Release Responsibility Gradually Over Time

As I ventured into classrooms the past few years armed with both reading and writing strategies for response to open-ended questions, I saw that teachers frequently did not differentiate between an initial lesson in a teaching sequence and a follow-up lesson. If we are serious about moving students to independence, a good first lesson to introduce an objective will look decidedly different from the ones that follow. Recognizing this distinction and designing lessons that require more and more student responsibility and accountability in later lessons is critical.

The teacher introduces the objective in Stage One via whole-class instruction, which, even for struggling readers, should only require a single lesson; the purpose of this lesson is solely to introduce the objective. Stage Two, with less teacher explaining and modeling and more student practice, should also represent a limited number of lessons (one or two) because at this point, the teacher is still doing the actual reading. Then instruction needs to be differentiated

Figure 6.5. Gradual Release of Responsibility: Moving Students Toward Independent Reading

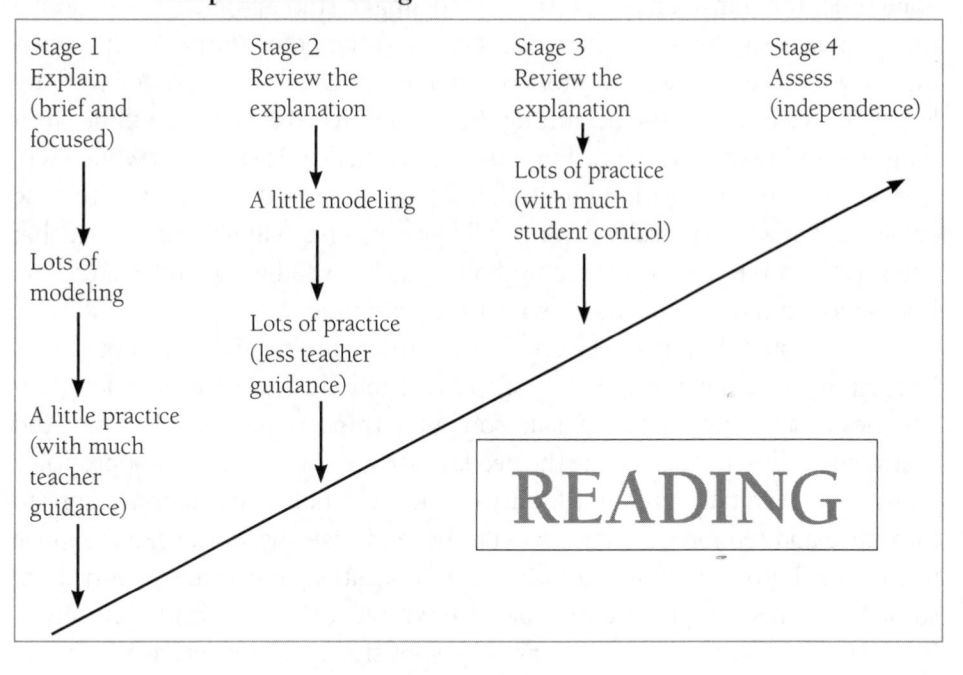

so that all students in the class, even struggling students, can do the reading themselves. This is Stage Three of the gradual release model and, for struggling students, this represents the greatest investment of time in their quest for competence.

Tomlinson (2001) clarifies for us that there are three instructional components that can be differentiated for learners: content, process, and product. For struggling readers, the content will generally be easy text. In order for students to be able to focus on comprehension at an instructional level, they need to be able to read the words with at least 95% accuracy (Morris, 2008). Some background knowledge on the topic also adds to their capacity to comprehend (Trabasso & Bouchard, 2002).

The instructional process for struggling students needs to be firmly guided. That means students will be most successful when the chunks of text they are asked to read are relatively short, with frequent opportunities for them to stop to monitor their thinking. For example, when the outcome is to be a written summary of a story, you might say to a small group, "In your head, read the first two paragraphs. Pause and consider whether you've found any story parts in those two paragraphs—and be prepared to tell us in your own words what you've found. For support, you can read the evidence aloud." This is a manageable task, and the accountability is clear.

After success with the first text chunk, students would move on to the next couple of paragraphs. Notice that there is no round robin reading. Notice that these struggling readers are not whisper reading the text while their teacher listens in. Notice that the requirements are for students to paraphrase the text (demonstrating their comprehension) as well as to justify their response by referencing the text. Over time, the chunks of text should become gradually longer along with increased requirements for internal monitoring because even struggling readers will need to arrive at independence at some point—or risk widening, rather than narrowing, the achievement gap.

Likewise, the products that struggling students generate will also need to move from supported to unsupported. It is our struggling students who will benefit most from those Answer Frames or Answer Organizers described earlier in this chapter when they initially respond to open-ended questions in writing. But the teacher needs to systematically move students to needing only a blank piece of paper because that's what independence means—at least for the purpose of assessment.

Stage Four of the Gradual Release model for both Reading and Writing is, in fact, more accurately about assessment, not instruction. When the goal is proficient written response to text, Stage Four of the Reading model converges with Stage Four of the Writing model (provided in Figure 6.5.)

Assess Students' Written Responses

Instruction in strategic reading and writing will produce written responses that demonstrate proficiency across four criteria: accuracy, elaboration, organization, and fluency. The first and second criteria (accuracy and elaboration) are addressed through instruction in strategic reading; the remaining two criteria are strengthened through instruction in writing strategies. Figure 6.6 provides teachers with a useful tool for assessing students' written responses using these criteria. Figure 6.7 converts the rubric descriptors to a simpler checklist format that is more manageable for struggling students as they reflect on their own performance.

Figure 6.6. Rubric for Assessing Students' Written Response to Comprehension Questions

WRITTEN RESPONSE RUBRIC

Student: _____ Date: _____

	2 Excellent	1 Developing	0 Deficient
Accuracy	The answer is completely accurate. The answer is clearly based on events in the text that really happened, correctly represents factual information, and formulates reasonable inferences.	The answer is partially accurate. The answer shows some confusion about events or information described in the text, and inferences may be "far-fetched" or not tied directly to the content of the reading.	The answer is clearly inaccurate and is well below the range of developmental level expectations. The answer does not indicate that the student has constructed basic meaning from the text, either explicitly stated information or inferred relationships among ideas. The answer may point to problems that go deeper than comprehension, perhaps insufficient word identification skills.
Elaboration	The answer is thorough according to grade-level expectations. The answer meets all criteria for details and elaboration specified for the response to a particular question, and the details show a close, careful reading of the text.	The answer is more general than specific. The answer contains some details and elaboration, but the student has missed or has neglected to include enough evidence from the text to sufficiently support a general statement or main idea.	The answer is vague or irrelevant and is well below the range of grade-level expectations. The answer may be so general, far-fetched, or so loosely tied to the text that it is hard to tell whether the student has even read the text.

(continued)

Figure 6.6. Rubric for Assessing Students' Written Response to Comprehension Questions (*continued*)

	2 Excellent	1 Developing	0 Deficient
Organization	The answer is logically organized. The answer follows the steps specified in the response criteria or uses another sequential structure that makes sense to the reader.	The answer is marginally organized. The answer may begin in a logical fashion but loses its focus, or the parts may all be present but are not well sequenced.	The answer has no organizational framework and is well below the range of grade-level expectations. The answer may be too sparse to provide a sense of organization, or it may be very long and repetitive, saying the same thing over and over in a variety of ways, or it may be largely incoherent with no sense of direction.
Fluency	The answer flows smoothly. The answer demonstrates grade-level appropriate competence with grammar, usage, writing conventions, vocabulary, and language structure.	The answer sounds somewhat "choppy." The answer is generally able to be read and understood but may show more carelessness or lack of proficiency in the use of grammar, usage, writing conventions, vocabulary, and language structure than is appropriate for a student at this grade level.	The answer is nearly incomprehensible because of written language deficits and is well below the range of grade-level expectations. It shows extreme lack of skill in communicating ideas in writing and may signal the need for interventions beyond the scope of written response instructional supports.

Developing a Logical Sequence of Objectives

As noted at the outset of this chapter, the very act of getting their thoughts about a text onto paper in a proficient manner demonstrates a level of thinking that is suitably high for struggling readers. But which objectives represent the construction of basic meaning about a text, and which ones reflect higher order thought processes, such as interpretation and critical thinking? State literacy

Figure 6.7. Student's Written Response Checklist

Name: _____   Date: _____

MY WRITTEN RESPONSE CHECKLIST

_____ My answer is completely **accurate** and is based on exact events or information in the text.

_____ My answer has plenty of **elaboration**. I looked for two details and even tried to find a quote to support my response.

_____ My answer is **organized**. I began with a topic sentence and wrote my sentences in an order that makes sense.

_____ My answer is **fluent**. It sounds good when I read it out loud. I was careful not to leave out any words.

---

frameworks do not necessarily provide us with a neatly sequenced hierarchy of objectives, leaving teachers guessing about what they should teach first and which objectives they should pursue later.

The National Assessment of Educational Progress (NAEP), which samples students' literacy performance from all 50 of the United States, identified the following three cognitive targets (National Assessment Governing Board, 2008, p. 14):

- Locate and Recall
- Integrate and Interpret
- Critique and Evaluate

The order of these targets implies to some extent that each successive target builds on the one that precedes it. But a more accurate view might be that these are not strictly levels of thinking; these are different ways of thinking. We can make these targets more concrete by identifying specific reading objectives that might fall within each one. These objectives are listed in Table 6.1. Regardless of where teachers teach, the same literacy objectives are likely to apply—organized

Table 6.1. Reading Comprehension Cognitive Targets and Possible Objectives

Locate and Recall

L/R-1: Identify the main idea when it is stated.

L/R-2: Identify characters, settings, problems, events, relationships, and details within a literary work.

L/R-3: Select and use relevant information from a written work in order to summarize events or ideas in the text.

L/R-4: Use specific information from the text to make a prediction based on what is read.

Integrate and Interpret

I/I-1: Use the structure or organizational pattern of the text to aid the construction of meaning.

I/I-2: Draw conclusions about the author's purpose for choosing a genre or for including or omitting specific details in text.

I/I-3: Use stated or implied evidence from the text to draw or support a conclusion.

I/I-4: Infer the main idea or theme when it is not stated.

Critique and Evaluate

C/E-1: Make connections between the text and outside experiences and knowledge.

C/E-2: Select, synthesize, or use relevant information from within a written work to write a personal response to the text.

C/E-3: Analyze and evaluate the author's craft, including use of literary devices and textual elements.

C/E-4: Select, synthesize, or use relevant information within a written work to extend or evaluate the work.

C/E-5: Demonstrate an awareness of an author's or character's customs and beliefs included in a text.

slightly differently perhaps—but we all tend to ask students to do the same kinds of things when they respond to a text.

If the intention is not to simply progress through these targets—Locate and Recall, Integrate and Interpret, Critique and Evaluate—then in what order should we teach them? I have developed a three-tiered approach for addressing all of these objectives that I feel builds foundational thinking skills in Tier I, develops deeper thinking in Tier II, and applies thinking critically and creatively in Tier III.

Tier I: The Foundations of Thinking: L/R-1, L/R-2, L/R-4, I/I-3, I/I-4

The most basic concept to constructing meaning is that of understanding story elements: characters, settings, problems, events, and solutions. Hence, you really need to start with L/R-2. Students will not get very far with comprehension unless they grasp these basics and can manipulate them to comprehend what they are reading. Also central to foundational understanding is the notion that behind most quality literature is some kind of big idea—a theme, main idea, or lesson learned. Thus, in order to analyze a text at a deeper level, students need to come to terms with the L/R-1 objective and I/I-4 objective. (Sometimes the main idea is stated; sometimes it must be inferred.) Two other objectives serve students well as they begin to make sense of text. They need to make reasonable predictions (the L/R-4 objective) that will help them monitor their comprehension, and they need to know how to retrieve specific evidence from text to support a conclusion (I/I-3). Armed with these skills, they can proceed to objectives that build on this foundation.

Tier II: Building on the Foundation: L/R-3, C/E-1, C/E-2, C/E-3

Summarizing text (L/R-3) is integral to comprehension, but it is impossible to summarize meaningfully without an understanding of basic text elements, story parts for narrative text, and main ideas and details for nonfiction. Hence, L/R-2 must precede L/R-3. Personal connections to text (C/E-1) and personal reactions (C/E-2) are almost always superficial if students don't have a sense of the big idea to which their connection should be made. The reason that students offer weak connections tied to insignificant details is because teachers attempt to get students to connect to a text before building their capacity to figure out the big idea (L/R-1 and I/I-4). Likewise, in order for students to notice authors' crafts (C/E-3) such as similes, imagery, personification, and so forth, they need to know what it means to look for evidence in a text (I/I-3).

Tier III: Extending Comprehension Through Critical and Creative Thinking: I/I-1, I/I-2, C/E-4, C/E-5

The most sophisticated comprehension skills revolve around an analysis of a text's structure, the extension of thinking beyond a text, and the application of thinking to understand values, culture, and customs. In order to understand the structure of a text (I/I-1), it helps to first be able to summarize it (L/R-3). Recognizing why an author included particular information (I/I-2) is contingent upon noticing not just the craft (C/E-3) but also inferring why the author chose those words and what those words represent. Extending the text through, for example, a journal entry, questions to ask the author, or points to include in a speech (C/E-4) all rely on your personal reaction to the text (C/E-2). Similarly, interpreting an author's or character's values or customs (C/E-5) is generated from one's personal connection to the text (C/E-1).

Teachers need to consider the logic of these three tiers as they strive to help struggling students comprehend and respond to text. While we might want to jump right in to making personal connections (C/E-1) at the beginning of the year because such connections typically cause students problems on state assessments, we really should back up a bit and lay the necessary foundation before we try to build on it.

Drilling Down Another Layer

To make these objectives more teachable and measurable, we ought to drill down one more layer. It is much easier to plan a lesson around an objective that is specific. For example, consider the I/I-1 objective: *Identify or infer the author's use of structure/organizational patterns*. This objective is so broad and abstract that it is virtually useless to a teacher planning a lesson: Exactly what should students know and be able to do to master this objective? And how will you know when they've achieved the desired outcome?

Now look at the more precise objectives that fall under this general category:

- **I/I-1a:** What caused _____ to happen in the story?
- **I/I-1b:** What happened at the beginning, in the middle, and at the end of the story?
- **I/I-1c:** Compare these two characters.
- **I/I-1d:** Can this part of the [story/text] be described as a description, an explanation, a conversation, an opinion, an argument, or a comparison? How do you know?

Any one of the objectives in this drilled down layer could be the focus of an excellent lesson. The task is clear, and for each one, it would be relatively easy to determine the criteria for a worthy response.

The specific objectives within each tier around which I develop my demonstration lessons are indicated in Table 6.2. Note that the related comprehension strategy is indicated next to each objective, as well as whether the objective is appropriate for fiction, nonfiction, or both. Powerful teaching is precise teaching! Note that other precise objectives could also be included under each of the general categories. These are simply samples of the kinds of comprehension tasks that students might have to perform.

Table 6.2. Specific Objectives for Comprehension Lessons

<u>Tier I Objectives</u>

L/R-1: Main idea and lesson when it is stated.
>   **L/R-1a:** What lesson does _____ learn in this story? (fiction) [figuring out]
>   **L/R-1b:** What is the main idea? (nonfiction) [figuring out]

L/R-2: Characters, problem/solution, setting.
>   **L/R-2a:** Using information in the story, write a brief description of how _____ felt when…. (fiction) [figuring out]
>   **L/R-2b:** What is _____'s main problem in the story? Give details from the story to support your answer. (fiction) [noticing]
>   **L/R-2c:** How did _____ solve his/her problem? Give details from the story to support your answer. (fiction) [noticing]
>   **L/R-2d:** How did _____ change from the beginning to the end of the story? (fiction) [figuring out]
>   **L/R-2e:** What is the setting of this story? Give details from the story to support your answer. (fiction) [noticing]

L/R-4: Predicting.
>   **L/R-4a:** Predict what will happen next in this story. (fiction) [guessing/predicting]
>   **L/R-4b:** If the author added another paragraph to the end of the story (or article), it would <u>most likely</u> tell about _____. Use information from the story (or article) to support your answer. (fiction, nonfiction) [guessing/predicting]

I/I-3: Use evidence from the text to support a conclusion.
>   **I/I-3a:** Prove that [character/person] is very _____. (fiction, nonfiction) [noticing]
>   **I/I-3b:** Which facts show that _____? (fiction, nonfiction) [noticing]

I/I-4: Infer the main idea or theme when it is not stated.
>   **I/I-4a:** What lesson does _____ learn in this story? (fiction) [figuring out]
>   **I/I-4b:** What is the theme of this story? (fiction) [figuring out]
>   **I/I-4c:** What is the main idea? (nonfiction) [figuring out]
>   **I/I-4d:** What would be another good title for this book/story? (fiction, nonfiction) [figuring out]

(continued)

Table 6.2. Specific Objectives for Comprehension Lessons *(continued)*

Tier II Objectives

L/R-3: Summarizing.

> **L/R-3a**: Briefly summarize this story. (fiction) [figuring out]
>
> **L/R-3b**: Summarize the main things that happened in this book. (fiction, nonfiction) [figuring out]
>
> **L/R-3c**: Briefly summarize this article/informational text. (nonfiction) [figuring out]

C/E-1: Connect the text to personal experience, another text, or the outside world.

> **C/E-1a**: Think about someone who was [helpful]. Tell how that experience was like the experience of _____ in the story. (fiction) [connecting]
>
> **C/E-1b**: Make a personal connection. Show how something that happened in the story is like something that happened in your own life. (fiction) [connecting]
>
> **C/E-1c**: Which character/person in the story/article would you like to know and why? (fiction, nonfiction) [connecting]
>
> **C/E-1d**: Using information in the story, explain whether you would ever want to _____. (fiction, nonfiction) [connecting]

C/E-2: Make a personal response to the text.

> **C/E-2a**: Which part of the story/article do you think was *most* important? Use information from the story to explain why you chose that part. (fiction, nonfiction) [connecting]
>
> **C/E-2b**: Which part of this story/article was most interesting or surprising to you? Why? (fiction, nonfiction) [connecting]
>
> **C/E-2c**: Did you like this story/article? Why or why not? (fiction, nonfiction) [connecting]
>
> **C/E-2d**: What was your first reaction to this text? Explain. (fiction, nonfiction) [connecting]

C/E-3: Examine the author's craft.

> **C/E-3a**: Choose [2] words from paragraph _____ that help you picture the _____ _____. (fiction, nonfiction) [picturing]
>
> **C/E-3b**: Choose a simile and explain why the author chose that simile. (fiction, nonfiction) [noticing]
>
> **C/E-3c**: How did the author create humor in paragraph _____? (fiction) [noticing]
>
> **C/E-3d**: Give an example of personification in paragraph _____. (fiction) [noticing]
>
> **C/E-3e**: Do you think the author made this story believable? Why or why not? (fiction) [figuring out]

Tier III Objectives

I/I-1: Identify or infer the author's use of structure/organizational patterns.

> **I/I-1a**: What caused _____ to happen in the story? (fiction) [noticing]
>
> **I/I-1b**: What happened at the beginning, in the middle, and at the end of the story? (fiction) [noticing]
>
> **I/I-1c**: Compare these two characters. (fiction) [noticing]

(continued)

Teaching Struggling Readers to Respond in Writing to Open-Ended Questions 155

Table 6.2. Specific Objectives for Comprehension Lessons (*continued*)

> **I/I-1d:** Can this part of the story/text be described as a description, an explanation, a conversation, an opinion, an argument, or a comparison? How do you know? (fiction, nonfiction) [noticing]
>
> **I/I-2: Draw conclusions about the author's purpose for choosing a genre or for including or omitting specific details in text.**
>
> **I/I-2a:** Why does the author include paragraph _____? (fiction, nonfiction) [figuring out]
>
> **I/I-2b:** Why did the author write a [poem/story/nonfiction book] about this? (fiction, nonfiction) [figuring out]
>
> **C/E-4: Extend the text.**
>
> **C/E-4a:** What two questions would you like to ask the author that were not answered in this text? (fiction, nonfiction) [wondering]
>
> **C/E-4b:** Imagine you are going to give a talk to your class about _____. What two points would you be sure to include in your speech? (nonfiction) [figuring out]
>
> **C/E-4c:** Using information in the text, write a paragraph that could have appeared in _____'s journal after _____ occurred. (fiction, nonfiction) [figuring out]
>
> **C/E-5: Show that you understand what was important to an author or character.**
>
> **C/E-5a:** How does the author/character show that _____ is important to him/her? (fiction, nonfiction) [noticing]
>
> **C/E-5b:** How are your customs different from the customs described in this story/article? (fiction, nonfiction) [figuring out]

High-Quality Instruction Is Key!

I began this journey over a decade ago, seeking stronger answers to open-ended comprehension questions from struggling readers because I knew they could do it! I believed that if I could just help them navigate the murky waters of written response—explaining what a good answer included, modeling the writing of my own good answer, providing them with useful graphic organizers to help them get their thoughts on to paper, and then gradually releasing responsibility until they achieved independence—all would be well in the world of written response evermore. I was partly correct; instruction in written response was exactly what some struggling students needed. Some students did, in fact, struggle solely with the act of getting their thinking down on paper, and my scaffolded system for supporting them brought about the expected improved performance.

What I did not anticipate was that the bigger issue in students' failure to write high-quality answers to open-ended questions wasn't about writing; it was about reading—specifically the *teaching* of reading. The basic misconception for too many teachers was that if they just asked the right question about the right book and handed out the right graphic organizer, amazing answers would magically pour forth from their students' pencils. Except it doesn't work that way. Between the question and the response is the not-so-small matter of instruction. First, there is the planning for instruction: choosing the right objective, guided by the data. Next, there is implementing today's lesson with all of the components that make teaching explicit. And finally, there is organizing instruction over time so that students achieve that independence that signals their success.

Just as I was convinced that students could write high-quality answers, I am likewise sure that teachers can deliver high-quality comprehension instruction. I hope this chapter will help teachers build on what they already know to move forward in the kind of focused teaching of comprehension that leads to more insightful thinking, not just for struggling students, but for all students. May the questions below guide you as you consider your own next steps in helping students become strategic readers and writers.

Struggling students are most likely to achieve higher levels of thinking on responses to open-ended comprehension questions when *all* components of quality instruction are in place, and when a sequence of reading lessons and written response scaffolds leads them to independence. Figure 6.8 identifies the action steps teachers must take in order for students, especially struggling students, to ultimately write a good answer to an open-ended question. It also provides a tool for teachers, coaches, and administrators to use to monitor and reflect on the implementation of all of these literacy best practices. The Action Plan (including a few hot tips) makes a useful guide for quick reference.

Figure 6.8. Protocol for Reflecting on Instruction for Written Response to Text

Teacher: _____ Date: _____

Instructional element	What to look for	Comment or ✓
Objective	A specific objective, like C/E-4c: *Using information in the text, write a paragraph that could have appeared in ____'s journal after ____ occurred.*	
Text	The text is selected to align with the objective and is appropriate for the reading/interest level of students.	
Making the reading strategic (explanation)	Teacher explains how she or he goes about finding the evidence to meet this objective in 3–5 minutes.	
	The hints may be applied to *all* texts, not just the current text. (*Look for the place in the text where the character's thinking changes.*)	
	Teacher may write the hints on a "target" sheet to provide visual cues to students.	
Finding the evidence in the text through teacher modeling	There are plenty of places where the evidence for meeting the objective can be noted in the text.	
	The teacher models sufficiently but not endlessly; there is a transition to more student accountability for the objective (5 minutes or less).	
Finding the evidence in the text through student practice	This is the longest portion of the lesson (about 7 minutes).	
	There are multiple opportunities for students to practice the objective (finding the evidence).	
	The teacher provides feedback and notes who gets it and who doesn't.	
Making the written response strategic	Oral discussion precedes written response.	
	Students complete the response independently.	
	Students flip the question and turn it into an answer stem.	
	Students write their response in approximately 2–3 minutes.	
	Students' answers demonstrate accuracy, organization, elaboration, and fluency.	
	Students demonstrate more independence each time they respond to a similar question.	

ACTION PLAN

- The teacher selects a clear lesson objective based on students' assessment data.

  Tip: The objective needs to be specific and measurable and should be determined by screening or progress-monitoring assessments.

- The teacher chooses an appropriate text.

  Tip: Texts used for shared lessons do not need to be at students' instructional levels because the teacher will do most of the reading. However, struggling students will need extensive practice applying the objective in their own reading with text they can read.

- The teacher explains the reading strategy for finding the best evidence to meet an objective.

  Tip: This is the most important lesson component for struggling readers; this is the part that shows them *how*.

- The teacher models the reading strategy to locate evidence for the objective.

  Tip: Some modeling that demonstrates how you apply the strategy efficiently to meet the objective is essential; too much modeling becomes counterproductive because students may stop listening.

- Students practice finding evidence in the text to meet the objective.

  Tip: You will need to prompt students initially as they look for evidence; eventually they should be able to find their own evidence without your guidance.

- The teacher scaffolds students' written responses with supports that gradually lead to independence (beginning with oral rehearsal of the response).

  Tip: You should begin with oral response, giving several students the opportunity to respond in full sentences that incorporate specific text evidence. Then move to written response, beginning with an Answer Organizer or Answer Frame if necessary. Eventually, all students will need to respond to the question in writing—independently.

QUESTIONS FOR STUDY AND REFLECTION

1. What appears to be causing your students the most trouble as they respond to open-ended comprehension questions? What is one thing you could try immediately that might help to alleviate this problem?

2. If you could observe a focused comprehension lesson, which instructional component would you particularly like to see?

3. What point(s) in this chapter need further clarification in order for you to move forward with explicit reading instruction leading to students' improved written responses?

4. Think about a comprehension lesson you taught recently. Using the Protocol for Reflecting on Instruction for Written Response to Text found in Figure 6.8, identify a couple of areas where your teaching was particularly strong. Is there an area that you feel could be stronger? How could you address this need?

5. Which comprehension objectives are most critical to students at your grade level? Select one of these objectives and think about strategies you could suggest to students that would help them find the best evidence for meeting this objective.

6. Getting students to independence in written response is so important to their future success. What could you do to get more students to this point?

REFERENCES

Badger, E., & Thomas, T. (1992). *Open-ended questions in reading* (ERIC Document Reproduction Service No. ED355253). Washington, DC: ERIC Clearinghouse on Tests Measurement and Evaluation.

Boyles, N.N. (2002). *Teaching written response to text: Constructing quality answers to open-ended comprehension questions.* Gainesville, FL: Maupin House.

Boyles, N.N. (2004). *Constructing meaning through kid-friendly comprehension strategy instruction.* Gainesville, FL: Maupin House.

Boyles, N.N. (2007). *That's a GREAT answer! Teaching literature response to K–3, ELL, and struggling readers.* Gainesville, FL: Maupin House.

Boyles, N.N. (2009). *Launching RTI comprehension instruction with shared reading: 40 model lessons for intermediate readers.* Gainesville, FL: Maupin House.

Durkin, D. (1978). What classroom observations reveal about reading comprehension instruction. *Reading Research Quarterly, 14*(4), 481–533. doi:10.1598/RRQ.14.4.2

Harvey, S., & Goudvis, A. (2000). *Strategies that work: Teaching comprehension to enhance understanding.* York, ME: Stenhouse.

Jones, F.H. (1987). *Positive classroom instruction.* New York: McGraw-Hill.

Keene, E.O., & Zimmermann, S. (1997). *Mosaic of thought: Teaching comprehension in a reader's workshop.* Portsmouth, NH: Heinemann.

Marzano, R.J., Pickering, D.J., & Pollock, J.E. (2001). *Classroom instruction that works: Research-based strategies for increasing student achievement.* Alexandria, VA: Association for Supervision and Curriculum Development.

Miller, D. (2002). *Reading with meaning: Teaching comprehension in the primary grades.* Portland, ME: Stenhouse.

Morris, D. (2008). *Diagnosis and correction of reading problems.* New York: Guilford.

National Assessment Governing Board. (2008). *Reading framework for the 2009 National Assessment of Educational Progress.* Washington, DC: Author.

National Institute of Child Health and Human Development. (2000). *Report of the National Reading Panel. Teaching children to read: An evidence-based assessment of the scientific research literature on reading and its implications for reading instruction* (NIH Publication No. 00-4769). Washington, DC: U.S. Government Printing Office.

Paris, S.G., & Winograd, P.W. (1990). How metacognition can promote academic learning and instruction. In B.J. Jones & L. Idol (Eds.), *Dimensions of thinking and cognitive instruction* (pp. 15–51). Hillsdale, NJ: Erlbaum.

Pearson, P.D., & Gallagher, M.C. (1983). The instruction of reading comprehension. *Contemporary Educational Psychology, 8*(3), 317–344. doi:10.1016/0361-476X(83)90019-X

Pressley, M., El-Dinary, P.B., Gaskins, I., Schuder, T., Bergman, J.L., Almasi, J., et al. (1992). Beyond direct explanation: Transactional instruction of reading comprehension strategies. *The Elementary School Journal, 92*(5), 513–556. doi:10.1086/461705

Pressley, M., & Harris, K.R. (1990). What we really know about strategy instruction. *Educational Leadership, 48*(1), 31–34.

Shanahan, T. (2008). Implications of RTI for the reading teacher. In D. Fuchs, L. Fuchs, & S. Vaughn (Eds.), *Response to intervention: A framework for reading educators* (pp. 105–122). Newark, DE: International Reading Association.

Tomlinson, C.A. (2001). *How to differentiate instruction in mixed-ability classrooms* (2nd ed.). Alexandria, VA: Association for Supervision and Curriculum Development.

Trabasso, T., & Bouchard, E. (2002). Teaching readers how to comprehend text strategically. In C.C. Block & M. Pressley (Eds.), *Comprehension instruction: Research-based best practices* (pp. 176–200). New York: Guilford.

Wilkinson, L. (1999). An introduction to the explicit teaching of reading. In J. Hancock (Ed.), *The explicit teaching of reading* (pp. 1–12). Newark, DE: International Reading Association.

LITERATURE CITED

Gardiner, J.R. (1980). *Stone fox.* New York: Scholastic.

Hoffman, M. (1991). *Amazing Grace.* New York: Scholastic.

Lowry, L. (1993). *The giver.* New York: Bantam Doubleday Dell.

Woodson, J. (2001). *The other side.* New York: Putnam Juvenile.

CHAPTER 7

A Step-by-Step Program for Developing Higher Level Skills in Struggling Readers

Thomas G. Gunning

Although most students achieve a basic level of literacy, approximately one out of every three has significant difficulty with higher level reading and writing tasks (Gunning, 2010b). To provide for the needs of students struggling with higher level literacy skills, a step-by-step program is recommended. As discussed in Chapter 2, the program will begin by finding out where students are in their literacy development and take them from there. Key elements of the program include the following:

- *Systematic instruction in strategies.* Although adept readers orchestrate a number of strategies, strategies would be introduced one at a time with ample opportunity for practice and application. Key skills would be taught for a significant amount of time, typically one a month. However, new skills would be integrated with previously taught skills so that eventually students would be using a host of skills simultaneously. Instruction would be intensive and systematic. Skills would be explained and modeled, and ample guided practice would be provided. Special attention would be paid to prerequisite skills. For instance, deriving main ideas requires the ability to categorize. If students lacked the ability to categorize, they would be taught categorizing skills before being taught how to derive a main idea.

- *Gradually build independence.* The program would be graduated. Students would be given maximum help in the beginning but would gradually take on more responsibility. Scaffolding would be provided in the form of modeling, explanations, and think-alouds. A variety of templates would be used to help students formulate responses. However, in keeping with the concept of gradual release of responsibility, scaffolding would be faded and students would take on more responsibility. As they grew in skill and understanding, they would be asked to select strategies to be used and explain their choices, and they would be responsible for constructing and self-evaluating their responses.

- *Provide brief, relatively easy selections for practice.* Although high-stakes tests and materials designed to develop higher level skills are typically written on grade level, struggling readers, by definition, are reading below grade level. A program designed to teach struggling readers higher level literacy skills needs to provide them with materials that are well within their grasp. It is essential that students be instructed on a level where they know just about all the words in the practice selections so they can focus on applying newly introduced comprehension strategies. Otherwise, they will be devoting their mental energy to decoding text and so will be unable to engage in higher level thinking. A program for struggling students should also start off with brief selections and gradually work up to longer selections.

- *Build language in general, vocabulary in particular, and background knowledge.* An important element would be selection of practice materials. One way of developing higher level skills is to build background. Students can think more deeply about things that they know well. Materials should be selected that build essential background information and also that are of interest to students. Along with building background, the program would build academic language so that students understand what they are being asked to do and also have the language to respond. Although this is especially important for English learners, it is also helpful to native speakers of English who struggle with the demands of higher level literacy.

- *Provide data-based instruction.* As suggested in Chapters 2 and 8, formal and informal measures would be used to assess students' comprehension. Instruction would be based on the data provided. Students' work would be carefully analyzed so that instruction could be geared to students' level of thinking and any confusion they might be having. Progress would be monitored so that the instructional program could be revised if students weren't making adequate progress.

- *Use a physical base to instruct and provide reinforcement to intensify the learning.* Physical activities, manipulatives, illustrations, and graphic organizers would be used whenever possible.

- *Personalize the approach.* It is easy to get lost in numbers, but the group of struggling readers is made up of individuals, each with his or her own particular needs and patterns of response to instruction. The details of a systematic program of skill building will be presented in terms of Eduardo, a struggling reader with whom I worked for a two-year period, and other struggling readers with whom I or my colleagues have worked. Eduardo was a fourth grader with excellent decoding skills but poor comprehension when we met; he was described in Chapter 2 along with assessment measures that were used to gather information about him.

- *Present skills systematically.* Skills and strategies would be presented from the easiest to the most complex.

- *Build responding skills.* Along with building comprehension skills and strategies, the needed oral and written responding skills would be developed so that struggling readers and writers have the tools to show what they know.

Scope and Sequence of Skills and Strategies: Building a Poor Comprehender's Textbase

What do higher level skills and strategies look like? Although there are a number of accounts of key skills and strategies, this text uses the 2009 NAEP Framework (National Assessment Governing Board, 2008). The 2009 Framework represents a cognitive approach to describing skills and strategies. It describes skills and strategies in terms of the cognitive process needed to implement the skill and includes three levels: Locate and Recall, Integrate and Interpret, and Critique and Evaluate. Key skills and strategies and their supporting skills are listed in Table 7.1. Perhaps the best way to understand this rather abstract listing of key skills and strategies is to see how poor comprehenders, such as Eduardo, struggle in their attempts to learn them.

Eduardo is a puzzle. Now a fifth grader, Eduardo has superb word recognition skills, but his comprehension is poor. Eduardo was slow to catch onto reading. In first grade, he was provided extensive one-on-one intervention for seven months. The good news is that because of the expert help he received and the extra time he spent reading materials on his level, Eduardo achieved a solid grasp of word-recognition skills and was able to read first-grade material with relative ease. The bad news is that, although Eduardo could pronounce

Table 7.1. Comprehension Skills and Strategies

Cognitive Dimension	Skills/Strategies
Locate and Recall	**Details** Recalling details Locating details Recognizing details that answer questions Locating supporting details Recognizing/determining important details Locating and describing explicit details in narratives, such as plot, setting, characters, story problem Making simple inferences
	Main idea/supporting details Recognizing stated main idea Recognizing implied main idea Constructing main idea (stated) Constructing main idea (implied) Noting supporting details
	Summarizing Retelling Summarizing orally Recognizing best summary Composing written summary Polishing written summary by combining and condensing
Integrate and Interpret	**Inferring/concluding** Recognizing inference Recognizing support for inference Given inference, locating support Given support, making inference Constructing inference and providing support Explaining support Judging inferences, conclusions
	Predicting Using background and text to predict Revising predictions Supporting predictions
	Imaging Constructing partial image Constructing fuller image Constructing concrete image Constructing abstract image

(continued)

Table 7.1. Comprehension Skills and Strategies (*continued*)

Cognitive Dimension	Skills/Strategies
Integrate and Interpret (*continued*)	**Questioning** Constructing general questions Constructing specific questions Constructing literal-level questions Constructing higher level questions
	Comparing/contrasting Noting differences Noting similarities Noting differences and similarities Determining key similarities and differences Comparing texts Comparing ideas across texts
	Connecting Noting general connections Noting key connections Justifying/explaining connections
Critique and Evaluate	**Identifying author's purpose** Identifying stated purpose Identifying implied purpose Identifying dual purpose
	Judging fairness/accuracy Distinguishing between facts and opinions Noting biased language Identifying biased/slanted language Identifying persuasive techniques Identifying assumptions Judging credibility of source
	Judging literary quality Identifying /evaluating elements of author's craft Judging effectiveness of literary techniques

Adapted from Gunning, T.G. (2008). *Developing higher level literacy in all students, Building reading, reasoning, and responding*. Boston: Allyn & Bacon, and National Assessment Governing Board (2008). *Reading Framework for the 2009 National Assessment of Educational Progress*. Washington, DC: Author.

the words with ease and with expression, he was not constructing the meaning behind the words. About three students out of a hundred are good decoders but poor comprehenders (Valencia & Buly, 2004). As the years passed and the reading material grew more complex, Eduardo's difficulty grew worse. By fourth grade, it was clear that Eduardo needed additional help beyond that provided by the classroom teacher.

Formal and informal assessments confirmed that Eduardo's difficulty was language based. He had difficulty comprehending material that he heard and also material that was read to him or that he viewed. His retellings of stories that he read and stories that he viewed on DVD were equally sketchy. Eduardo was also classified as a storyteller (Wade, 1990). Storytellers construct retellings that are based more on personal background knowledge than on actual events in the story they have read. Much of his retelling was based on his own background. Eduardo picked up a few details in stories or expository selections but didn't grasp the overall picture. Perhaps because it was difficult for him to process text or to organize the information so that it could be retold, Eduardo created his own version of what he had read, which didn't closely correspond to the author's version. It was clear that Eduardo needed to build a textbase.

An intervention program that focused on comprehension was planned. The program would involve building background, building skills and strategies, developing reasoning and language skills, and developing responding skills. The program was also designed to engage Eduardo. Students comprehend best when the material they are reading is of interest to them. Because Eduardo has an interest in animals, the topic of animals was chosen. To help develop Eduardo's background knowledge and reasoning skills, a theme or big idea was selected: Animals have a number of ways to keep themselves safe. A series of brief, well-constructed passages that developed the theme were chosen. The idea was to practice skills and strategies on easy-to-read paragraphs so that the focus could be on constructing meaning rather than on decoding words. Because Eduardo had a weak textbase, especially when it came to getting the big picture or seeing main ideas, instruction was initiated at the Locate and Recall level.

Locate and Recall

At this level, students are creating a textbase. Students identify main ideas, supporting details, and essential elements in a story, such as characters and setting. They make simple inferences and note causal relationships. Locating information, which is sometimes known as a "lookback," entails going back over a selection to find supporting details or other information. Students also monitor for meaning.

The process of deriving a main idea, which is the key skill in Locate and Recall, involves the following steps. Steps can be skipped if the student has mastered them, and some steps can be combined.

- Classifying words
- Classifying sentences
- Identifying topic sentences
- Selecting the main idea when directly stated in the paragraph
- Constructing the main idea when it is not directly stated
- Using titles, headings, and subheadings to construct the main idea
- Using a graphic organizer to depict the main idea and supporting details
- Using a frame to state main idea and details
- Stating the main idea and details

Deriving a Main Idea

Deriving a main idea is a foundational step in developing higher level skills for two reasons. First of all, it provides students with a framework for comprehending a passage. Once the main idea of a passage is known, it can be used to organize the supporting details. Second, deriving or even recognizing a main idea requires essential thinking skills. The main idea is the idea that includes all the other ideas. To derive a main idea, the readers must be able to detect similarities and then classify the similarities. In a sense, a main idea statement is a category label for a set of related details.

Instruction in deriving main ideas can be initiated by having students classify related words: *cottonmouth, water moccasin, copperhead, rattlesnake* (snakes, poisonous snakes, poisonous snakes of North America). Once students have caught on to the idea of classifying, they can classify sentences, as in the following example, where students select the sentence that includes all the others:

Anteaters are built for hunting and eating ants and termites.
Anteaters have very sharp claws, which they use to dig up termite or ant nests.
Anteaters have long snouts for poking into the nests.
With their long sticky tongues, anteaters can pick up hundreds of ants or termites.

Model the process and explain how you picked the main idea sentence (Anteaters are built for hunting and eating ants and termites.) because it includes the ideas expressed by all the other sentences. This can be a difficult process for some students. They might need lots of modeling, explanation, and practice. However, if students have a grasp of the process of categorizing words and sentences, move onto the next step. In trials with fifth graders, about half the group had no difficulty categorizing sentences, but the other half needed careful instruction. Eduardo, who had difficulty identifying the main idea, did not do well with printed exercises but showed considerable improvement when the sentences were placed on cards so that they could be manipulated. An essential component of the exercises was to have Eduardo explain how each sentence fit into the topic sentence.

After becoming adept at categorizing, students can select the topic sentence in brief paragraphs, select from four choices the sentence that expresses the main idea, identify a directly stated main idea, or construct a main idea when one is not directly stated.

Constructing the Main Idea

To construct a main idea, students can use either a whole-to-part or part-to-whole strategy. In a whole-to-part approach, students use the title, headings, graphics, and apparent topic sentence to hypothesize the main idea. They then check their hypothesis by seeing if the details support it. In a part-to-whole approach, readers construct a main idea by noticing the key details and seeing how they are related (Afflerbach, 1990; Afflerbach & Johnston, 1986). Struggling readers may find it easier to build a main idea from the bottom up by looking at the details and seeing what they add up to. Because the paragraph below about the screaming frog has no title, heading, or topic sentence, a bottom-up approach would be the better strategy to use for deriving the paragraph's main idea:

> When it is threatened, the Screaming Budgett's Frog puffs up its body so that it will look big and scary. Then it does just what its name says it does. It screams. Its scream is very loud. Many would-be attackers turn and run away when they see its scary body and hear its loud scream.

The following steps in deriving a main idea begin as a top-down process but transition into a bottom-up process if the top-down approach doesn't work. If a title or heading is available, students might use the following steps to select a stated main idea or construct a main idea if it is not stated. Post these steps or an adaptation of them in your classroom (Gunning, 2010a, p. 319):

1. Use the title or heading to make a hypothesis (careful guess) as to what the main idea is.

2. Read each sentence and see whether it supports the hypothesis. If not, revise the hypothesis.

3. If you can't make a hypothesis as to what the main idea is, see what all or most of the sentences have in common or are talking about.

4. Select a sentence or make a sentence that tells what all the sentences are about.

Using Manipulatives

Given systematic, controlled instruction, Eduardo showed some improvement. However, he was still evidencing difficulty retelling and comprehending key elements in selections that he read. An experimental approach known as indexing was tried. Indexing is based on the premise that comprehension has a motor base. According to Bruner (1964), we make sense of our environment through three modalities: enactive representation (action), iconic representation (imagery), and symbolic representation (language). Glenberg, Gutierrez, Levin, Kaschak, and Japuntich (2004) propose an indexical hypothesis of language comprehension. According to the indexical hypothesis, a first step in comprehending language is indexing, or relating the words to their objects or referents. Manipulating objects assists the indexing process and improves the student's ability to create a representation of the text. Thus, if the story said, "The horses ran out of the barn and into the corral," the reader would use toys to show the horses running out of the barn and running into the corral. In experiments, students who manipulated objects after reading sentences outperformed students who simply read the sentences twice by a 1.39 and 0.81 effect size for recall and question answering (Glenberg et al.). Even students who simply viewed the manipulations had improved comprehension. As the researchers conclude,

> Meaning arises from simulating the content of sentences. This simulation requires indexing words to the objects and actions those words represent, deriving affordances (how those objects can be manipulated), and meshing those affordances as directed by the syntax of the sentence. The manipulation condition required children to explicitly index the words to objects and to align the objects as directed by the syntax of the sentence. Thus, the manipulation condition guaranteed meaningful comprehension as described by the Indexical Hypothesis. (Glenberg et al., p. 435)

To foster comprehension when students don't seem to be reading for meaning, when they are just saying the words, or when they can't seem to understand the simplest of texts, you might have them use manipulatives to show the action in a story. For instance, if the story says that "The boy put a dish of milk at the bottom of the tree. The cat climbed down from the tree and lapped up the milk," the reader may show a toy boy placing a play dish on the ground and the cat climbing down. After students have mastered this ability, you could move into imaging. Then, instead of manipulating the action in the story, students imagine it, mentally picturing the action in the story.

It is not necessary to have each sentence manipulated. You might use an arrow or other symbol to indicate which sentences you want students to manipulate. Students might work individually, in pairs, or in a small group. Students benefit almost as much by watching the objects being manipulated as they do by actually manipulating them (Glenberg, Brown, & Levin, 2007). This technique resulted in very large gains in comprehension for the students who manipulated the objects but also for those who watched the manipulations. In the following paragraph, figures of animals and trees were used to simulate the actions or ideas expressed in the sentences preceded by an asterisk. Eduardo read the paragraph and used the toy figures to show what the marked sentences were portraying.

Giraffes
Giraffes are tall animals. *A giraffe is taller than an elephant. *A giraffe is so tall that it can eat the leaves on the tops of trees. Giraffes have many enemies. *Lions, hyenas, and Nile crocodiles hunt giraffes. Because they stand tall and have excellent eyesight, giraffes can see far away. *A giraffe can see a lion or hyena that is a mile away.

For the first stopping point, Eduardo placed the giraffe next to the elephant to show that the giraffe was taller. For the next, he showed a giraffe eating from a toy tree. For the third, he chose from a group of animals and showed the lions, hyenas, and Nile crocodiles hunting giraffes. For the last sentence, he showed a giraffe looking at a lion and hyena that were a distance away. He correctly portrayed the essence of each marked sentence

Just as the research had suggested, the manipulative exercise worked quite well. Using the manipulatives, Eduardo was able to show what the article described, and his retelling was accurate and detailed. Indexing was highly engaging. It got Eduardo's full attention. Perhaps most important of all, indexing demonstrated that Eduardo was able to comprehend and retell when provided with the right stimulus and scaffolding. Indexing was then used with more complex articles and also with narratives.

One limitation of indexing is that it requires objects that can be manipulated. Obtaining toy animals was relatively easy. Commercially produced sets of farms, homes, garages, and airports can be purchased. You might put out a request for old sets of toy objects and toy buildings. You might also construct or have students construct dioramas or use cardboard depictions of objects. Care needs to be taken that students don't view the activity as being too immature. Because the animals that Eduardo worked with were realistic replicas, he didn't view them as being beneath him. For older students, you might use sports figures, race cars, or other objects that would appeal to them. Or you might use illustrations instead of objects. Colleagues have used illustrations instead of objects and have also reported a high degree of success, engagement, and enthusiasm on the part of the struggling readers with whom they were working. One colleague reported that two students who typically had a great deal of difficulty staying on task stayed focused and remarked how much they liked the activity. Another colleague had struggling readers place objects in a bowl designed to represent a bog to show the contents of a bog. She reported that "The improvement in comprehension after doing this was amazing!" Of all the techniques used with Eduardo, indexing was easily the most effective.

Because comprehension is complex and there are many possible reasons why a student has difficulty comprehending, the key is to find a way in, an approach that reaches them. The success of indexing revealed a way in to helping Eduardo, whose puzzling comprehension difficulty had confounded his teachers for nearly four years. Providing a physical foundation improved Eduardo's comprehension. Eduardo did better when he could physically manipulate objects or language. In subsequent lessons, imaging, graphic organizers, and manipulatives were used whenever possible. For complex passages describing processes, diagrams were drawn.

Scaffolding Written Responses

Although indexing helped improve Eduardo's oral responses, he experienced difficulty translating his oral responses to written ones. Answer organizers and frames were used to guide Eduardo's responses. Answer organizers, such as that shown in Figure 7.1, use prompts to help students respond, such as What is the main idea? What are all the sentences talking about? What details support

Figure 7.1. Example Main Idea Organizer

What is the main idea? (What are all the sentences talking about?) Write the main idea below.	What details support the main idea? (Which details are giving examples of the main idea? See if you can find two. Be sure to explain how each way of keeping safe works.) Write the details below.
_____	1. _____ 2. _____

the main idea? Frames, such as that shown in Figure 7.2, provide even greater assistance. They supply a portion of the expected response and blanks where the student fills in the missing part. Initially, the frame might contain almost all of the expected response so that the student need only supply a word or two. Over time, the student provides a greater proportion of the response until eventually frames are phased out. Frames are especially helpful to English learners because the frames provide the language and the structure needed to complete responses. Note in Figures 7.1 and 7.2 how an answer organizer and a frame are used to help students note the main ideas and supporting details in the practice paragraph "Keeping Safe."

After students have become adept at identifying main ideas in brief, well-constructed paragraphs, introduce longer works and model for them how to use heads and subheads as clues to main ideas. A subhead can be thought of as a hypothesis as to what the main idea is. If the details don't support the subhead, the readers can revise the hypothesis.

Brief, well-controlled paragraphs provide controlled practice. Help students transfer skills learned to their content area texts. Show them how they can use their ability to identify and construct main ideas to better understand their content area texts. Through modeling, you might show students how they can turn subheads into questions and then read to answer questions, Survey Question Read Recite Review (SQ3R)–style.

Also make use of graphic organizers. Tie the graphic organizers to the kind of organization and thinking involved. Webs of semantic maps, with their main idea in the center and supporting details arranged web style, work well with

Figure 7.2. Example Main Idea Frame

Keeping Safe

Some fish have unusual ways of keeping themselves safe. When puffer fish are in danger, they fill themselves with water or air. They puff themselves up to twice their size. This makes the puffer fish look frightening. It makes them harder to eat, too. Porcupine fish also double their size by gulping water or air when attacked. But a porcupine fish is covered with needles. These needles lie flat until the porcupine fish swells up. Then they stick out. Any enemy who tries to bite a porcupine fish gets a mouthful of cuts.

Fill in the frame answers based on the passage above. Use the Main Idea Organizer to help you.

The main idea of this article is that some fish _____

_____ .

The main idea is supported by information from the article. The article explains that the puffer fish can _____. This helps the puffer fish because _____ .

The porcupine fish can_____ . This helps the porcupine fish because _____ .

Adapted from Gunning, T.G. (2010b). *Reading Comprehension Boosters: 100 Lessons for Building Higher Level Literacy for Students in Grades 3–5.* San Francisco: Jossey Bass.

a main idea-detail organization. Eduardo responded well to the use of webs to show the main idea and supporting details. At first he completed partially composed webs. Later he used Kidspiration software to create webs. Because Eduardo seems to do best when learning has a physical basis, he illustrated his webs with clip art.

Extend the concept of main idea into writing. Have students develop topic sentences, create titles for their written pieces, and also use subheads for their longer expository pieces. Also extend the idea of seeing likenesses and differences and categorizing whenever the opportunity presents itself. Help students develop themes, big ideas, and connections.

Summarizing

When researchers analyzed studies in the use of strategies to determine which strategies resulted in the greatest gains in comprehension, they concluded that summarizing was the most powerful strategy (Pressley, Johnson, Symons, McGoldrick, & Kurita, 1989). Summarizing enables students to organize information, but it is also a check on understanding. Difficulty summarizing is a sign that comprehension is deficient and corrective action is called for. Building as it does on the ability to determine the main idea and supporting details, summarizing requires the ability to select the most essential information and the ability to condense and paraphrase. The following activities can be used to develop the ability to summarize:

- Identifying the best summary
- Using frames to summarize
- Using answer organizers to summarize
- Using graphic organizers to summarize
- Using visualizations to summarize

Although different from retelling because summarizing entails selecting the most important information, retelling can be a good preparation for summarizing. You can, for instance, encourage students to retell only the most important information. A summary should begin with a statement of the main idea and then include essential supporting details. Once students can provide a main idea and key details, they can proceed to condensing by combining related details. The shorter the summary, the more combining will have been used. Shorter summaries also require a greater degree of generality.

To introduce summarizing, relate it to everyday activities. Talk over how students might provide their parents a summary of their activities at school or give friends a summary of a movie they have seen, a TV show they have watched, or a game they have played. After a discussion or demonstration, show how you would summarize the key ideas. Then involve students in helping you to create summaries. After explaining the value of summarizing as a tool for comprehending and monitoring comprehension, do a think-aloud as you read an expository passage and then summarize it. To help students compose summaries, provide frames. Also use graphic organizers as summaries.

Students can practice writing summaries by having them complete quickwrites, in which they respond to a prompt for about five minutes, or by asking them to write the most important things they learned in class. By imposing a time limit as in quickwrites, students naturally tend to summarize. Being limited to write about the three most important things they learned fosters the selection of essential details. Students also summarize when they work in groups in which one person is asked to tell what the group has discovered or decided.

Eduardo experienced difficulty summarizing but did better when the task was more concrete and more constrained, when, for instance, he was asked to tell about the three most important facts he learned about Komodo dragons. Because summarizing was obviously difficult for him, extra time was also spent in an activity that involved selecting from three choices the one that was the best summary and discussing why that summary was best. Creating a graphic organizer was also helpful. Steps for composing a summary are as follows:

1. Determine the main idea.
2. Write the main idea.
3. Write the most important details that support the main idea.
4. Shorten the summary. Combine ideas. Get rid of ideas that are not important. Get rid of unnecessary words.
5. Read over the summary. Make sure that it has the main idea and key details. Make sure that it is clear.

Because of past difficulties when asked to summarize, Eduardo expressed some reluctance when the strategy was mentioned. However, perhaps intrigued by the title, he responded favorably to the summarizing task titled "Somebody–Wanted–But–So," which is a way of summarizing the key elements in a piece of fiction or a biographical selection (Beers, 2003). Four columns are drawn and are headed Somebody, Wanted, But, and So. *Somebody* is the main character. *Wanted* is the story problem or what the main character wants. *But* is the problem or conflict that the main character faces. *So* is the resolution of the problem. Figure 7.3 shows an example of a Somebody–Wanted–But–So organizer. For informational text, students might also use a traditional graphic summary in which they list the main idea and supporting details, as in Figure 7.4.

Have students stop occasionally while reading and summarize what they have read. If they have begun their reading with a question, they can see if they can answer that question. After summarizing, they might evaluate the summary or make connections.

Figure 7.3. Somebody–Wanted–But–So Summary

Somebody	Wanted	But	So
Jason	To make the team	He missed a lot of his shots.	He practiced every day.

Figure 7.4. Graphic Summary

Main Idea	Possible results of global warming
Supporting Details	Rising seas and flooding
	Expansion of deserts
	Changes in weather patterns
	Changes in farming yields

Integrating and Interpreting

Interpreting entails going beyond the textbase. At this level, readers integrate background knowledge with information from the text. They infer, draw conclusions, create images, compare and contrast, and make connections to other texts they have read or to personal experiences. For instance, as students read about porcupine fish, they might visualize what the fish looks like; they might also connect the way a porcupine fish defends itself with the way that a puffer fish defends itself: The puffer fish bluffs, but the porcupine fish has a genuine weapon. The students might think back to a science class in which animal defenses were discussed.

Inferencing

In their everyday lives students are constantly making inferences. For instance, they can infer from a friend's actions when the friend is angry or upset. However, when reading a story they might not infer how the main character is feeling or what kind of a person the main character is. Characters in a story are more abstract than people in real life. Students need to apply what they know about real life to what they read about. Students might also be very literal readers. They might not realize that inferring is required or even allowed. To introduce inferencing, place single sentences on the board and have students make inferences based on them. Ask students, What did that sentence lead you to infer? What makes you infer that? (Yuill & Oakhill, 1991). Emphasize that inferences may vary but should be logical. The following are sample sentences you could use to teach inferencing:

> Nobody expected Juan to get a hit, much less smack the ball over the fence.

> (Students might infer that Juan is a boy, that baseball is being played, that Juan is not a good hitter, and that Juan hit a home run.)

At last we were home.

I should have studied more.

Next time I'll make sure I get on the right train.

QAR. Bogged down in decoding issues or literal comprehension, struggling readers might not realize that not all of the answers to questions are in the text. They might not be aware that, for certain kinds of questions, they need to integrate information from text with background knowledge to make inferences and draw conclusions. On the other hand, some struggling readers, perhaps because processing text has been difficult for them, answer questions based solely on their background knowledge, even though that might conflict with what the text says. One device for focusing students' attention on the sources of answers to questions is Question-Answer Relationship (QAR; Raphael, 1984, 1986). The types of answers in this strategy include the following:

Right there: Answer is contained within a single sentence in the text.

Putting it together: It is necessary to put together information from several sentences to obtain an answer.

On my own: The answer is part of the student's prior knowledge.

Author and me: The reader must combine personal knowledge with information from the text to construct an inference.

To introduce QAR, you might place a paragraph similar to the following on the board and ask the questions that follow. Discuss students' responses. Emphasize using the appropriate source for answering each question.

The wind had picked up. After three windless hours, they were moving once more. The sun was straight overhead. It was noon. If the winds kept up, the travelers would reach port by six o'clock, just in time for dinner.
What time of day was it? (Right there)
About how much longer will it take the travelers to reach port? (Putting it together)
What is the travelers' means of transportation? (Author and me)
What is your favorite way of traveling? (On my own)

Macro Cloze. Macro cloze is also an excellent device for providing practice with inferencing. In macro cloze, students integrate information from the text and background knowledge to supply deleted sentences in a passage (Yuill & Oakhill, 1991), as in the following examples:

1. I didn't know the zoo was closing.

_____

_____

You have no idea how happy I was when I saw the zookeeper opening up next morning.

2. My Aunt Betty was right.

_____

_____

Next time I'll follow the recipe exactly.

Mystery Passages. Wade (1990) created think-alouds in which the main idea or topic is not revealed until the last sentence. Although Wade's think-aloud was designed to be used as an assessment, it can also be used as an instructional tool (Smith, 2006). The student is told that she or he will be reading a story in segments and, after reading a segment, will be asked to tell what the whole story is about. The mystery passage is read in portions consisting of one to four sentences. After each segment the student is asked, What do you think this is about? The student's response is followed by the prompt, What makes you think that? After the student has worked her or his way through the passage, the student is asked to reread the passage before engaging in the retelling of the whole passage. The mystery passage works well because each segment is like a riddle and challenges the reader to respond. The clues are cumulative. The student must relate the segments to one another, something that poor comprehenders often fail to do. Because the mystery subject isn't revealed until the last segment, it leads the student to use background knowledge and information from the article to guess the identity of the subject. By asking the student to explain each response, you get insight into the student's thinking, and you also require him or her to think about the response rather than to just hazard an easy guess. The following is an example of a mystery paragraph:

> It is a very large animal. When fully grown, it might weigh up to 1,500 pounds or even more.
>
> It is a powerful swimmer. It can swim for ten hours or more.
>
> It is a fast swimmer. It can swim six miles in an hour's time.
>
> It doesn't mind the cold. It swims in icy water and sometimes floats on large sheets of ice.
>
> It has a built-in lifejacket. It has two coats of hair. The inner coat is made of fine white hair and keeps it warm. The outer coat is made up of longer hairs that are hollow and are like tiny life jackets or tubes.

The two coats of hair help keep the polar bear on top of the water. (Gunning, 2010b, p. 121)

You might have the student jot down her or his response after each segment with the challenge being to guess the identity of the subject in as few segments as possible.

It Says–I Say–And So Charts. A catchy way to explain the process of making inferences is with It Says–I Say–And So charts (Beers, 2003; see Figure 7.5). The chart has three columns for students' input: It Says, I Say, and And So are written by the teacher or student at the head of the columns. *It Says* is what the text states. *I Say* is what the reader's background tells him or her. *And So* is the inference that might be drawn by putting together text details and reader background as shown in Figure 7.5.

Predicting

Predicting is also known as forward inferencing. Readers make predictions about what might happen or what they might learn from expository text. Predicting is more difficult because the reader has only a title and maybe an illustration to use as the basis for making a prediction.

To improve students' prediction skills, show them how to preview. Explain how to use the title, subheads, illustrations, and overview—if there is one—to get a sense of what an expository text might contain or what might happen in

Figure 7.5. It Says–I Say–And So Chart

Question	It Says	I Say	And So
Read the question.	Find information from the text that will help you answer the question.	Think about what you know about the information from the text.	Put together what the text says with what you know.
What kind of a person is Ryan?	When Ryan heard that he didn't have enough money for a well, he said, "I'll just have to do more chores."	It takes persistence to keep on trying when your plans don't work out.	Ryan is a persistent person. He just worked harder when his plan didn't work out.

Adapted from Gunning, T.G. (2010b). *Reading Comprehension Boosters: 100 Lessons for Building Higher Level Literacy for Students in Grades 3–5.* San Francisco, CA: Jossey Bass.

a story. Stress the importance of using background knowledge along with any clues from the survey to make a prediction. So that they base their predictions on a consideration of text clues, ask students to justify their predictions. Also emphasize flexibility.

Some struggling readers have the mistaken idea that a prediction is like a quiz question: It's either right or wrong. Emphasize that predictions are based on a careful consideration of what the survey suggests and that if a prediction does not appear to be working out, it can be changed.

The value of predicting is threefold. It gets the struggling reader to activate background knowledge, create a purpose for reading, and be a more active reader. Students might work in pairs to predict. Figure 7.6 shows how a prediction might be scaffolded. The prediction is based on a short article about Ryan, who collected money to dig a well in Jimmy's village in Africa. Students might also use a Prediction Chart such as that shown in Figure 7.7. The Prediction Chart emphasizes the concept that predictions are tentative and should be changed if

Figure 7.6. Example Supporting a Prediction Chart

What do you predict will become of Ryan and Jimmy's friendship? Support your prediction with information from the article.	
Prediction Write your prediction here. *I predict that Ryan and Jimmy's friendship will grow stronger.*	Support Give at least one reason for your prediction here. *Both boys were sad when Ryan had to leave.*

Figure 7.7. Example Prediction Chart

What is my prediction?	What led me to make this prediction?	What did the text actually tell?	As I read the text, what changes, if any, did I make in my prediction?
The article will tell about a new kind of glue.	*The title of the article is "A Sticky Invention."*	*The article told how Post-It Notes came to be invented.*	*I predicted the article would tell how sticky notes came to be used by many people.*

additional information points in a new direction. Once students get in the habit of making predictions, phase out the prediction chart, or else it will become tedious.

Imaging

Creating nonverbal representations can dramatically increase understanding and retention. According to dual coding theory, we have two main ways of storing information: through words and through images (Paivio, 1986). If knowledge is stored both verbally and in images, retention is greatly strengthened. One advantage of imaging is that it is a technique that is not often used, so therefore it will be a novelty for struggling readers. It will be different from other approaches that they were taught and might have negative associations with. It offers the promise of a fresh start and a new approach. Relatively uncomplicated, imaging has a fast payoff.

To introduce imaging, do a think-aloud as you read a high-imagery passage, and describe how you form an image and how forming the image helps you to get a deeper understanding of the passage. Stress the fact that images vary because our background and experiences vary. Guide the class as students create images after reading such passages. Encourage students to explain how visualizing helps them understand the passage. Once students have grasped the concept of imaging, have them complete the following activities:

- Students mark passages where they visualize
- Students share images with a partner.
- Students write a high-imagery passage. They might write about their favorite meal or their favorite time of day.
- Students bring in high-imagery passages and share them.

Characters and settings in fiction pieces lend themselves to imaging. For instance, before reading "All Summer in a Day," a story by Ray Bradbury about life on Venus where the sun only comes out for one hour every seven years, the teacher is encouraged to set the scene by turning off the classroom lights, having students close their eyes, and having them supply the sound of rain by drumming their fingers on their desks. The students are asked to imagine they are on Venus, sitting in their classroom on the day the sun comes out for only one hour. They are asked to describe how they might feel as they sit there and suddenly the rain stops, the clouds part, and the sun comes out. The students are asked to describe what the sun feels like and looks like.

Making Connections

Students can make connections between portions of the text, with other texts, with personal experiences, or with what's happening in the world. The most valuable connections are those that contribute to an understanding of the story. An ideal connection occurs when something the student is reading touches him or her personally. Perhaps the story of a young person who feels lonely after transferring to a new school brings to the fore a time when the reader had a similar experience, and so the response becomes an affective one. As Collins (2004) explains,

> Besides teaching children about different ways that readers can connect to their texts I also want to extend or deepen their connections in a way that helps them to better understand the text. Instead of simply saying, "This reminds me of..." my students can go further by adding "and this connection helps me to understand the story, character, part, page because...." (p. 176)

Some possible connection questions include the following:

- Does this story remind you of anything that has happened in your life?
- Are any of the characters like anyone you know or anyone that you have read about?
- Has anything like this ever happened to you?
- Do you know anyone like the main character?
- Does this story remind you of any other stories that we have read?
- How does the information in this article compare with the information in your textbook?
- In what way is what happened in the story similar to what is going on in the world?

Model making connections for your students. In modeling a connection, discuss how it is similar to or different from the incident or person in the story. Explain how your connections help you to understand the story a little better or deepen a feeling that the story is eliciting. Encourage students to mark connections in their reading and share connections they have made.

Figure 7.8. Connection Chart

What the Text Said	Text-to-Self Connection	Text-to-Text Connection	Text-to-World Connection
Puppy raisers take care of their puppies for 14 to 18 months. During that time the puppy raisers learn to love their puppies. They feel sad when they have to give their puppies back to the seeing eye organization.	I remember when I had to give my dog up when we moved. It was like losing a friend.	This reminds me of a book about hearing ear dogs. People had to raise the puppies until they were ready to be trained.	There was a guy in our old neighborhood who had a seeing eye dog. His dog helped him to go all kinds of places, even on planes. I guess if you figure you were raising a puppy that would grow up to be a seeing eye dog and make a difference in somebody's life, you would feel proud and sad at the same time when the puppy left.

Ask them to describe a character or incident in a story and describe their connection. Stress making connections that are substantive and help them to understand a story better. Students might use a connection chart such as the one shown in Figure 7.8.

Elaborative Interrogation

Elaborative interrogation was also used to build Eduardo's comprehension. This technique, as its name suggests, is questioning that is designed to have the student seek an expanded or extended response. Elaborative interrogation is simply asking a *why* question that prompts students to make use of background knowledge to make information that one is reading more understandable and also more memorable (Menke & Pressley, 1994). For instance, after reading the sentence, "Giant squid live at the bottom of the sea," the reader asks, "Why do giant squid live at the bottom of the sea?" Asking why worked as well as having students create images. The technique works especially well with text that has a lot of facts.

Comparing and Contrasting

As Terman (1916), who is regarded as the father of cognitive testing in the United States, has noted,

> Thinking means essentially the association of ideas on the basis of differences or similarities. Nearly all thought processes, from the most complex to the very simplest, involve to a greater or lesser degree one or the other of these two types of association.... Intellectual development is especially evident in increased ability to note essential differences and likenesses. (p. 202)

As Terman comments in his testing manual, it is easier to detect differences than it is to note likenesses. Therefore, students may need more scaffolding to note similarities. Begin instruction with subjects that are fairly well known to students and that have obvious similarities and differences. For instance, students might compare the hippopotamus and the rhinoceros or Bactrian camels and dromedary camels. They might also compare characters in stories or stories by the same author. In fact, most topics lend themselves to some sort of comparison. One of the most effective ways to foster the ability to see likenesses and differences is to include compare and contrast questions in discussions and writing activities.

Graphic organizers are especially helpful in noting comparisons and contrasts. In comparing and contrasting, students are required to identify and organize similarities and differences. Venn diagrams are frequently used to display comparisons and contrasts. In a Venn diagram, two overlapping circles are drawn. Similarities are listed where the circles overlap. Differences are listed where there is no overlap, as shown in Figure 7.9.

Although relatively easy to construct, Venn diagrams have several shortcomings. Characteristics of items being compared are not grouped or categorized. Only two or three items can be compared. In most situations, a frame matrix (see Figure 7.10), sometimes known as a compare–contrast map, would be more effective. A frame matrix map is recommended because it presents a side-by-side comparison and allows comparison of a virtually unlimited number of elements. A frame matrix has two components: a frame, which lists essential categories of information—such as location, area, population, average income—and the matrix. The matrix consists of the elements being compared. Two or more elements may be compared.

To construct a frame matrix, decide on the important categories of information for a topic. Then note how each category might be subdivided. If you

Figure 7.9. Venn Diagram for Camels

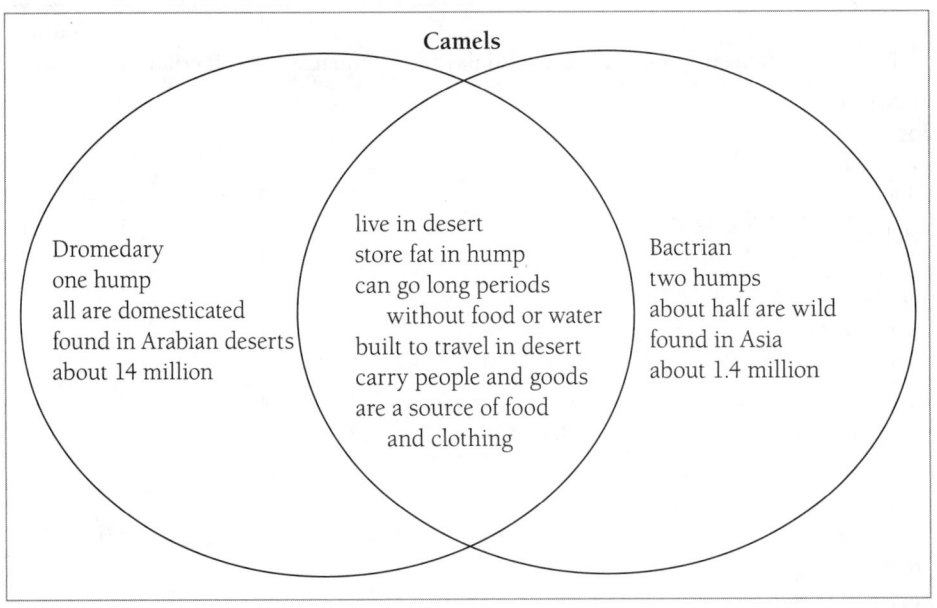

Camels

Dromedary
one hump
all are domesticated
found in Arabian deserts
about 14 million

live in desert
store fat in hump
can go long periods
    without food or water
built to travel in desert
carry people and goods
are a source of food
    and clothing

Bactrian
two humps
about half are wild
found in Asia
about 1.4 million

are familiar with a topic, you might set up a tentative frame and then verify it by checking the text that students are about to read (Armbruster, 1991). You might also check the topic in an encyclopedia. Encyclopedias often organize their articles around major topics or questions. Possible frame matrix elements for a chapter or a book on weather disasters might include main characteristics, causes, damage, how it's forecast, signs of, protection against, and examples of.

A frame matrix helps students see relationships. Students can see at a glance what entities are being compared and what the major categories of information are. Making comparisons is facilitated because categories being compared are lined up side by side. The matrix also makes it obvious when information is missing (Heiman & Slomianko, 1986). A shortcoming of the frame matrix is that differences and similarities are not highlighted as well as they are in the Venn diagram. To highlight similarities and differences, include a similarities column and only list differences in the other columns. To foster connections, students might include their own experiences in the matrix. To foster drawing conclusions, students might complete a block that asks them to supply a "so what" statement (Ellis, 2004). In the "so what" statement, students draw conclusions about the comparisons they have made. After completing the frame

Figure 7.10. Frame Matrix

TIGERS	Bengal	Indochinese	Malayan	Sumatran	Siberian	South China
Countries or areas where they live						
Habitat (kinds of places where they live)						
Size						
Life expectancy (how long they live)						
Estimated population						

matrix for tigers, they might conclude that tigers differ in size and preferred habitat according to subspecies.

Critique and Evaluate

In the Critique and Evaluate phase, the reader makes judgments about the text. For fiction, the reader might make aesthetic judgments about the quality of the writing, the plausibility of the plot, the development of the characters, the development of a theme, or the appropriateness of the setting. For nonfiction, the reader might make judgments about the fairness and accuracy of the information and the clarity of the writing. Skills range from judging the fairness of the language used to evaluating the credibility of sources.

Judging the Words

Evaluating might begin at the word level. Words are used in four main ways: to describe, to evaluate or judge, to point out, and to interject (Wilson, 1960).

The words *car*, *look*, and *piano* describe objects or actions. The words *sly* and *deceive* evaluate; they express a judgment. Some words both describe and evaluate. *Shock*, *steal*, and *junk* describe objects and actions, but they also incorporate unfavorable evaluations. Struggling readers might not realize that a word being used to describe is also being used to judge and sway opinion. It's the choice of words that signal originality in a piece of writing or bias in an expository piece. Exercises, such as the following, might be used to help students become aware of ways in which words are used. Students discuss whether the underlined words are used to describe or to judge.

It was a <u>rainy</u> day.

It was a <u>miserable</u> day.

The turtle <u>snapped</u> at me.

The owner of the store <u>snapped</u> at me.

Anna <u>bragged</u> about her trip.

Anna <u>discussed</u> her trip.

The hyena is a <u>cowardly</u> animal.

The hyena is a <u>swift</u> animal.

In a related exercise, students select the words in a sentence that make an action, person, or thing sound better.

Our team was (defeated, crushed).

The game was (boring, slow moving).

The players made several (careless, stupid) plays.

The coach (bawled out, corrected) the players after the game.

Students can also underline words that make an action, person, or thing sound worse.

Anna is (determined, stubborn).

She (always wants her own way, is independent).

Anna usually (convinces, orders) other people to do what she wants them to do.

Anna becomes (furious, upset) when no one listens to her.

Applying this skill to the real world, students might discuss words that advertisers use to sell their products: These include words such as *new, improved, extra, bonus, adventure, excitement, value,* or *quality.* Students should extend their skills by picking out judgmental language in practice paragraphs such as the following one about feral pigs, but ultimately they should apply this skill to their textbooks and other materials that they read and also to the media.

Feral Pigs
Feral pigs are a menace. Feral pigs live in the wild. Wild pigs in Hawaii gobble up berries, seeds, grasses, and crops planted by hard-working farmers. Greedy feral pigs trample young plants in fields and destroy valuable orchards. Vicious feral pigs have also attacked innocent horses, dogs, and even people.

Determining Fact and Opinion

Although distinguishing between facts and opinions is sometimes listed under Interpret and Integrate, it seems to be more a matter of evaluating. Determining whether a statement is a fact or an opinion requires stepping back and taking a critical look at the statement, especially if it is cleverly worded. Although included in literacy curricula at the earliest stages, distinguishing between a fact and an opinion involves making a judgment as to whether a statement can be verified. Facts can be verified by empirical or analytical means. A fact can be verified empirically by measuring, counting, weighing, or observing. A fact can be verified analytically by examining the language of the statement. "There are 12 items in a dozen" can be proved by examining the language. A *dozen* means 12, so the statement is factual. Opinions are statements that express an attitude or a value. Opinions can be convincing and supported with examples and reasons but cannot be proved.

The terms *fact* and *opinion* can be confusing. The word *fact* indicates something that can be proved with empirical evidence, but it has the connotation of something that is true. As used in the curriculum, *fact* means an empirical statement, something that can be verified with objective evidence.

The word *fact* is sometimes used to indicate the strength of an opinion, as in the statement, "Our team is better than yours, and that's a fact." Of course, it isn't a fact. It's an opinion. To avoid students' confusing the two meanings of the term, you might use the phrase *factual statement*. At one time it was said that Mt. Everest was 29,141 feet high. That is an empirical, or factual, statement. It can be proved by measuring Mt. Everest. Using an improved measuring technique, scientists recently found Mt. Everest to be higher. This doesn't mean that the first statement is no longer factual. It is still factual—it can be verified empirically— but it has been shown to be inaccurate.

To introduce the concept of factual statements as being verifiable as opposed to opinion statement, that express personal preferences or values, have students discuss sentences such as the following:

There are more than 500 students in our school.

Our school has 25 classrooms.

Our school's outside walls are made of red brick.

Our school is the best in the state.

Lead students to see that the first two sentences can be verified by counting and the third by observing, so those are factual statements. Point out that factual statements are ones that can be proven right or wrong. However, note that the fourth sentence is an opinion; it simply tells how someone feels about the school. Reasons and facts can be given as to why the school is judged to be the best, but the statement cannot be proven right or wrong. Then discuss sentences in which the information is verifiable but incorrect:

There are more than 25 students in our class (There are just 25.)

Our classroom is green. (It is another color.)

Help students to understand that these sentences are factual because the first can be proved wrong by counting, and the second can be proved incorrect by observing. Emphasize that any statement that can be proved right or wrong is factual. Discuss the importance of being able to tell whether a statement is a fact or opinion. Note that in many advertisements and political speeches, opinions are presented as facts. Being able to tell an opinion from a fact can help us make better judgments and decisions.

Present exercises such as the following in which students note whether the statement is a fact or an opinion. If the statement is classified as being a fact, students should say how it might be verified or proved right or wrong.

Bills and advertisements make up most of the mail delivered to homes.

Bills should be paid on time.

Advertisements are annoying.

Because of e-mail, people aren't sending as many letters.

E-mail is better than regular mail.

Students should apply this skill to any reading, viewing, or listening that they do. During discussion, talk over whether key statements in a selection are facts or opinions. Have students note whether they are using facts or opinions in their writing and whether they are supporting opinions with facts.

Judging Sources

Never has the ability to judge sources been more critical. Leu and Hartman (2006) recount an experiment in which seventh graders read an article at a hoax site on the Internet about a species of octopus that lives in trees. Incredibly, all but one of the students believed what they read. With the proliferation of television and radio commentators, the popularity of blogs and Tweets, and the openness of the Internet, students need to be able to judge sources more than ever. When checking sources, students should ask themselves three questions:

1. Is the source of information a competent authority? What are the source's credentials?

2. Is the information up to date? Fortunately, many Internet sites note when they were last updated. Some sites are more than a decade old.

3. Is the source unbiased? Does the source have anything to gain by convincing me of the source's position? Obviously, a commercial site has a product to sell or point of view to make the corporation look good. For the Internet, one helpful bit of information is the URL. A URL ending with *.com* indicates a commercial site. A URL ending in *.org* indicates an organization, but this is no guarantee that the source is unbiased. Websites with other endings, such as *.gov* for government and *.edu* for education, are less likely to be biased. You might have students consult the American Library Association (2009) for criteria for choosing websites and its list of recommended sites.

As an ongoing activity, have students evaluate the sources of information, whether the source is a TV program, newspaper, magazine, textbook, trade book, Internet site, blog, or something else. Students should view, listen, and read with a critical eye, ear, and mind. Model how you judge sources. As part of classroom discussions of sources of information, discuss their credibility and reliability.

Using Language With Care

As part of evaluating sources of information, students should use language in a responsible, accurate fashion. A virtually universal misuse of language is the use of absolutes: "You always break your promises." "You never say 'thank you.'" "Everybody thought the test was too difficult." The antidote for erroneous absolutes is to apply the concept of verifying statements or clarifying them. What do you mean when you say that the test was "too difficult"? The speaker's idea of too difficult might not be the same as yours and might more readily fit in with the idea that the test was "comprehensive" or "challenging." Of course, defining what is meant by "too difficult" introduces another thinking issue. Clarifying statements is an essential thinking skill. If asked to verify the statement, it might turn out that "everybody" is the student who complained and his or her best friend.

Developing Aesthetic Judgment

Fiction is judged in terms of character development, plot, theme, author's style, and setting. When judging fiction, students should consider the following about these criteria:

- **Character development**. Does the character seem like a real person? Is the character too good or too bad to be true? Does the character develop throughout the course of the story?
- **Plot**. Is the plot interesting or exciting but also plausible? Is the plot original or is it predictable? Can you guess from the opening incident what is going to happen?
- **Theme**. Is the theme a genuine one or is it a thinly disguised message or moral? Does the theme have significance?
- **Author's style**. Is the style original and engaging? What kinds of literacy devices does the author use? How effectively are these devices used?
- **Setting**. How appropriate is the setting to the story? How vividly has the author described or presented the setting? Can we picture where the action is taking place and when it is taking place? Has the author managed to transport us to another time or place?

Captain Underpants to the Rescue

Reading was not Eduardo's favorite activity. Perhaps, because of his initial struggle to learn to read, he viewed reading as an unpleasant task. He wouldn't read voluntarily. Because he struggled to develop basic reading skills, Eduardo was provided with a series of easy-to-read books that reinforced the skills he had been taught. This is a research-based best practice, and it worked. When he was provided with extra help and lots of practice, Eduardo mastered basic decoding skills. However, the practice materials that he had been provided were dull. Although Eduardo had learned needed skills, he had not learned that books can make you laugh out loud, put you on the edge of your seat as you wonder if the hero is going to survive, root for the underdog, and transport you to fascinating new worlds. Eduardo's parents struggled each night to fulfill his homework assignments to read for 20 minutes. Fortunately, Eduardo's teacher knew from past experience that the Captain Underpants series by Dav Pilkey was a favorite read for fourth-grade boys and recommended it. With its two antiheroes, fourth graders George and Harold, and constant mention of unmentionables, Captain Underpants is an almost sure bet to capture the attention of the most reluctant of male readers.

Intrigued by the cover and title, Eduardo gave Captain Underpants a try. Soon, Eduardo's parents were faced with a new dilemma. Eduardo went well past the 20 minutes of required reading time and in fact read until his nine o'clock bedtime. Eduardo's parents were faced with the novel task of getting Eduardo to stop reading! Eduardo's retelling skill was also bolstered as Eduardo regaled his younger brother with the antics of George and Harold. Later on in the year, Eduardo discovered Jeff Kinney's Diary of a Wimpy Kid series. Again, Eduardo needed no prodding to read or discuss. He spent many hours discussing the books with his classmates and friends.

Learning is intensified when students are engaged. Although the brief paragraphs were helpful in building Eduardo's basic comprehension skills and strategies, it was essential that these skills and strategies be applied in the kinds of materials that he would be reading in and out of school. Ideally, the skills and strategies students are taught will be applied in all their content areas. Eduardo was asked to tell what kind of things he liked to read about and was provided with a choice of library books written at his independent level. Books were also chosen that reinforced the skills being taught. For instance, in connection with the main idea unit, Eduardo read a book about monitor lizards. Eduardo had cited the Komodo dragon as an animal in which he was interested. Fortunately, the books available on the Komodo dragon had titles and subheads that could be used to help determine main ideas. The books also built background and allowed for sustained reading on a single topic.

ACTION PLAN

- If you haven't already done so, as suggested in Chapter 1, list a scope and sequence of skills and strategies that would have the greatest impact on students' ability to engage in higher level literacy tasks and that are based on students' needs, the texts they will encounter, the school or district's curriculum, and the kinds of skills that will be tested.
- Focus on six to eight skills and strategies.
- Decide on the teaching techniques that you will use to teach the skills and strategies. Also select materials that you plan to use.
- As a rule of thumb, you might allocate a month's time for each skill or strategy. However, also allow time for review of previously taught skills and strategies.
- Plan introductory lessons for each skill or strategy.
- Also plan extra teaching and practice lessons for students who need added instruction and reinforcement.
- Decide on ways to help students transfer and apply skills and strategies taught to the content areas and to outside reading and viewing.

QUESTIONS FOR STUDY AND REFLECTION

1. How does the comprehension curriculum explored in this chapter fit in with the curriculum you are currently teaching?
2. What changes might you make in your current curriculum?
3. Which of the techniques described in this chapter might you use or adapt?
4. Try out one or more techniques that you think would be of most benefit to your students. Reflect on the effectiveness of the technique and share your reflection with the group.

REFERENCES

Afflerbach, P. (1990). The influence of prior knowledge on expert readers' main idea construction strategies. *Reading Research Quarterly, 25*(1), 31–46. doi:10.2307/747986

Afflerbach, P., & Johnston, P.H. (1986). What do expert readers do when the main idea is not explicit? In J.F. Baumann (Ed.), *Teaching main idea comprehension* (pp. 49–72). Newark, DE: International Reading Association.

American Library Association. (2009). *Using primary sources on the web.* Available at www.ala.org/ala/mgrps/divs/rusa/resources/using primarysources/index.cfm

Armbruster, B.B. (1991). Framing: A technique for improving learning from science texts. In C.M. Santa & D.C. Alvermann (Eds.), *Science learning: Processes and applications* (pp. 104–113). Newark, DE: International Reading Association.

Beers, K. (2003). *When kids can't read: What teachers can do: A guide for teachers 6–12.* Portsmouth, NH: Heinemann.

Bruner, J.S. (1964). The course of cognitive growth. *American Psychologist, 19*(1), 1–15. doi:10.1037/h0044160

Collins, K. (2004). *Growing readers: Units of study in the primary classroom.* Portland, ME: Stenhouse.

Ellis, E.S. (2004). *Comparison frames.* Northport, AL: Masterminds Publishing. Available online at graphicorganizers.com/resources.html

Glenberg, A.M., Brown, E.M., & Levin, J.R. (2007). Enhancing comprehension in small reading groups using a manipulation strategy. *Contemporary Educational Psychology, 32*(3), 389–399. doi:10.1016/j.cedpsych.2006.03.001

Glenberg, A.M., Gutierrez, T., Levin, J.R., Kaschak, M.P., & Japuntich, S. (2004). Activity and imagined activity can enhance young children's reading comprehension. *Journal of Educational Psychology, 96*(3), 424–436. doi:10.1037/0022-0663.96.3.424

Gunning, T.G. (2008). *Developing higher-level literacy in all students: Building reading, reasoning, and responding.* Boston: Allyn & Bacon.

Gunning, T.G. (2010a). *Creating literacy instruction for all students* (7th ed.). Boston: Allyn & Bacon.

Gunning, T.G. (2010b). *Reading comprehension boosters: 100 lessons for building higher level literacy for students in grades 3–5.* San Francisco: Jossey Bass.

Heiman, M., & Slomianko, J. (1986). *Methods of inquiry.* Cambridge, MA: Learning Skills Consultants.

Leu, D.J., Jr., & Hartman, D. (2006). *Integrating the new literacies into your classroom: Ten steps for equipping students with the Internet comprehension skills of today and tomorrow.* Paper presented at the Annual Convention of the International Reading Association, Chicago.

Menke, P.J., & Pressley, M. (1994). Elaborative interrogation: Using "why" questions to enhance the learning from text. *Journal of Reading, 37*(8), 642–645.

National Assessment Governing Board. (2008). *Reading framework for the 2009 National Assessment of Educational Progress.* Washington, DC: Author.

Paivio, A. (1986). *Mental representations: A dual coding approach.* New York: Oxford University Press.

Pressley, M., Johnson, C.J., Symons, S., McGoldrick, J.A., & Kurita, J.A. (1989). Strategies that improve children's memory and comprehension of text. *The Elementary School Journal, 90*(1), 3–32.

Raphael, T.E. (1984). Teaching learners about sources of information for answering comprehension questions. *The Reading Teacher, 27*(4), 303–311.

Raphael, T.E. (1986). Teaching question answer relationships, revisited. *The Reading Teacher, 39*(6), 516–522.

Smith, L. (2006). Think-aloud mysteries: Using structured sentence-by-sentence text passages to teach comprehension strategies. *The*

Reading Teacher, 59(8), 764–773. doi:10.1598/RT.59.8.4

Terman, L.M. (1916). *The measurement of intelligence: An explanation of and a complete guide for the use of the Stanford revision and extension of the Binet-Simon Intelligence Scale.* Boston: Houghton Mifflin.

Valencia, S.W., & Buly, M.R. (2004). Behind test scores: What struggling readers really need. *The Reading Teacher, 57*(6), 520–531.

Wade, S.E. (1990). Using think alouds to assess comprehension. *The Reading Teacher, 43*(7), 442–451.

Wilson, J. (1960). *Language and the pursuit of truth.* Cambridge, England: Cambridge University Press.

Yuill, N., & Oakhill, J. (1991). *Children's problems in text comprehension: An experimental investigation.* Cambridge, England: Cambridge University Press.

CHAPTER 8

Beyond Strategy Instruction: Looking at Person, Situation, Task, and Text Variables

Irene W. Gaskins and Emily Phillips Galloway

N ine-year-old Liam (a composite of many students we have taught) sits disengaged from the reading group activities, while the other three group members ponder how the story will end. Liam has been struggling to revise his previous story prediction in light of the information from the page he just read. Unable to do this, he sits with his head in his hands. Unfortunately, this is not the only difficulty that Liam has encountered during daily reading group instruction. Often, he seems unable to apply an alternative reading strategy when his previous strategy fails, despite the fact that he has been explicitly taught and guided through the use of additional strategies. In other instances, it is evident that Liam has not monitored his reading for sense, as he frequently concludes that the text itself is nonsensical. Paradoxically, when read to, Liam has little difficulty with comprehension and, when asked to read words in isolation, Liam exhibits no difficulty reading at sight (or decoding) unknown words at his beginning-of-second-grade instructional level. Moreover, Liam possesses a rich tapestry of background knowledge that should enrich his understanding of text, although he often needs cueing to make appropriate connections between the text and his lived experience. Diagnosed by his home school district as having a reading problem, Liam has his summer session teachers perplexed about how to provide meaningful instruction that addresses his disparate difficulties, including his growing disengagement.

Ruling out poor decoding skills, lack of comprehension strategies, and inadequate background knowledge as the primary causes of Liam's poor response to instruction, his teacher and her literacy coach are wrestling with why Liam is not responding to what, for the other reading group members, seems to be excellent reading instruction. It appears that for Liam to become an engaged reader who actively constructs meaning, his reading instruction will need to take into consideration more than just decoding and comprehension—but what else should be considered? There are few available tools to guide his teachers in making this complex instructional decision. What seems to be needed, as suggested by Shepard (2000), is an array of assessments that address not only the cognitive product the teacher is trying to achieve (reading with understanding) but also the process of achieving it, namely, the habits of mind and dispositions needed for reading success. Shepard recommends that educators expand "the armamentarium for data gathering" (p. 8) to include, among other things, observational data. Yet how to use these data to bring about meaningful action in the classroom has rarely been addressed.

In this chapter, we explore using a summary instrument to catalog classroom observations and to identify patterns in students' habits of mind and behaviors that may impede reading progress but that are not usually measured on formal reading assessments. This observation summary, the Interactive Learner Profile (see Appendix on pp. 223–229), allows for specific learner characteristics to be identified within the context of tasks, texts, and situations that are authentic and frequently occur in the classroom. Similar to Afflerbach (2007), we believe that assessment that is situated in the observations that educators make as students engage in routine reading, writing, and classroom activities is crucial to designing the differentiated instruction struggling readers need. The observations of educators over time and in various contexts (e.g., in the classroom, on the playground, when the student is engaged in independent reading activities) become those data that inform completion of the Learner Profile. This summary of learner characteristics can then be used to focus attention on the particular needs of each student, including those needs related to the affective (usual emotional tendency) and conative (motivational and volitional) processes of achieving the cognitive product, and it can inform teaching practices and contribute to teachers' making changes in the instructional environment. As Stewart (2002) suggests, teachers are "architects" who craft the character, the intentions, and the goals of the instructional context to meet the learning needs of the diverse children they teach. Yet if teachers are to master this art of teaching, we must add tools to their instructional arsenal that help them recognize the needs of the learners in their classrooms beyond the presenting academic profile.

We begin by discussing current conceptions of the connection between reading difficulties and learner characteristics and examine the issues that arise from currently dominant forms of assessment. Next, we suggest a schema for understanding learner characteristics and their interaction with task, text, and situation variables. Finally, we highlight the patterns of difficulty faced by one struggling reader, Liam, and discuss the ways in which knowledge of a pattern of learner characteristics informed our teaching practices and brought about changes in the instructional environment to help Liam become a more successful and confident reader.

Reading Difficulties, Learner Characteristics, and Current Assessments

Although low-level reading processes (e.g., phonemic awareness, decoding) are related to a child's acquisition of reading (National Institute of Child Health and Human Development, 2000), researchers also note that other learner characteristics play an important role in acquiring reading proficiency (e.g., Gaskins, 2005; Keogh, 2003; Sternberg & Grigorenko, 2003; Strickland, Ganske, & Monroe, 2002). These reports are supported by the finding that a significant number of struggling readers who have received appropriate interventions in the primary grades and have attained grade-appropriate decoding skills continue to experience reading difficulties (Pressley, 2006; Snow, Porche, Tabors, & Harris, 2007). This suggests that such interventions fail to address the broad nature of reading difficulties (Gaskins, 2010). In addition to decoding, phonemic awareness, fluency, vocabulary, and reading comprehension, research suggests that reading involves a wide range of cognitive and noncognitive functioning such as attention (Olson & Byrne, 2005), executive functioning (Meltzer, 2007), memory (Ehri & Snowling, 2004), self-regulation (Zimmerman & Campillo, 2003), and motivation (Snow et al., 2007), among others.

Need to Address Learner Characteristics Related to Reading Difficulties

In a meta-analysis of the learning disabilities literature in which reading problems were pervasive, Swanson (1999) discusses how two learner characteristics, inefficient information processing and difficulty with self-regulation, distinguished LD students from their more successful peers. This finding is bolstered by those of Strickland et al. (2002), who assert that instruction for struggling readers should emphasize self-monitoring and control over one's own learning.

It appears that to become successful readers struggling readers may require instruction that targets specific learner characteristics.

The need for students to develop both literacy skills and the specific learner characteristics demonstrated by successful learners is highlighted in a recent longitudinal study conducted by Snow et al. (2007). They examined the paradox of students who do well on reading tests in fourth grade and beyond but who are not successful academically within the context of middle school and high school. They concluded that, teaching students to read is not sufficient to ensure academic success and that in addition to literacy skills, other factors influence the degree to which students can succeed in school. Similar to the researchers discussed earlier, Snow and her colleagues note the importance of executive functioning skills, such as goal setting, to achieving success in school.

On the positive side, other studies have suggested that instruction that addresses person variables enhances students' chances for success. For example, although many successful learners, when presented with challenging cognitive tasks, will engage in metacognitive regulation, this is often not the case with struggling readers (Meltzer, 2007; Zimmerman & Campillo, 2003). The good news is that cognitive strategies emphasizing thinking skills for strategic behavior, self-reliance, and flexibility in learning have been shown to be quite teachable and associated with better learning (Borkowski, Carr, & Pressley, 1987; Halpern, 1996). Thus, by addressing person variables, teachers are better able to help students harness their power as learners. To accomplish this, educators benefit from understanding students' cognitive and metacognitive strengths and challenges as well as the affective, motivational, volitional, and situational factors that mediate learning.

We, like Ackerman and Beier (2003; 2006), propose that ability (in this case, reading ability) involves more than raw cognitive power. Instead, reading ability, like other abilities, is a complex of cognitive, conative, and affective variables (Snow, Corno, & Jackson, 1996) that interact with task, text, and situation variables in determining how well a person will learn to read (Gaskins, 2005; RAND Reading Study Group, 2002). These variables interact and may either facilitate or impede progress in reading. As an example, initial failure in learning to read words may lead to a decrease in associated reading interests and the traits that support reading acquisition, such as adaptability or active learning. This decrease in interest and supportive learner traits may lead to a decrease in cognitive investment in acquiring new knowledge about decoding or comprehension strategies. In view of our multidimensional and interactive conception of ability as proposed in Gaskins's work (e.g., Gaskins, 2005), it would appear that a summary of teachers' observations of cognitive/affective/conative traits would indicate a student's disposition toward or away from particular learning tasks and be helpful to teachers in planning supportive interventions.

Related to this proposal, Ackerman and Beier (2003) suggest that an assessment of personal trait complexes can be useful in identifying students at risk for academic failure. Based on such an assessment, educational interventions can be developed and focus "on the entire complex of traits that are indicators of an avoidance of domain-knowledge acquisition" (p. 25). Ackerman and Beier recommend a multiple-pronged intervention that addresses most or all of these traits.

Reading Tests and Reading Programs Assess and Teach to Limited Learner Variables

Ackerman and Beier (2003) join a chorus of educators who for many decades have attested to the multifaceted nature of reading difficulties (Doehring, 1968; Gaskins, 1984; Gates, 1941; Koppitz, 1971; Robinson, 1946; Strickland et al., 2002; Ysseldyke & Taylor, 2007). Despite these research findings, many commonly used reading assessments evaluate only a few variables which account for a small percentage of the variance in learning to read. For example, witness the focus of dozens of standardized tests and state-mandated reading assessments on low-level reading skills to the exclusion of assessments that seek broader explanations for reading success or difficulty. Notably, ability profiles resulting from test scores highlight only a "fraction of the significant propensities" (Corno et al., 2002, p. 191) that may lead to reading failure. In response to these limited ability profiles, there has been a proliferation of approaches and programs to remedy students' failure to test well on basic reading skills (Elmore, 2002), with the result that teachers spend enormous amounts of time teaching the skills that will be tested in a high-stakes arena. Furthermore, often only one instructional approach, even if it is evidence based, is employed to remediate the deficit areas identified by the test (Allington, 2006). Using a single approach often fails to provide opportunities for differentiated instruction or to address the characteristics of individual learners that are contributing to their struggles in reading (Al Otaiba & Fuchs, 2006; Gaskins, 2010; Valencia & Buly, 2004). All of this occurs despite research evidence that preparation for specific tests of reading subskills does not result in better readers (Klein, Hamilton, McCaffrey, & Stecher, 2000;

Linn, 2000) and that one instructional approach does not work for all students (Allington, 2006).

The failure of programs that address only basic reading subskills to remediate poor reading has resulted in a call for instruction that focuses on the specific needs of individual readers (Valencia & Buly, 2004). Furthermore, researchers and practitioners alike seek tools that provide a systematic approach to assess not only cognitive strengths and challenges of struggling readers but also the other important noncognitive aspects of reading (Afflerbach, 2007). These include affective, motivational, and situational factors that mediate learning. A student's inability to demonstrate successful grade-level appropriate reading in a mainstream classroom often results from, or is exacerbated by, these "other" factors (Gaskins, 1984; Gaskins & Baron, 1985; Prawat, 1989; Schmeck, 1988). Despite the fact that noncognitive factors are recognized as central to reading success, Afflerbach (2007) notes that "they are largely neglected from an assessment viewpoint, thus their designation as 'the other'" (p. 153).

A Model for Understanding Learner Characteristics and Their Interactions

Educators are keen "kid watchers," and the knowledge gained through observation serves to inform many of the instructional decisions made in the classroom. It is a not-uncommon practice for educators to record observations about students in a daily or weekly log, to take running records, or to chronicle student growth by collecting work samples (Alexander, 2006). When viewed as individual pieces of information such data may be helpful, but we contend that the true power of such observational data rests in its ability to be viewed as an aggregate to reveal trends and patterns of learning facilitators and impediments.

To acknowledge the validity of teacher observations and to better serve the school's struggling readers, the community of educators of which the authors are members worked collaboratively to create a systematic rubric that would serve as a summary instrument for observational data. This summary instrument takes into account not only cognitive factors that influence school success but also these "other" factors: conative, affective, and physiological. In addition to addressing these within-the-person variables, the Interactive Learner Profile situates learning facilitators and impediments within the context of external variables. Using a Likert scale, teachers reflect on each student's functioning within the context of everyday learning tasks. By attending to a student's thoughts and actions outside of the context of formal assessments, educators are able to identify factors that facilitate or impede learning. This knowledge informs teaching practices and stimulates changes in the instructional environment. The Interactive Learner Profile also provides a means for tracking progress in Response to Intervention and for differentiating instruction. As one example, the Interactive Learner Profile was employed to gain a better understanding of Liam, the student who was introduced earlier. An analysis of Liam's learning profile will be discussed later in this chapter.

In this chapter, the discussion of struggling readers is contextualized within a theory of reading that seeks to connect challenges and successes in gaining reading proficiency with internal (person) and external (text, task, and situation) variables that operate interactively (Gaskins, 2005). The Interactive Learner Profile operationalizes the model outlined in this section.

Internal Variables

Theory and research (e.g., Snow, Corno, & Jackson, 1996) suggest that there are at least four broad categories of person variables that affect learning: affective, conative, cognitive, and physiological. A plethora of studies (e.g., Biggs, 1987; Dweck, 1999; Deci & Ryan, 2002) have identified person variables (e.g., locus of control, self-esteem, general disposition toward learning, learning style, goal-setting ability) that impact an individual's capacity and propensity to respond to instruction. The Interactive Learner Profile provides a tool for teachers, parents, and students to consider systematically the person variables that facilitate or impede learning.

External Variables

External (text, task, and situation) variables interact with person variables to impact literacy acquisition in developing readers. For example, it has long been known that using appropriately leveled materials (Pinnell & Fountas, 2007; Washburne & Morphett, 1938), as well as providing explicit strategy instruction (Gaskins, 2005; Pressley, 2006), can aid struggling readers in comprehending text. Within the context of this discussion, task variables refer to the requirements of a particular learning activity, for example, if the assignment consists of 5 or 40 pages of reading or an activity is long term and has complex components or is a routine homework assignment due the next day. Text variables refer to characteristics of the text itself—the ratio of known sight words to unknown words on each page or the density of new concepts presented in the chapter. Situation variables include sociocultural factors and pedagogical factors (e.g., classroom setting, level of teacher knowledge). Both can facilitate or impede the learner's ability to complete the task at hand. A mismatch between a student's person variables and instruction (pedagogical factors) often results in a student being unresponsive to instruction. Within classrooms, many of the task, text, and situation variables are under the control of educators who plan and initiate learning activities. Yet despite an educator's ability to engineer many external variables, internal person variables are less easily manipulated. It is often these person variables that surprise and delight, as well as continually challenge teachers to tailor instruction to the individual's unique learner characteristics.

Application of the Model and the Interactive Learner Profile

As documented by the research of Valencia and Buly (2004), the term *struggling reader* should not evoke a monolithic profile of person variables, but rather it should embrace the understanding that for each student so labeled, there is a unique combination of person variables that facilitates or impedes reading progress. For the purpose of illustrating the use of the Interactive Learner Profile, we have chosen to discuss one student, Liam. Although our composite presented through Liam's case cannot be generalized to all struggling readers, the function of the Interactive Learner Profile as a tool to identify patterns of facilitators and impediments as well as to shape instruction is easily generalized to students who exhibit a variety of person variables.

Liam, a Caucasian male, was 9 years old and completing third grade when his mother enrolled him in our summer reading program. When we first met Liam at his presession screening, he was struggling to keep pace with his peers in reading, despite the fact that he was receiving one-on-one, twice-weekly, pull-out sessions with a reading specialist in his public school. When discussing his reading experiences in third grade, Liam commented that reading was "too hard," although he claimed that he could often read the words.

We came to know Liam as a learner through daily observations of him at work in our classroom and through his written work, as well as through conversations with his mother. The second author also engaged in conversations with Liam about his reading experiences. As a part of the responsive teaching occurring in the classroom, careful lesson notes as well as running records (Clay, 1993, 2001) from each session with Liam were kept to document observable behaviors.

The Interactive Learner Profile is intended as a rubric upon which to consolidate and summarize observational data collected by teachers. The method of collecting observational data may vary by teacher. In this case, Liam's teachers wrote daily narrative notes; however, data in another format, such as a chart or goal card, could have been employed in the same way. Therefore, the way in which teachers collect data is less central than the fact that data are collected on a regular basis to ensure that the patterns identified by completing the Interactive Learner Profile are in fact representative of a student's typical functioning and are not merely fascinating, but infrequent, anomalies. Our experience using the Interactive Learner Profile suggests that the resulting graphic, which depicts clusters of facilitating and impeding person characteristics that influence learning, improves teacher efficiency by more clearly guiding instructional efforts toward capitalizing on students' strengths and helping students manage characteristics that interfere with learning.

Internal Variables—Initial Observations of Liam

Liam brought tremendous strengths to the classroom. For example, he was well liked by his peers in large part because he was a kind child with a pronounced ability to form positive social connections. Liam exhibited a wealth of background knowledge about science and World War II fighter planes and enjoyed sharing what he knew with his classmates. His expressive language skills were age appropriate, as was his vocabulary, and he exhibited an uncommon wit.

During our first few sessions together, Liam attempted to avoid reading tasks and appeared lethargic, frequently resting his head on his book. Although the books and writing tasks were at Liam's instructional level, when reading silently he often had difficulty decoding words accurately and monitoring for sense. This was evidenced by the sporadic, decoding-centered queries Liam posed to the teachers in the classroom and the difficulty he sometimes experienced when asked to verbally summarize what he had read. Initially, we felt that Liam was simply experiencing difficulty with decoding, so we provided him with additional decoding support. Yet when Liam was asked to whisper read a text at his instructional level to one of his teachers, he often was able to decode words with automaticity but was unable to construct a retelling of what he had read. Conversely, when text was read to him, constructing an accurate retelling posed no difficulty. Initially, in our daily notes we frequently recorded "poor decoding?" and "poor comprehension?" next to various activities. The question marks suggested that we were confused by Liam, who did not consistently have difficulty with either decoding or meaning making.

Our program focused on explicitly teaching strategies for reading, writing, and learning. Liam seemed to struggle in the first weeks of the program to flexibly switch from using one strategy when reading, such as using a known word to decode an unknown word, to another, such as using context and the initial consonant of a word when the first strategy did not work. A similar pattern was evident with respect to comprehension, such as applying his knowledge of story elements to gain a deeper understanding of the story. This lack of cognitive flexibility was most apparent when Liam was asked to choose a new strategy when his previous strategy had failed. Liam was able to recite reading strategies but seemed unable to apply them independently. Yet when provided with a strategy suggestion, he was able to make progress.

In addition, despite the highly structured classroom, Liam appeared to be extremely disorganized. Furthermore, he acted with very little agency in attempting to manage the text, task, and situation variables that he encountered, especially when he was assigned what he perceived to be a difficult task, a boring text, or a novel situation. On such occasions, he simply would cease to be engaged. It appeared by his pleasant affect that Liam truly wanted to please his teachers and meet with success. However, for some reason, he was unable to engage in behaviors that would bring about that success. As a result, Liam became increasingly withdrawn and exuded boredom when confronted with reading tasks.

The daily notes we kept about Liam's struggles with reading and writing during his first few weeks in our classroom seemed to indicate no consistent pattern that would suggest why he was experiencing difficulty or what would be the best focus of instruction. However, once we reflected on our observation data and completed the Interactive Learner Profile, a pattern did emerge from the seemingly contradictory information we had gathered (i.e., reads words correctly, has excellent background knowledge, experiences difficulty understanding what he reads) and, as a result, we were able to craft instruction that addressed Liam's pattern of difficulty. This experience reminded us that there is more to remedying reading and writing difficulties than teaching the skills and strategies of reading and writing, especially if the difficulties in reading and writing emanate from a common source.

External Variables—Liam's Classroom

The summer reading program consisted of 25 daily small-group sessions each lasting 105 minutes. We worked with Liam in a class of nine students, cotaught by two reading clinicians. The second author served as the lead teacher. Within the context of the classroom, external variables (text, task, and situation) were tailored to meet the individual needs of each student. Texts used in Liam's classroom were leveled appropriately for each student based on the informal reading inventory conducted at the outset of the program and on daily monitoring of student progress. Each text was chosen with the chronological age and interests of the student in mind. Task variables were similarly managed in that students were only asked to complete tasks for which they had been taught the strategies to enable success. As an example, students read only fiction texts for which strategies to manage the story elements had been taught. The classroom schedule was strictly followed to create predictability and structure for the students. Each day began with a 20-minute read-aloud, followed by a writing strategy lesson, and then independent journal writing. Students attended reading group, visited the library, and engaged in independent reading accompanied by a written response-to-reading activity.

Data Summary on the Interactive Learner Profile (ILP)

Completing the Interactive Learner Profile helped solidify our understanding of Liam and allowed us to recognize that, although Liam had initially presented as a struggling reader, it was neither just decoding nor simply comprehension that was at the root of his reading difficulties. In fact, the sections of the ILP with the most notations of "sometimes demonstrated proficiency" or "rarely demonstrated proficiency" were the two components of conation (motivation and volition) and, more specifically, processes of volition. Conative abilities refer to the processes that allow students to engage in ongoing, goal-directed behavior by harnessing the power of motivation and volition (Denckla, 1996; Eslinger, 1996; Meltzer, 2007). Generally, we have found that the young struggling readers we teach are motivated but often lack the ability or disposition to take deliberate action to manage (volition) the cognitive resources required to achieve learning goals, including goal-setting, planning, prioritizing, organizing, self-regulation, and monitoring, which all mediate the enactment of goals and intentions.

Educational theorists have linked conative processes with a broad array of reading skills (e.g., Meltzer & Krishnan, 2007). For example, struggling readers, especially at the early levels, must toggle between decoding unknown words and managing cognitive resources to construct meaning. These readers often experience difficulty simultaneously carrying out both processes and therefore appear to be either poor decoders or erratic meaning makers when in reality, as in Liam's case, these skills in isolation pose little difficulty.

In further analyzing the observation data entered on Liam's Interactive Learner Profile, we also saw several cognitive style issues (persistence and adaptability), which undoubtedly interacted with conative variables to compound difficulties in responding to instruction. As noted above, Liam struggled with adaptability when faced with the competing cognitive demands of simultaneously reading words and constructing meaning. Meltzer (2007) notes a similar pattern when prior knowledge must be flexibly integrated with novel information presented in the text. In a similar vein, the task of prioritizing which story events are of the greatest importance can pose a difficulty to students who struggle with motivation and volition, especially when exacerbated by cognitive style issues. Although deficiencies in low-level reading skills may appear to be at the root of these readers' difficulties, upon deeper analysis, the role of conative functioning difficulties often becomes apparent as these difficulties interact with not only cognitive style issues but with a student's identity as a reader and his or her more general concept of self. For Liam, this was the case.

After five sessions together, Liam still demonstrated little interest in being identified as a reader. As his classmates began to anticipate with excitement the beginning of each day's reading group, Liam still exuded boredom. His past history as a struggling reader and the way he had been positioned in juxtaposition to "readers" in his former classroom seemed to contribute to Liam's inability to identify himself as a reader and seemed to play a role in his poor level of motivation and inadequate volition. Students like Liam increase a teacher's awareness that creating a reader is not only about teaching reading skills and strategies but also about responding to learner characteristics and creating a reading identity.

The Interactive Learner Profile provided a systematic and graphic way to examine and organize the person variables that facilitated or impeded Liam's reading development. Additionally, the ILP's final section listed possible supports that his teachers might put in place to help Liam deal with the task, text, and situation variables that interact with person variables to facilitate or impede reading progress. The ILP orchestrated for Liam's teachers a process of reflection regarding the facilitators or impediments that were interacting to create Liam's response to instruction, and it provided the foundation upon which his teachers could build in designing an instructional program that addressed his learning needs.

Addressing the Interaction of Internal and External Variables

Liam's volitional and cognitive style impediments suggested to us that an important element of his differentiated instructional plan should be learning metacognitive strategies for managing cognitive processes. Thus, one of our instructional goals was to teach Liam how to think metacognitively and, in so doing, teach him how to learn (Meltzer, Pollica, & Barzillai, 2007). We planned to accomplish this by employing explicit strategy instruction, teacher modeling, and cognitive behavior modification, all within the context of authentic reading, writing, and learning tasks. Further, we would be conscious of maintaining a nonthreatening, convivial learning environment in which Liam could identify himself as a reader.

According to McCarthey and Moje (2002), an individual's identity as a reader is cemented through shared group affiliation (readers and nonreaders) and reinforced when a shared purpose for reading exists. In classrooms with struggling readers, there exists a need to help students join the "literacy club," for when students come to identify themselves as readers, they begin to believe that they will become like the more experienced readers in the group (Smith, 1997). Thus, becoming a reader for Liam would not simply be about providing him with the skills and strategies to engage in decoding and meaning making; it would also be about initiating him into the club of readers.

Coaching Liam to Set and Achieve Learning Goals

Like most children with volitional difficulties, Liam struggled to engage in goal-directed behavior. In addition to establishing a common goal for the class, we also developed goals for each student in the classroom. To begin to overcome Liam's lack of engagement, a weekly goal card was created for him (see Figure 8.1). In the course of each session, we would have "goal checks" during which students were asked to evaluate the degree to which they had met their individual goals. Initially, we would pause with each student to help him or her

Figure 8.1. Liam's Goal Card

Liam's Goal Card

My Goal: *I will participate six times in reading group by asking for clarification, by answering questions, and by working with a partner.*

Monday	Tuesday	Wednesday	Thursday	Friday
✓ ✓ ✓	✓ ✓ ✓	✓ ✓ ✓	✓ ✓ ✓	✓ ✓ ✓
✓ ✓ ✓	✓ ✓ ✓	✓ ✓ ✓	✓ ✓ ✓	✓ ✓ ✓

✓ signals number of times Liam participated in reading group.

evaluate if he or she had accomplished the goal. This was done by asking the student questions that promoted reflectivity: What did you do to meet your goal? What did it look like when you were (participating, being an active learner)? Eventually, as our students grew in their abilities to self-assess, each student would independently place a check on his or her card to signify that the goal for that day was accomplished. Therefore, goal cards became a graphic, tangible representation of progress.

Initially, with teacher coaching, Liam chose goals that were action centered: "I will participate twice." This type of goal was easily measured, and as Liam succeeded, he began to choose goals that emanated from his growing ability to think metacognitively. During our 15th session, Liam chose the goal "To take action when reading doesn't make sense." Each time Liam took action he would place a check on his goal card, and as our work together continued, there were more and more occasions when Liam succeeded and was able to place checks on his goal card. In the process, he sometimes commented that he was becoming a more competent reader, and we saw him take action to apply the strategies that he was being taught. By implementing a tangible instructional tool in the form of a goal card, Liam was assisted in engaging in the type of thinking that successful readers employ when reading. Furthermore, Liam was supported by frequent positive feedback that focused on specific behaviors over which we hoped Liam would take ownership. Often this feedback would establish Liam as an "expert" by asking him to share with his peers his developing understanding of the connection between smart effort and reaching his reading goals. For example, we might say, "Liam, I like how you stopped and reread when you became confused. I wonder what it was that helped you know that your reading had become confusing." When Liam received praise, which provided him the opportunity to share his developing capacities, his face would light up with delight. Liam was not only beginning to think metacognitively, he was helping his peers to do so as well, and he was beginning to see himself as a reader.

Coaching Liam to Manage Text Variables by Realistically Assessing Reading Level

After completing the Interactive Learner Profile, Liam's teachers were more attuned to his difficulty with simultaneously decoding and constructing meaning. Through responsive teaching, his teachers observed that Liam was most successful when the books he chose to read were "easy books" below his instructional reading level. Liam was coached to realistically assess if the books he was selecting for his nightly reading were at his independent level. He was taught to open to a page in the book and read the page to himself. If there was more than one word per page that he could not decode automatically, he was to consider choosing another book. By reducing Liam's need to decode, he was better able to accomplish word reading and meaning making simultaneously. By exerting control over this aspect of text, Liam slowly began to see himself as more competent. Liam was familiar with fiction texts, and he was explicitly instructed in the use of story elements to organize story events and to identify the internal structure of the stories he read. Often we would observe Liam in the library as he selected his books. Initially, like most students, he made his selections based on the attractiveness of the book cover or the boldness of the illustrations. After we began to instruct Liam about how to choose fiction books at his independent reading level, it was instructionally beneficial to Liam and diagnostically effective for us to ask him, "Why did you choose this book? What things did you consider?" Eventually, Liam strode up to his teachers in the library and boldly queried, "Would you believe that this book is both at my easy level *and* a fiction story?" The modeling of self-talk that we had been providing for Liam had become his own, which is the ultimate goal of metacognitive coaching.

Coaching Liam to Manage Task and Situation Variables by Providing Organizational Frameworks

The nature of Liam's volitional challenges meant that there was a need for his teachers to foster a nurturing classroom culture in which organization was a priority. Liam was taught to recognize when he had become disorganized and was provided with charts to help him organize his materials systematically. In addition, he was given time for reorganizing during transitions.

Completing the Interactive Learner Profile helped us recognize that Liam's inability to organize materials, as well as his evident lack of an organizational framework to determine when to use a reading strategy as a component of goal-directed behavior, emanated from poor conative functioning abilities. This realization alerted his teachers that just as Liam needed a process to follow when organizing materials, he also needed a process to guide him in taking strategic action with respect to comprehension. Initially, Liam was often unaware that he did not understand what he had just read. To assist Liam in overcoming this impediment, his teacher would model a statement that he might say to himself to monitor understanding, such as, "My purpose question was..., and the answer is...." If he was unable to complete this statement by the time he finished reading the assigned section of text, Liam was coached to take action by rereading. In working with struggling readers, we have discovered that it is important to explicitly teach and model strategies for thinking about text, for it is rare for these students to figure out comprehension strategies on their own until they have been taught a few strategies that they can implement successfully (Gaskins, 1998). In keeping with this realization, Liam's teachers would often model self-talk. This modeling would take the form of a think-aloud in which the teacher would position rereading as an activity in which all readers engage, even experienced readers like the teacher. For example, the teacher might model self-talk in this way: "Based on my background knowledge, I was thinking that [...] was going to happen, but based on what I just read, my prediction doesn't seem possible—I guess I'd better reread to see whether I read something incorrectly and to help me revise my prediction." This process of teacher self-talk can position rereading as a hallmark of what members of the reading club do, as well as normalize the rereading action taken by the reader. During our 10th class session, Liam began to engage in rereading voluntarily, which signaled that we could gradually release the responsibility for using this strategy to Liam.

Coaching Liam to Take Charge of Person Variables by Setting a Purpose for Reading

Although we did not initially link Liam's poor recall of story events to his difficulty integrating meaning making with decoding, the identification of conative functioning difficulties via the Interactive Learner Profile helped us understand what was at the root of Liam's disengagement in reading group. In keeping with the conative difficulties highlighted by the Interactive Learner Profile, Liam struggled to keep in mind his purpose for reading and to locate segments of the text that he could use to justify his opinions during reading group discussions. The simple instructional tool of a sticky note provided Liam with a means to hold his purpose in mind when reading and developed into an even more elaborate strategy that helped Liam recall what he read. Curiously, Liam not only wrote his purpose for reading on a sticky note, which he placed in the margin of the text, but also he began to write detailed story-element notes on them. When he was questioned about why he wrote so many notes, Liam removed the sticky notes from his book and placed them neatly on the story-element chart that we had created on the board. Liam had produced a summary of the story in a unique way and had fashioned a method that compensated for his difficulty in recalling story events. The ability to put exterior supports into place to assist with internal processes suggested that Liam was becoming cognizant that he could independently compensate for his weak executive functioning skills by developing the habits required to engage in purposeful, goal-directed behavior.

Coaching Liam to Independently Orchestrate Variables

During reading group, we were able to provide support to Liam more readily than when he was working independently at his desk. Therefore, one of our goals was to guide Liam in developing tools that he could use independently to cue himself to employ strategies. To achieve satisfactory comprehension in these independent situations, Liam would need to self-assess his understanding of what he was reading and apply appropriate fix-up strategies when needed. Early in Liam's experience in our classroom when he was reading on his own, he would become confused about what he had just read and simply stop reading. To counteract this tendency, Liam was coached to stop and talk to himself about what he had read. For example, he might say, "First the story said…, but now it seems to be saying…; that doesn't make sense. Guess I'd better reread to see if I misread something." If rereading didn't help, Liam told himself to read ahead and, if he was still confused, he instructed himself to ask a peer or teacher for clarification. When he was coached by a teacher, this process helped Liam to make sense of what he was reading, but he struggled to hold this fix-up process in mind when he was reading independently. Therefore, his teachers created a laminated bookmark for Liam that listed the talk-to-yourself steps (see Figure 8.2).

Often Liam would sit completing his independent response to reading with his small, chubby index finger poised over the step on his bookmark that he was completing; his lips would be moving as he talked to himself about what he should do next. Diagnostically, this observation of Liam as he worked independently suggested that, when given tools that provided an external framework to direct his actions, he was able to take control of goal-directed behaviors.

In recognition of the fact that struggling readers like Liam who suffer from conative impediments often are not aware of the habits of mind and behaviors

Figure 8.2. Liam's Bookmark

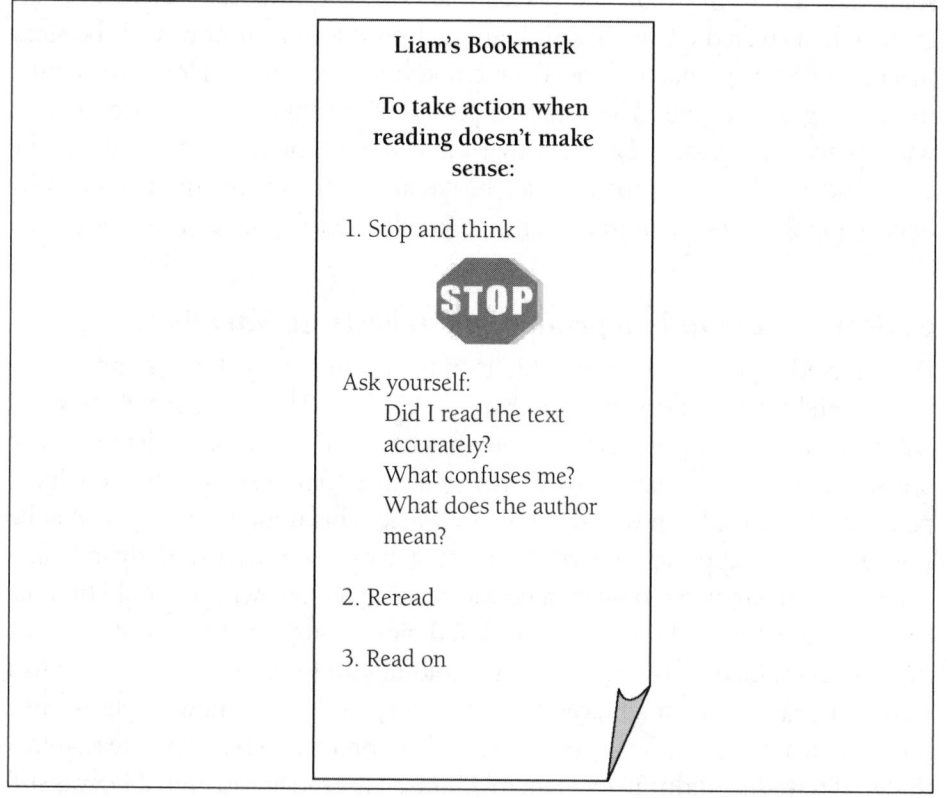

that enhance learning, these things were explicitly taught and modeled. Liam was explicitly taught strategies for being actively involved in learning, such as repeating directions to himself, summarizing to monitor understanding when listening and reading, and asking for clarification when he felt confused. At the onset of the summer program, Liam's learner profile suggested a pattern of disengagement (i.e., he slumped in his chair, looked about the room as instructions were given, and failed to ask the questions he needed to ask) and did not capture the competence he often revealed when working one-on-one with a teacher. Liam's self-defeating beliefs regarding his competence, beliefs that often accompany conative and executive functioning difficulties, needed to be addressed. This was accomplished by teaching Liam the habits of mind and behaviors that underpin learning. For example, when we saw Liam begin to disengage during discussion, we would draw him into the conversation (e.g., "Liam, you always have interesting questions that are helpful to everyone; do you have a question?") As Liam asked more questions, he was more successful. Therefore, Liam's success served as the evidence to prove that habits of mind and behaviors, such as persistence and active involvement, paid off in successful learning. As we confronted Liam with the overwhelming evidence of his competence as a learner ("When you ask questions, you do such good work"), Liam began to internalize these learning behaviors.

The Key to Reading Success: Looking at the Interaction of Person, Situation, Task, and Text

When we first encountered Liam, his general inertia around reading and writing tasks masked his low level of self-belief about his competence, a self-belief shaped in the forge of persistent failure as a reader. As Liam began to take control of person, text, task, and situation variables, he began to experience success, which resulted in the volitional know-how that Liam needed to join the reading club. Gaskins (2005) suggests that motivation is a desire to meet goals whereas volition is the ability to enact self-regulation and to employ executive control skills to mediate the enactment of goals. Our job was to guide Liam in becoming aware of and taking control of his ample cognitive resources.

We believe that Liam, like all struggling readers, had the desire to be a reader. Presenting Liam with large amounts of "easy" reading and the strategies to be successful allowed him to develop the initial confidence he needed to see himself as a reader. After seven sessions together Liam commented that he "had these books down." This sense of mastery fueled Liam's volition to accomplish the goal of reading for understanding, which presented initially as a major area of difficulty. The use of goal cards and other external aids was central in this process. Creating an external metric (the goal card) to visually measure his own success seemed to encourage Liam to employ the executive control skills and strategies he was taught. Liam was also taught to use self-talk to provide encouragement for himself as he attempted to accomplish his goals. At our 10th session together, we discussed the story of the little engine that could and how this could be a model for how we could talk ourselves through reading that was difficult by keeping in mind the mantra, "I think I can, I think I can...." Five sessions later, as Liam sat at the reading group table, he was asked to explain to the others what he had done when he became confused when reading. He explained that at first, he had wanted to give up and stop reading, but he remembered the little engine that could and he reread the text.

What We Learned From Liam

This chapter rests on the research-supported assertion that it is not instructional programs that most aid struggling readers in gaining proficiency, but rather it is knowledgeable educators who make the difference (Allington, 2006; Gaskins, 2010; Pressley, 2006). Yet if teachers are to be able to match instructional interventions to children's unique characteristics as learners, they must be equipped with an understanding of how learner characteristics impact reading acquisition and with tools, such as the Interactive Learner Profile, that provide a systematic way to look at readers holistically and to identify patterns of facilitators and impediments. Liam's story illustrates how information gathered outside the parameters of formal assessment situations can inform teaching practices.

The use of the Interactive Learner Profile guided us in identifying the multiple variables that contributed to Liam's reading difficulties and, in so doing, helped us create powerful, student-centered interventions. Once we were aware of the patterns of difficulty that Liam faced, we could address these conative impediments with strategy instruction. It was our belief that as Liam gained agency over the process of reading, his self-concept would improve. Through the course of our sessions together, we attempted to help Liam revalue reading by providing him with the tools he needed to be successful. The student that emerged in the course of this process is reflected in his final journal entry of the summer in which he wrote, "I am a smart reader." Liam's transformation was the result of a focus not only on basic reading processes but also on Liam's learner characteristics and the way in which these characteristics interacted with task, text, and situation variables.

In sum, this chapter advances the argument for responsive, whole-child-centered teaching and suggests that the use of tools that examine the entire learner, such as the Interactive Learner Profile, can aid educators in accomplishing this type of instruction. By viewing students ecologically and by creating instruction that accounts for their variation in person variables, students may be taught to value and to understand the distinct ways in which they each learn.

ACTION PLAN

To try the techniques described in this chapter, complete the Interactive Learner Profile for a specific student to gain greater insight into how text, task, situation, and person variables are affecting the student's acquisition of reading skills. Armed with this new information, you will be better able to differentiate instruction and measure Response to Intervention. To accomplish this, engage in the steps that follow:

- Select a student in your classroom who appears to be struggling with decoding or comprehension or who exhibits a lack of engagement with reading instruction.

- Identify opportunities during your day to gather anecdotal data (e.g. observational notes, student work samples) about this student's decoding and comprehension abilities as well as general behavior during reading.

- Complete the Interactive Learner Profile after one to two weeks of data collection.

- Analyze the information you have entered on the ILP to identify the learner characteristic that most relate to the student's difficulty in reading (these characteristics will have received the most check marks in the far right-hand column).

- Set goals to help this student address the learner characteristics identified on the ILP with the most checks in the far right-hand column. These goals will help this student to manage text, task, situation, and learner variables that impede progress in reading.

- Continue collecting anecdotal data and using the ILP as a way to measure Response to Intervention and to aid in goal setting.

QUESTIONS FOR STUDY
AND REFLECTION

1. Explain your point of view regarding the following statement: There is more to teaching reading than teaching strategies for decoding and comprehension.

2. Describe how you would collect and analyze data related to person, situation, task, and text variables.

3. Explain your understanding of an interactive model of teaching.

REFERENCES

Ackerman, P.L., & Beier, M.E. (2003). Trait complexes, cognitive investment, and domain knowledge. In R.J. Sternberg & E. Grigorenko (Eds.), *The psychology of abilities, competencies, and expertise* (pp. 1–30). New York: Cambridge University Press.

Ackerman, P.L., & Beier, M.E. (2006). Determinants of domain knowledge and independent study learning in an adult sample. *Journal of Education & Psychology, 98*(2), 366–381. doi:10.1037/0022-0663.98.2.366

Afflerbach, P. (2007). *Understanding and using reading assessment, K–12.* Newark, DE: International Reading Association.

Al Otaiba, S., & Fuchs, D. (2006). Who are the young children for whom best practices in reading are ineffective? An experimental and longitudinal study. *Journal of Learning Disabilities, 39*(5), 414–431. doi:10.1177/00222194060390050401

Alexander, P.A. (2006). *Psychology in learning and instruction.* Upper Saddle River, NJ: Pearson Education.

Allington, R.L. (2006). *What really matters for struggling readers: Designing research based programs* (2nd ed.). Boston: Pearson Education.

Biggs, J.B. (1987). *Student approaches to learning and studying.* Melbourne, VIC: Australian Council for Educational Research.

Borkowski, J.G., Carr, M., & Pressley, M. (1987). Spontaneous strategy use: Perspectives from metacognitive theory. *Intelligence, 11*(1), 61–75. doi:10.1016/0160-2896(87)90027-4

Clay, M.M. (1993). *Reading recovery: Guidebook for teachers in training.* Portsmouth, NH: Heinemann.

Clay, M.M. (2001). *Change over time in children's literacy development.* Portsmouth, NH: Heinemann.

Corno, L., Cronbach, L.J., Kupermintz, H., Lohman, D.F., Mandinach, E.B., Porteus, A.W., et al. (2002). *Remaking the concept of aptitude: Extending the legacy of Richard E. Snow.* Mahwah, NJ: Erlbaum.

Deci, E.L., & Ryan, R.M. (Eds.). (2002). *Handbook of self-determination research.* Rochester, NY: University of Rochester Press.

Denckla, M.B. (1996). Biological correlates of learning and attention: What is relevant to learning disability and attention-deficit hyperactivity disorder? *Journal of Developmental and Behavioral Pediatrics, 17*(2), 114–119. doi:10.1097/00004703-199604000-00011

Doehring, D.G. (1968). *Patterns of impairment in specific reading disability: A neuropsychological investigation.* Bloomington: Indiana University Press.

Dweck, C.S. (1999). *Self-theories: Their role in motivation, personality and development.* Philadelphia: Taylor & Francis.

Ehri, L.C., & Snowling, M.J. (2004). Developmental variation in word recognition.

In C.A. Stone, E.R. Silliman, B.J. Ehren, & K. Apel (Eds.), *Handbook of language and literacy: Development and disorders* (pp. 433–460). New York: Guilford.

Elmore, R.F. (2002). Testing trap. *Harvard Magazine, 105*(1), 35.

Eslinger, P.J. (1996). Conceptualizing, describing, and measuring components of executive function: A summary. In G.R. Lyon & N.A. Krasnegor (Eds.), *Attention, memory, and executive function* (pp. 367–395). Baltimore: Paul H. Brookes.

Gaskins, I.W. (1984). There's more to a reading problem than poor reading. *Journal of Learning Disabilities, 17*(8), 467–471. doi:10.1177/002221948401700806

Gaskins, I.W. (1998). There's more to teaching at-risk and delayed readers than good reading instruction. *The Reading Teacher, 51*(7), 534–547.

Gaskins, I.W. (2005). *Success with struggling readers: The Benchmark School approach.* New York: Guilford.

Gaskins, I.W. (2010). Interventions to develop decoding proficiencies. In R.L. Allington & A. McGill-Franzen (Eds.), *Handbook of reading disabilities research.* Mahwah, NJ: Erlbaum.

Gaskins, I.W., & Baron, J. (1985). Teaching poor readers to cope with maladaptive cognitive styles. *Journal of Learning Disabilities, 18*(7), 390–394. doi:10.1177/002221948501800704

Gates, A.I. (1941). The role of personality maladjustment in reading disability. *The Journal of Genetic Psychology, 59*(1), 77–83.

Halpern, D.F. (1996). *Thought and knowledge: An introduction to critical thinking.* Mahwah, NJ: Erlbaum.

Keogh, B.K. (2003). *Temperament in the classroom: Understanding individual differences.* Baltimore: Paul H. Brookes.

Klein, S.P., Hamilton, L.S., McCaffrey, D.F., & Stecher, B.M. (2000). *What do test scores in Texas tell us?* Santa Monica, CA: RAND.

Koppitz, E.M. (1971). *Children with learning disabilities: A five-year follow-up study.* New York: Grune & Stratton.

Linn, R.L. (2000). Assessments and accountability. *Educational Researcher, 29*(2), 4–14.

McCarthey, S.J., & Moje, E.B. (2002). Conversations: Identity matters. *Reading Research Quarterly, 37*(2), 228–237. doi:10.1598/RRQ.37.2.6

Meltzer, L. (Ed.). (2007). *Executive function in education: From theory to practice.* New York: Guilford.

Meltzer, L., & Krishnan, K. (2007). Executive functioning difficulties and learning disabilities: understandings and misunderstandings. In L. Meltzer (Ed.), *Executive function in education: From theory to practice* (pp. 77–105). New York: Guilford.

Meltzer, L., Pollica, L., & Barzillai, M. (2007). Executive functioning in the classroom: Embedding strategy instruction into daily teaching practices. In L. Meltzer (Ed.), *Executive function in education: From theory to practice* (pp. 165–193). New York: Guilford.

National Institute of Child Health and Human Development. (2000). *Report of the National Reading Panel. Teaching children to read: An evidence-based assessment of the scientific research literature on reading and its implications for reading instruction* (NIH Publication No. 00-4769). Washington, DC: U.S. Government Printing Office.

Olson, R., & Byrne, B. (2005). Genetic and environmental influences on reading and writing ability and disability. In H.W. Catts & A.G. Kamhi (Eds.), *The connection between language and reading difficulties* (pp. 152–174). Mahwah, NJ: Erlbaum.

Pinnell, G.S., & Fountas, I.C. (2007). *The continuum of literacy learning, grades K–8: Behaviors and understandings to notice, teach, and support.* Portsmouth, NH: Heinemann.

Prawat, R.S. (1989). Promoting access to knowledge, strategy, and disposition in students: A research synthesis. *Review of Educational Research, 59*(1), 1–41.

Pressley, M. (2006). *Reading instruction that works: The case for balanced reading* (3rd ed.). New York: Guilford.

RAND Reading Study Group. (2002). *Reading for understanding: Toward an R&D program in reading comprehension.* Santa Monica, CA: RAND.

Robinson, H.M. (1946). *Why pupils fail in reading.* Chicago: University of Chicago Press.

Schmeck, R.R. (1988). An introduction to strategies and styles of learning. In Schmeck, R. (Ed.), *Learning strategies and learning styles* (pp. 3–12). New York: Plenum.

Shepard, L.A. (2000). The role of assessment in a learning culture. *Educational Researcher, 29*(7), 4–14.

Smith, F. (1997). *Reading without nonsense* (3rd ed.). New York: Teachers College Press.

Snow, C.E., Porche, M.V., Tabors, P.O., & Harris, S.J. (2007). *Is literacy enough? Pathways to academic success for adolescents.* Baltimore: Paul H. Brookes.

Snow, R.E., Corno, L., & Jackson, D. (1996). Individual differences in affective and conative functions. In D.C. Berliner & R.C. Calfee (Eds.), *Handbook of educational psychology* (pp. 243–310). New York: Macmillan Library Reference.

Sternberg, R.J., & Grigorenko, E.L. (Eds.). (2003). *The psychology of abilities, competencies, and expertise.* New York: Cambridge University Press.

Stewart, M.T. (2002). *"Best practice"? Insights on literacy instruction from an elementary class-room.* Newark, DE: International Reading Association.

Strickland, D.S., Ganske, K., & Monroe, J.K. (2002). *Supporting struggling readers and writers.* Portland, ME: Stenhouse.

Swanson, J.L. (with M. Hoskyn & C. Lee). (1999). *Interventions for students with learning disabilities: A meta-analysis of treatment outcomes.* New York: Guilford.

Valencia, S.W., & Buly, M.R. (2004). Behind test scores: What struggling readers *really* need. *The Reading Teacher, 57*(6), 520–531.

Washburne, C., & Morphett, M.V. (1938). Grade placement of children's books. *The Elementary School Journal, 38*(5), 355–364. doi:10.1086/462185

Ysseldyke, J.E., & Taylor, B.M. (2007). Understanding the factors that allegedly contribute to students' reading difficulties. In B.M. Taylor & J.E. Ysseldyke (Eds.), *Effective instruction for struggling readers, K–6* (pp. 1–18). New York: Teachers College Press.

Zimmerman, B.J., & Campillo, M. (2003). Motivating self-regulated problem solvers. In J.E. Davidson & R.J. Sternberg (Eds.), *The psychology of problem solving* (pp. 233–262). Cambridge, England: Cambridge University Press.

BENCHMARK SCHOOL INTERACTIVE LEARNER PROFILE

Summary Checklist of Teacher, Parent, and Student Observations

Student's Name _____LIAM_____ Date _June 27, 2008_

Check no more than three areas of the presenting academic profile that most interfere with the student meeting grade-level expectations.

Presenting Academic Profile			
Phonemic Awareness		Written Expression	
Decoding	x	Written Mechanics	
Sight Vocabulary		Written Ideas	
Reading Comprehension		Content Areas	
Literal	x	Content Area Reading	
Interpretive		Content Area concepts	
Vocabulary (word meaning)		Listening Skills	x
Fluency		Mathematics	

The Benchmark School Interactive Profile is based on the theory and research discussed in Gaskins (2005) and is intended to promote an understanding of person, task, text, and situation variables that interact to determine a student's academic success.

Key

Demonstrates proficiency: Student consistently demonstrates awareness of and control over this characteristic almost all of the time (on approximately 9 out of 10 occasions).

Often demonstrates proficiency: Student demonstrates awareness of and control over this characteristic on at least 7 out of 10 occasions.

Demonstrates proficiency half of the time: Student demonstrates awareness of and control over this characteristic on at least 5 out of 10 occasions.

Sometimes demonstrates proficiency: Student demonstrates awareness of and control over this characteristic on at least 3 out of 10 occasions.

Rarely demonstrates proficiency: Student demonstrates awareness of and control over this characteristic on approximately 1 out of 10 occasions.

NA: Not applicable—not a current expectation.

(continued)

Appendix. Benchmark School Interactive Learner Profile (*continued*)

	Person Variables				
	Demonstrates Proficiency (9 out of 10 occasions)	Often Demonstrates Proficiency (7 out of 10)	Demonstrates Proficiency Half of the time (5 out of 10)	Sometimes Demonstrates Proficiency (3 out of 10)	Rarely Demonstrates Proficiency (1 out of 10)
Cognitive Style One's characteristic mode of attending, perceiving, or thinking.					
Attention					
Stays focused during instruction as demonstrated through physical behaviors				X	
Demonstrates attentiveness through ability to follow teacher instructions			X		
Demonstrates attentiveness through appropriate and timely written and verbal responses			X		
Reflectivity					
Takes time to think before responding and responds in a thoughtful way			X		
Demonstrates ability to reflect by using feedback productively			X		
Expresses awareness of cognitive style factors that require conscious control					X
Active Learning					
Participates in whole-class discussion				X	
Participates in small-group discussion				X	
Asks for appropriate clarification			X		
Asks for feedback			X		
Persistence					
Sustains appropriate effort				X	
Completes tasks to expectations			X		
Adaptability					
Considers the perspective of another		X			
Adjusts pace to satisfactorily meet task demands				X	
Makes smooth transitions				X	
Accepts change			X		

(continued)

	Consistently (9 out of 10)	Often (7 out of 10)	Half the time (5 out of 10)	Sometimes (3 out of 10)	Rarely (1 out of 10)
Demonstrates awareness of alternate possibilities for solving a problem				X	
Demonstrates willingness to accept feedback and to try alternate approaches				X	
Organization					
Manages time effectively				X	
Uses assignment book appropriately	X				
Paces completion of long-term projects to meet deadlines	X				
Turns in assignments on time	X				
Keeps track of possessions	X				
Speaks in an organized way		X			
Writes in an organized way			X		
Cognitive Abilities **One's thinking ability.**					
Reasoning/Higher Level Thinking					
Demonstrates understanding of abstract concepts by using concepts appropriately			X		
Makes evaluative comments, which suggests analysis of information			X		
Demonstrates recognition of patterns by noting similarities			X		
Generates new understandings by making appropriate connections			X		
Demonstrates ability to solve problems strategically			X		
Memory					
Recalls previously presented information				X	
Holds in mind and manages several thoughts (cognitive demands)					X
Recalls how to use strategies and procedures taught in previous years				X	
Oral Language (Expressive and Receptive)					
Articulates sounds correctly		X			

(continued)

	Consistently (9 out of 10)	Often (7 out of 10)	Half the time (5 out of 10)	Sometimes (3 out of 10)	Rarely (1 out of 10)
Speaks with age-appropriate language		X			
Expresses ideas in an understandable way		X			
Expresses ideas fluently in an academic setting		X			
Listens with understanding		X			
Pace					
Processes information at an appropriate pace			X		
Works at an appropriate pace—not too quickly/not too slowly				X	

Affective Factors
One's usual emotional tendencies.

Social Awareness					
Speaks respectfully		X			
Observes the rights and responsibilities that the class has generated		X			
Forms positive relationships with peers		X			
Relates appropriately to adults		X			
Works cooperatively		X			
Responds appropriately to social cues		X			
Self-awareness					
Advocates for self at an appropriate developmental level			X		
Demonstrates ability to manage emotions at an appropriate developmental level		X			
Assesses self realistically			X		
Maintains control in less structured situations		X			
Handles frustration appropriately		X			

Conative Abilities
The aspect of mental processing or behavior directed toward goal setting, will, and action. Conation is comprised of motivation (wishing or wanting) and volition (the will to take action, which involves self-regulation of effort and action).

Motivation					
Expresses satisfaction with his/her level of connectedness with the school community			X		

(continued)

Appendix. Benchmark School Interactive Learner Profile *(continued)*

	Consistently (9 out of 10)	Often (7 out of 10)	Half the time (5 out of 10)	Sometimes (3 out of 10)	Rarely (1 out of 10)
Appears to believe that classroom expectations, instruction, and curriculum are valuable			X		
Exhibits an orientation to learn, rather than being satisfied to meet minimum requirements				X	
Sets realistic and meaningful goals				X	
Connects strategic effort to academic success					X
Expresses or demonstrates accurate assessment of his/her ability level				X	
Uses his/her own progress as a benchmark to measure growth				X	
Voices belief in his/her ability to take control of situations, rather than feeling controlled by them				X	
Volition					
Takes appropriate action to establish and maintain connections with peers				X	
Takes appropriate action to establish and maintain connections with faculty			X		
Demonstrates comfort with his/her level of competence by willingly completing assignments at an appropriate level of challenge (not too hard or too easy)					X
Believes that assignments are doable if appropriate strategies are employed					X
Self-regulates appropriate level of effort when working in groups or independently					X
Verbalizes appropriate self-talk for taking charge					X
Acknowledges the relationship between actions and results by accepting responsibility			X		
Makes an effort to find something interesting about topics and assignments				X	

(continued)

Appendix. Benchmark School Interactive Learner Profile (*continued*)

	Consistently (9 out of 10)	Often (7 out of 10)	Half the time (5 out of 10)	Sometimes (3 out of 10)	Rarely (1 out of 10)
Demonstrates personal commitment to tasks and goals that he/she has chosen to complete				X	
Demonstrates self-regulation in setting and executing realistic academic goals					X
Sets and monitors goals to take charge of emotions				X	
Sets and monitors goals to take charge of cognitive style factors					X

Physiologic Factors One's physical and health factors. Check items that apply to the student.	
Demonstrates no signs of hearing impairment	X
Demonstrates no signs of vision impairment	X
Demonstrates gross motor control	X
Demonstrates fine motor control	X
Demonstrates graphomotor control	X
Demonstrates stamina	?
Reflects good health through regular school attendance	X

Sociocultural Variables Check items that apply to the student.	
Good background knowledge	X
High level of parental support for academics	X
Supportive and nurturing home environment	X
Home language does not differ significantly from school language	X
Other caretaker's language does not differ significantly from school language	X

A Few Possible Person, Text, Task, and Situation Supports Check classroom supports in place for this student and/or add additional supports.	
Person Variables	
Regular goal-setting mini-conferences as needed to set and evaluate cognitive style goals	
Goal-setting card checked by student to monitor specific cognitive style goals	X
Frequent Every Pupil Response (EPR) and Think-Pair-Share activities used to keep student actively involved	
Reflectivity encouraged by activities such as Ready, Set, Show and Take Five	X
Regular self-assessments after the completion of tasks	X
Coach for strategies to self-regulate cognitive style, affective factors, cognition, motivation, and volition	X
Daily teacher check of accurate entry of assignments in assignment book	
Support of completion of a checklist of items to take home each day	X
Assistance in making a plan for completing homework and long-term assignments	
Explicit instruction and support for becoming a self-advocate	
Modeling of self-talk student can use to take charge of person, text, task, and situation variables	X

(continued)

Appendix. Benchmark School Interactive Learner Profile (*continued*)

Explicit modeling and instruction of strategies for making connections and remembering information	
Instruction to support student's need for belonging, meaningfulness, competency, and autonomy	X
Explicit instruction and support for strategies for self-regulation of smart effort	X
Encouragement and praise for asking for clarification when confused	X

Text Variables	
Support in decoding unknown words	
Support with understanding story elements, genre elements, text structure	X
Support in developing sight vocabulary	
Cue use of metatext (illustrations, diagrams, charts, maps, subheads)	X
Support with reading texts in the content areas	
Texts appropriately leveled	X
Use of taped books	

Task Variables (elements involved in accomplishing academic tasks)	
Support in developing knowledge of sound-symbol relationships	
Support in developing background knowledge	
Support in managing space and materials	X
Extra time for tasks	X
Extra time for making transitions	X
Support in understanding directions and requirements of a task	X
Coach for tests (helps the student understand the requirements of the task/question)	
Scribe for tests (writes/formats what the student dictates)	
Coach for how to apply strategies to meet task demands	X
Use of computer	
Support provided in establishing academic and personal goals	X

Situation Variables	
Positive relationship is fostered between the student and teacher	X
Explicit explanations are provided	X
Support is provided to integrate student into the classroom community	X
Support is provided to engage student in learning activities	X
Support is provided to foster competency-related motivation	X
Support is provided to foster autonomy-related motivation (such as providing student choice)	X
Support is provided to foster appropriate self-talk to promote motivation and goal achievement	X
Support is provided to foster appropriate self-talk to manage academics, emotions, and behavior (self-regulation)	X
Student is taught using multiple instructional methods/strategies	X
Support is provided for students to discover strengths and talents	X

© 2009 Benchmark School. Reprinted with permission.

CHAPTER 9

Strategy Instruction and Lessons Learned in Teaching Higher Level Thinking Skills in an Urban Middle School Classroom

Karen C. Waters

I returned to my former district as a visiting professor to implement "Book Bistro," a literacy project emphasizing classroom conversation as a context for improving higher level thinking in struggling seventh-grade readers. Just a few months earlier, I had retired from public school education after 31 years of service to take a full-time position as a clinical assistant professor within the Department of Education at a nearby university. This university–school partnership permitted a productive and reciprocal collaboration to flourish and provided a great opportunity for my continual self-reflection as a practitioner.

On my first day back in the classroom I began with an interactive read-aloud using the semi-autobiographical text *Thank You, Mr. Falker* (Polacco, 1994), a story about a young girl's struggle to learn how to read. I had dutifully placed sticky notes at natural junctures in the narrative where I had intended to pause and have the students "turn and talk" (Calkins, 2001; Harvey & Goudvis, 2005). Wanting to impart the significance of the jar of honey in the story as a metaphor for the sweetness of knowledge, and hoping to induce conversation, I held up such a jar and asked the students to turn to a partner and talk about their thoughts. Their confusion was obvious as they quietly shook their heads.

Subsequently, when asked to turn and talk during natural breaks in the story, the students just sat silently, not even looking at one another, generally slumped over the desk with one arm outstretched, the other dangling over the side. To my complete surprise, in a classroom where students seemingly had no difficulty discussing the latest hip-hop artists, urban fashion, or their attitudes about homework, they simply did not utter a sound. Hoping to instill a sense of the theme within the group, I asked the class, "Have you ever given up on trying to do something when you didn't think that you could achieve it?" Still, there were no volunteers.

At the conclusion of the reading when I asked the students to explain to a partner the symbol of the jar of honey in the story, I learned that not one student in the class had ever tasted honey. I was presumptuous in expecting them to be able to explain its significance in the story. It was humbling to acknowledge that my years of urban experience were suddenly being challenged. Accompanying this realization was the lesson that a well-articulated theoretical understanding of the pedagogy does not necessarily translate into a model lesson. After the students had left for the day, I turned to their teacher in desperation, who informed me that they were, in fact, unaccustomed to talking about what they were learning.

This chapter will consider the critical importance of mediated dialogue in the classroom, not only as a means by which students practice to acquire skills that are mandated through curriculum and legislation, but also as the context for building foundational skills through research-based strategies that enable them to think critically about text while becoming valuable members of a social community. Research states that for effective classroom discourse to occur, it is necessary to establish a supportive atmosphere that pushes student thinking, uses scaffolding as an instructional strategy, anticipates and provides explicit instruction when needed, and challenges and respects the learner (Damico, 2005; Desai & Marsh, 2005; Goldenberg, 1993).

How was I going to help this group of struggling readers when they did not interact with one another in text-based conversation? Franklin (2005) states that "engaging students in oral and written extended responses to reading should not be ephemeral occurrences that dawn and fade only in light of NCLB testing" (p. 48). Before teaching the students the comprehension strategies that would stimulate higher level thinking, I realized that first I had to immerse them in reading, thinking, and talking about a variety of genres. Therefore, a scaffolded framework that treated classroom dialogue as a skill in helping students perceive subtle meanings, resolve controversies, and respect alternative viewpoints must be at the core of the project.

This is the story of one teacher's journey in helping to motivate a group of struggling adolescent readers to advance their reading achievement through strategy-based instruction that gently nudges the student to an elevated state of thinking. In a context of rich and varied fiction and nonfiction text, intensive instruction, and structured opportunities for students to practice the skills, I offer an explanation and theoretical rationale for each of the identified strategies. Table 9.1 provides an instructional scaffold for the teaching of the strategies before, during, and after reading, and is aligned with both the current and the 2009 NAEP reading frameworks.

Table 9.1. An Instructional Scaffold for Strategies in Teaching Higher Level Thinking

Strategy	Current NAEP Frameworks/ State Frameworks	2009 NAEP Frameworks	Before Reading	During Reading	After Reading
1. Concept of Definition	Forming a General Understanding Context Clues Reinforcing and extending vocabulary knowledge and concepts.	Monitoring/ Taking steps to construct appropriate meaning	A framework for organizing conceptual information in the process of defining a word. Information is organized in terms of three relationships: general category in which the concept belongs, properties of the concept, and examples of the concept. Can be used before, during, or after reading.		
2. Discussion Web	Developing Interpretation	Integrate and Interpret Generalize and draw conclusions based on facts, details, and examples. Support Inferences and conclusions.			A graphic organizer that requires students to examine both sides of an issue, draw conclusions through think-pair-share, and generate a piece of writing in which opinions are anchored through evidence from the text.
3. Pointed Reading	Rereading	Monitoring/ Rereading for meaning		A strategy to increase fluency and accuracy in oral reading.	

(continued)

Table 9.1. An Instructional Scaffold for Strategies in Teaching Higher Level Thinking (*continued*)

Strategy	Current NAEP Frameworks/ State Frameworks	2009 NAEP Frameworks	Before Reading	During Reading	After Reading
4. Probable Passage	**Forming a General Understanding** Making Predictions.	**Preparing** Previewing, Activating Prior Knowledge, Setting Purposes for Reading.	A story map template used to categorize key words that serve as predictions for characters, setting, problem, outcome, etc.		Can be used as after reading strategy to compare written predictions to actual text.
5. Semantic Feature Analysis	**Making Connections (comparing and contrasting)**	**Critique and Evaluate** Select essential elements for comparisons, Justify/explain connections.		A grid is used to help students analyze similarities and differences among the related concepts. A topic is selected, words related to that category are written across the top of the grid, and features shared by some of the words are listed with a "+" or a "−."
6. Story Impressions	**Forming a General Understanding** Making Predictions, Anticipate story content.	**Preparing:** Setting Purposes, Activating Prior Knowledge **Integrate and Interpret:** Base predictions on text and background.	Phrases are used to develop an anticipated story prior to the actual reading.		Can be used as an after reading strategy to compare written story guesses to actual text.
7. Tea Party	**Forming a General Understanding** Making Predictions, Anticipating story content.	**Preparing, Integrate and Interpret:** Base predictions on text and background.	Sentences extracted from a reading selection are read during structured encounter with other students for the purpose of discussing anticipated story content.		Can be used as an after reading strategy to compare oral predictions to actual text.

First Steps: Classroom Conversation

Ellen, a veteran teacher with nearly 20 years' experience, graciously offered her classroom as a lab site for project implementation and was intrigued by the concept of classroom discussion as a format for focused and mediated dialogue that might elicit full participation within a discourse community. She viewed our collaboration as an opportunity to enhance her teaching repertoire and gain expertise in her instructional delivery of literacy.

The art of classroom discussion, steeped in dialectic tradition, originates from Socratic dialogue where students were challenged to seek truth through questions that encouraged dissenting perspectives, demanded substantiation, and stimulated moral development. Embedded within that ancient tradition of open-ended questions that required students to extend and elaborate their thinking, classroom discussion has become a goal of artful instruction that has assumed a variety of labels over the years; all are rooted in theories of communication that represent the essence of discourse (Cazden, 2001; Coulter, 2001; Nichols, 2006).

Today, whether referred to as reciprocal teaching (Palincsar & Brown, 1984), accountable talk (Resnick, 1999), instructional conversations (Goldenberg, 1993), collaborative discussions (Chinn & Anderson, 1998), or comprehension through conversation (Nichols, 2006), high-quality classroom discussion has become a context for shared understanding, negotiated interpretation of text, purposeful talk, and alternate opinions (Nichols, 2006). My hope for this group of seventh-grade readers was that through well-designed lessons, students would see themselves as valuable contributors to a discourse community with opportunities to practice the very skills they would use beyond the classroom.

After my failed initial read-aloud experience, I concluded that the students would require procedural instruction in the art of communication as part of an intensive literacy program of strategy instruction. Ellen and I initiated the concept by modeling discussions of our own that focused on essential themes with which the students could connect using both narrative text and informational text. This way the students would be able to see discourse in action. In addition to teaching skills that would facilitate higher level thinking, we had to establish the ground rules that would govern lively but respectful conversations (McVittie, 2005).

Using short, informational selections, I taught the students how to employ self-monitoring or fix-up strategies, using *The Comprehension Toolkit* (Harvey & Goudvis, 2005) as my inspiration and mentor text. All the students in the class were reading approximately three to four years below grade level. I encouraged students to articulate the reasons they might have difficulty in making sense of text. As they engaged in the brainstorming process about "why meaning breaks down" (Harvey & Goudvis, 2005, p. 17), their teacher wrote down their responses on an anchor chart, which is demonstrated in Figure 9.1 (Harvey & Goudvis, 2005). Subsequently, after a minilesson on the features of nonfiction text, I asked students again to recall some of the elements of informational text as their teacher charted their responses on a genre chart (see Figure 9.2). Ellen posted the chart on the walls so that the students could reference these elements in the reading and writing process.

I purchased a subscription of *Time for Kids* magazine for the classroom so that the students would have a steady supply of current informational text. They began to discuss the roles of women in India, the historical significance of a woman *and* an African American as candidates in a presidential election, and the differences between the colonial penal system and the United States judicial system today (Masoff, 2000a). They talked about the characters in the graphic novel version of *The Prince and the Pauper* (Clemens, 2005), engaged

Figure 9.1. Anchor Chart

Monitoring Comprehension	
Why Meaning Breaks Down	**Fix-Up Strategies**
Really tired	Reread; ask questions
Text is boring	Keep reading
Brain distraction	Refocus
Lose interest	Try to connect; chunk it out
Can't pronounce a word	Ask questions; use background knowledge
Too hard	

Figure 9.2. Genre Chart

Nonfiction Text	
Features	**Purpose**
Picture	Helps understanding
Caption	Helps you "see" it
Title (entire)	Gives information
Table of contents	Kind of information
Headings	Location of information
Boldfaced print	Main ideas of sections

in higher level thinking in debating the themes of courage and cowardice in *The Red Badge of Courage* (abridged version, Hutchinson, 1998), and compared the layers of meaning in the classic poem "Sympathy" (Dunbar, 1899) with the current rhythm and blues interpretation of "Caged Bird" (Keyes, 2001). The students learned how to interact with a partner in turning and talking (Calkins, 2001; Harvey & Goudvis, 2005) during interactive read-alouds with excerpts from *The Boy in the Striped Pajamas* (Boyne, 2006), a powerful story of the Holocaust, and *Maniac Magee* (Spinelli, 1990), a story whose theme of racial prejudice elicited full participation. In reading about the historical events of American Colonialism, students shared opinions about whether the pillory should be resurrected as a form of punishment for lawbreakers (Masoff, 2000a). They debated the fairness of an early American educational system that gave priority to boys' schooling (Masoff, 2000b). They compared colonial practices to current educational inequality in third-world countries and the efforts of UNICEF to change antiquated practices that still give preference to boys (*Time for Kids*, 2005, cited in Harvey & Goudvis, 2005). Gradually, students began to recognize the critical elements of bias, perspective, and unanchored opinion as they readily connected with the themes of their culture unleashed through stories and music about turbulent times in a world fraught with injustice, social inequality, oppression, and death.

Rosenblatt (1978) referred to the reader's aesthetic response, which emanates from the experiences and mental attitude that the reader brings to the text and is manifested through a course of action following the reading of a selected piece. Sometimes the tender release of feelings that accompanies the reading of a text cannot be foreseen. Occasionally, a spontaneous reaction cannot be suppressed and must simply run its course, and even the wisest teacher is summoned to task in dealing with an unexpected situation engendered through the reading of a text, as the following example will illustrate.

One day the students were engrossed in reading, coding, and discussing a passage in *Maniac Magee* (Spinelli, 1990). Then it was time to share their markings with their partners. Andre began to read aloud the words that he coded: "Maniac went over. He shook the old man. It was cold. '*Grayson!*'" (p. 115). Andre stopped reading, and very quietly he murmured to his partner, "This reminds me of my grandfather. I'm sorry. I can't..." and his voice broke. This part of the story clearly hit a raw nerve with him, and he was quite inconsolable for the rest of the reading workshop. At first I wondered what we could have done differently to avert such a strong reaction from this student.

After Andre's initial withdrawal from partner reading, his participation in class discussions gradually increased, as did the quality and amount of his writing. Andre's written response to "Juicy" (Notorious B.I.G., 1994), a piece of contemporary prose, elicited another type of personal reaction:

> The poem is saying how he was when he was nothing. People used to [misjudge] him and his landlord was being mean to him and people thought that he was a fool because he dropped out of school. The thing that surprises me was when he was in high school he dropped out of school but he still made it big. Sometimes I wish I could make it big but not drop out of school. (Andre, 2007)

Ellen and I attributed this change in Andre to his personal connection with the other students in feeling part of a community that collaborated on projects, shared ideas with an audience, and laughed and learned together. In short, Andre's catharsis was made possible because his teacher had created an environment that supported him not only as a learner but as a valuable member of a learning community.

However, the safety of the classroom would not be enough to sustain student motivation for any length of time. As the weeks wore on, I noticed that students were making only half-hearted attempts to work with me. They were reluctant to participate in classroom conversations that focused on the essential or controversial questions in social studies or literature, or to undertake written tasks that corresponded with discussion topics. Concerned, I spoke with Ellen, who admitted that she, too, had seen evidence of growing apathy, which she attributed to the students' impoverished living conditions, destitute home situations, absence of one or both parents, and family unemployment. Even though I used books from the glossiest and newest reading programs, I had failed to consult the students about relevance.

I began to struggle with the idea of using hip-hop music and the lyrics of rap songs to engage the students in higher level thinking in the exploration of essential themes from the middle school curriculum, recognizing that this particular genre of music often contains language that is inappropriate for the classroom. I spoke with Ellen, who was also understandably concerned about deviation from the standards and warned me to proceed with caution. Desai and Marsh (2005) conclude that teachers must be willing to surrender control to inspire and allow for the emergence of student voices; thus, I chose to take a calculated risk that would not invite opposition from the educational hierarchy.

When I began to sprinkle the literacy lessons with carefully selected edited versions of contemporary prose written by musical artists, including Notorious

B.I.G., Tupac Shakur, and Mos Def, my group of struggling readers literally picked up their heads from their desks, found their individual and collective literary voices, engaged in acceptable outlets in speaking out against social injustice through dialogue and writing, shared their own stories, and ultimately bonded with me (Desai & Marsh, 2005). After reading the biographical words from "Me Against the World" (Shakur, 1998), Brice, a troubled young man who had been a reluctant participant, responded to the artist's prose with his own version:

> When all these problems get me/what would happen after I die/When I die I wonder if I'm going to heaven or hell/when will my problems go away/the people that have lots of stuff/I steal from the rich and give to the poor/the message that I said/do your work and do good in school. (Brice, 2007)

Fisher, Jackson, and Kinloch's study (2005, as cited in Desai & Marsh, 2005) reveals "the spoken word [rap] provides the teachers and students the opportunity to create meaningful relationships that lead to academic achievement" (p. 72). Until that time, Brice had not completed one written assignment since the start of school, and he had been recalcitrant with his partner during strategy instruction. However, when asked to rewrite Tupac's words using his own language, Brice approached this task vigorously and seriously, with a fierce concentration seen in athletes in training. Although Brice was not the only one in the class who had been transformed, he was the most extreme example of the change that Ellen and I witnessed.

By bringing their world into the classroom, the students no longer felt neutralized by an educational system that demanded subordination or by teachers who submitted to the constraints of an inflexible curriculum and high-stakes assessments. Desai and Marsh (2005) state that by using rap, students "can reflect and articulate their lived experiences while envisioning new possibilities" (p. 72). In using discourse to interpret and analyze the prose of the hip-hop culture, homage was paid to the lives of our students, thereby allowing them to look beyond their current existence to create dreams that transcended the classroom. Is that not really the foundation for creating social transformation?

With renewed enthusiasm for literacy lessons, these struggling adolescent readers allowed me to lead them through the strategies, this time using *their* prose to address curriculum objectives that encouraged them to engage in higher level thinking through reading, talking, and writing. In responding to the lyrics of the artists and the other students through dialogue and writing, students demonstrated an ease and ownership of content that was unique to them alone. Subsequently, we proceeded with strategy instruction that elevated students' thinking. They talked and wrote about racial discrimination, poverty, and drugs, and ultimately became members of a discourse community (McVittie, 2005), where they were required to cite evidence for an assertion, extend and build upon a previously stated idea, submit alternative viewpoints in a respectful way, and evaluate the merit of an argument. In short, they practiced the behaviors of higher level thinkers.

From Comprehension to Higher Level Thinking

What follows is a blend of evidence-based strategies that were revisited and revised to accommodate the needs of this special group of diverse adolescent students and to build in higher level thinking skills that would transcend the classroom and serve them throughout their lives. For each of the strategies listed, I offer an explanation of purpose and a simple implementation plan including modeling, guided and independent practice, and application where appropriate. The first strategies discussed in this section require the reader to anticipate story content using a schematic of story grammar and limited information. The strategies are Story Impressions, Probable Passage, and Tea Party. Both Probable Passage and Story Impressions entice the reader with bits of significant information and offer a framework for synthesizing the main ideas, drawing logical conclusions, and summarizing the events of a story, all requisite evaluative skills for higher level thinking. Students are required to take a critical stance on a controversial topic in Discussion Web, while Pointed Reading focuses on improving fluency and accuracy in oral reading.

Story Impressions

I used the Story Impressions (SI; Denner, McGinley, & Brown, 1989) strategy to engage students in appropriate activities to construct meaning before and after reading. In SI the reader uses significant phrases that have been extracted from the text to compose a story while relying on his schema of story grammar to make meaning. A story grammar refers to narrative story structure—the main characters, setting, problem, events, solution, and resolution. The purpose of the strategy is not only to establish purposes for reading as with other prereading strategies but also to enhance the student's ability to comprehend specific information garnered from the narrative through a series of related clues that pertain to the main idea(s) that have been established at the outset.

Specifically, the SI strategy is used to assist students in anticipating textual content by requiring them to make inferences using bits of related information that have been sequenced into an organizational framework that serves as a macrostructure for constructing meaning.

Modeling. I placed a transparency of phrases from the song lyrics of "Paid in Full" (Eric B. & Rakim, 1987) on the overhead projector while my group of seventh graders was poised with ill-concealed anticipation. I told them that we were going to use these clues to develop written stories that would serve as their predictions. I explained that we would do the first set of phrases together and then they would have an opportunity to engage in composing their own story guess, predictions that are written as a narrative (Denner, McGinley, & Brown, 1989). I modeled the construction of the first sentence by adding words that would expand the phrase into a sentence to show how the event connected with the sequence of the other phrases in the chain. (See Figure 9.3.)

Fig. 9.3. Story Impressions Graphic Organizer

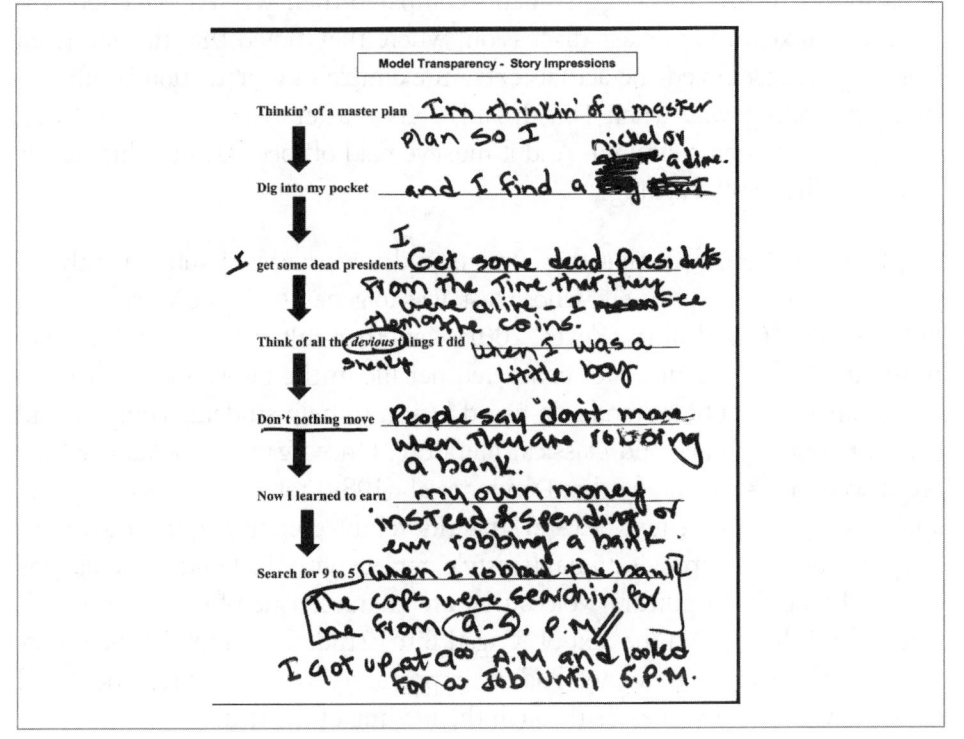

Guided Practice. Subsequently, my students and I collaborated to compose a paragraph from the rest of the phrases, which resulted in the following:

> I'm thinkin' of a master plan so I dig into my pocket/and I find a nickel or a dime/I get some dead presidents from the time that they were alive/I see them on the coins/I think of all the devious things I did when I was a little boy/People say "don't nothing move" when they are robbing a bank/Now I learned to earn my own money instead of spending other peoples' money and robbing a bank.

In an effort to resolve divided class opinion, the class offered two conclusions:

> Conclusion 1: When I was robbing the bank, the cops were looking for me from 9:00–5:00.
>
> Conclusion 2: I got up at 9:00 a.m. and looked for a job from 9:00–5:00.

I read aloud the composition that we coconstructed before distributing copies of the actual text, an edited excerpt from "Paid in Full" (Eric B. & Rakim, 1987). Students recognized the contemporary prose, an autobiography sung through what Desai and Marsh (2005) refer to as "spoken word" (or rap). Using SI as an after-reading strategy, students compared their written perceptions to the actual text through class discussion, where they noted that the contrived story closely resembled the actual text. An example of a prediction confirmed through reading was when David said, "His master plan was not robbing banks—he was going straight. And it must've paid off because he achieved the American dream by earning it."

Application. Confident that they understood the process, I subsequently divided the group into partners, whose task was to generate their own story using phrases from "Caged Bird" (Keyes, 2001)—another culturally relevant piece of prose in which the songwriter compared her life in the public eye to that of a caged bird—in another standards-based lesson to help students compare and contrast contemporary and classical literature. Once again, students used the sequenced phrases to craft what Denner et al. (1989) refer to as a "story guess" about the events in the text. Several students volunteered to perform their written predictions in improvisational freestyle, replete with the hand gesticulations and well-modulated guttural voices that are characteristic of the hip-hop culture. After I distributed the text of "Caged Bird," students compared their written perceptions to the lyrics and had the opportunity to validate predictions and confirm written story guesses through the reading of the text.

The next day I asked students to make text-to-text comparisons between Paul Lawrence Dunbar's (1899) poem "Sympathy" and Keyes's "Caged Bird" in yet another lesson with the objective of comparing and contrasting contemporary and classical literature while acknowledging how the reader is influenced by "social, cultural and historical contexts" (Connecticut State Department of Education, 2006, p. 2). In doing so I was able to facilitate student dialogue around themes through literacy lessons that empowered students to speak out against social injustices, preserved the classroom as a refuge for personal confession and testimony, and respected the language of their culture.

Probable Passage

Probable Passage (Beers, 2003) is a before-reading strategy that encourages the reader to anticipate story content by categorizing a list of keywords according to their perceived function in a story as depicted on a template using story map terminology. Using their schema for narrative story structure and background knowledge of the keywords selected for categorization, students create written predictions in the form of a main idea or "gist statement." Probable Passage can also be used as an after-reading strategy to compare initial perceptions with the actual text.

Modeling. Using keywords from the predictable poem "Haunted" (Silverstein, 1996, p. 94), I placed a transparency on the overhead and asked the students to assist me in placing the keywords in the appropriate categories of characters, setting, problem, and outcomes. I modeled the placement of *ghost* and *Howlin' Hill* through think-alouds: "I am thinking that the ghost must be the main character because there doesn't seem to be anyone else mentioned, and Howlin' Hill has to be the setting because it refers to a place or location."

Guided Practice. After modeling the strategic placement of the words *ghost* and *Howlin' Hill*, the students took a few minutes to complete the rest of the activity in small groups while Ellen and I circulated the room to offer help as needed (see Figure 9.4 for an example of a completed Probable Passage organizer). The students unanimously decided that an *axe in your head* was a problem. After considerable discussion, others realized that they needed more information about *ragged cobwebs* and concluded that the main idea or gist of the poem was the following: Someone lived in the house before it was haunted. Now it is abandoned. The owner got killed—there is an axe in his head.

Figure 9.4. Probable Passage

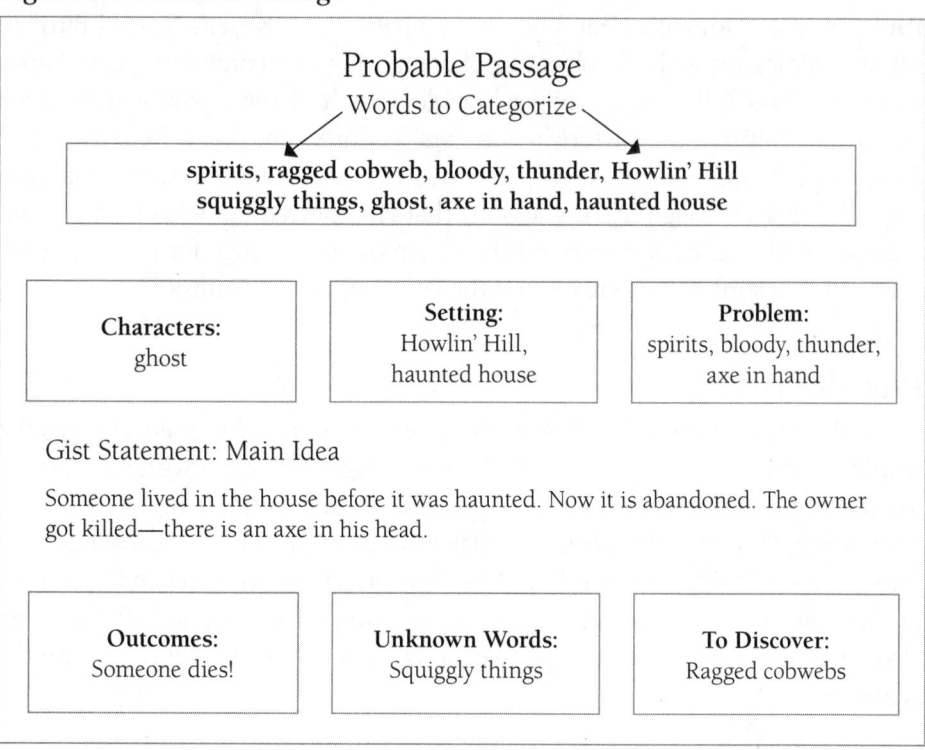

Probable Passage
Words to Categorize

> spirits, ragged cobweb, bloody, thunder, Howlin' Hill
> squiggly things, ghost, axe in hand, haunted house

Characters: ghost	**Setting:** Howlin' Hill, haunted house	**Problem:** spirits, bloody, thunder, axe in hand

Gist Statement: Main Idea

Someone lived in the house before it was haunted. Now it is abandoned. The owner got killed—there is an axe in his head.

Outcomes: Someone dies!	**Unknown Words:** Squiggly things	**To Discover:** Ragged cobwebs

Application. This time I gave each student a copy of the probable passage template and a choice in selecting lists of words to be categorized in small groups from two hip-hop songs: "Juicy" (Notorious B.I.G., 1994) and "Me Against the World" (Shakur, 1998), the titles of which were not revealed until after the completion of the activity. Giving them choice not only motivated the students to complete the activity but also heightened their anticipation of the text not chosen. Later, when I presented both hip-hop selections so that the students could validate predictions, Jose said, "Miss, you had to do research so that you could do this activity with us."

I smiled at his acknowledgment. If he had only known how true his statement was! The research to which he referred consisted of lengthy discussions with my then 22-year-old son, an expert on hip-hop music, who served as my personal musical consultant and interpreter for the development of the rap-infused literacy lessons.

Tea Party

Here again the reader is asked to anticipate story content while interacting with his or her classmates using critical bits of information to make sense of text. Ten to 15 phrases or sentences extracted from the text are placed on sentence strips or index cards in this before-reading strategy (Beers, 2003); only those phrases that advance the story line are selected. One sentence strip is distributed to every student in the class, so several sets of phrases may be used so that every student receives a phrase. (For example, two sets of 10 phrases will accommodate 20 students). Students circulate the room for several minutes, interacting with one another as if they were at a tea party, reading the sentence or phrase that has been written on their sentence strip and listening to others read their sentences. Back in cooperative groups the students use the limited pieces of information that they have acquired during the socializing activity to attempt to construct a meaning for the text through discussion. Predictions are written either on an overhead transparency or interactive whiteboard and shared with the class before the teacher provides access to the text.

Modeling. I modeled the Tea Party strategy using approximately seven different phrases from the graphic novel version of *The Prince and the Pauper* (Clemens, 2005) to accommodate the number of students in the class. Each student received one sentence strip on which one of the phrases had been written.

Guided Practice. I directed the students to mingle with one another by reading the phrase on the sentence strip while Ellen and I circulated the room to make sure that the students used accumulated evidence in discussing their predictions about the story content.

Application. For another lesson, I distributed phrases from the edited version of the contemporary hip-hop song "Respiration" (Kweli & Def, 1998) and directed the students to mingle with one another to read their sentence strips aloud and construct meaning from the strategic pieces of information. Students reconvened in cooperative groups to make logical inferences about the text prior to reading it. One of the results was the prediction that "New York is a violent town and even the cops have no heart sometimes," derived from phrases that included the words *the metropolis, Shiny Apple,* and *cops.*

Discussion Web

The Discussion Web (DW) adapted from Alvermann (1991) is both a framework for thinking and writing and a cooperative learning procedure for evaluating alternative viewpoints in coming to consensus about an issue, a question, or a scenario related to a piece of fiction or nonfiction. In a Discussion Web, students have opportunities to grapple with issues of morality and societal mores while questioning personal beliefs in an interactive format that encourages the burgeoning of students' ideas and dissenting opinions. As a graphic aid, the completed DW is a tool that represents multiple perspectives on an issue.

In DW, I posed a question that required the students to evaluate the pros and cons of an issue through group discussion. Students read the text using sticky notes to identify the metacognitive strategies (R = reminds me of, T-S = text to self, T-T = text to text, T-W = text to world, ? = question, G = gist, E = evidence, BK = background knowledge, P = prediction) while forming opinions about the issue, linking new information to background knowledge, discussing their perceptions with a partner, and writing down their thoughts on the DW graphic organizer. Students formed groups of four to arrive at consensus on the issue at hand through discussion and respectful argumentation that could be substantiated through textual evidence and connected to personal experience and background knowledge.

Reporters from each group stated the conclusions that evolved as a result of the consensus-building activity. My role became that of facilitator or scribe and mediator in converting oral conclusions to written statements on a master chart or transparency.

A follow-up to the procedure involved a response-to-literature activity to encourage students to retain their individual voices and safeguard opinion through extended writing, even after partner and group conversations had disbanded. We displayed the student work on the bulletin board so that individual thinking could be celebrated and published

Modeling. I began the lesson by asking the students if boys should play with dolls. Reactions from both the boys and the girls were strong and instantaneous, and in some cases unprintable within the parameters of a scholarly text: "Miss, you've got to be kidding. That's whacked!" I smiled and asked them to keep an open mind as I distributed the text *William's Doll* (Zolotow, 1972), a simple piece of prose about a boy's desire to have a doll and his father, who responded by giving him trains, basketballs, and tools. Ultimately the grandmother, who sees the value in preparing William for his eventual role as a father, gives her grandson a doll, despite the father's protestations that William is going to become a "sissy."

Guided Practice. Following the reading of the text I posed the question once more: Should boys play with dolls? I directed them to talk in partners, which was an established routine by this time in our work together, and to write down both the pros and cons of having boys play with dolls on the DW graphic organizer provided.

The next step was to form groups of four and to continue the discussion using the same question, this time coming to consensus on the issue. Upon completion of this next step we came together as a group and constructed a collaborative response that considered both sides to the question (see Figure 9.5). Through group discussion and textual support, the students concluded (albeit with reservations) that boys should be allowed to play with dolls. I posed another question to them following the completion of the collaborative discussion web: "Was the grandmother right in giving William a doll?"

Figure 9.5. Discussion Web

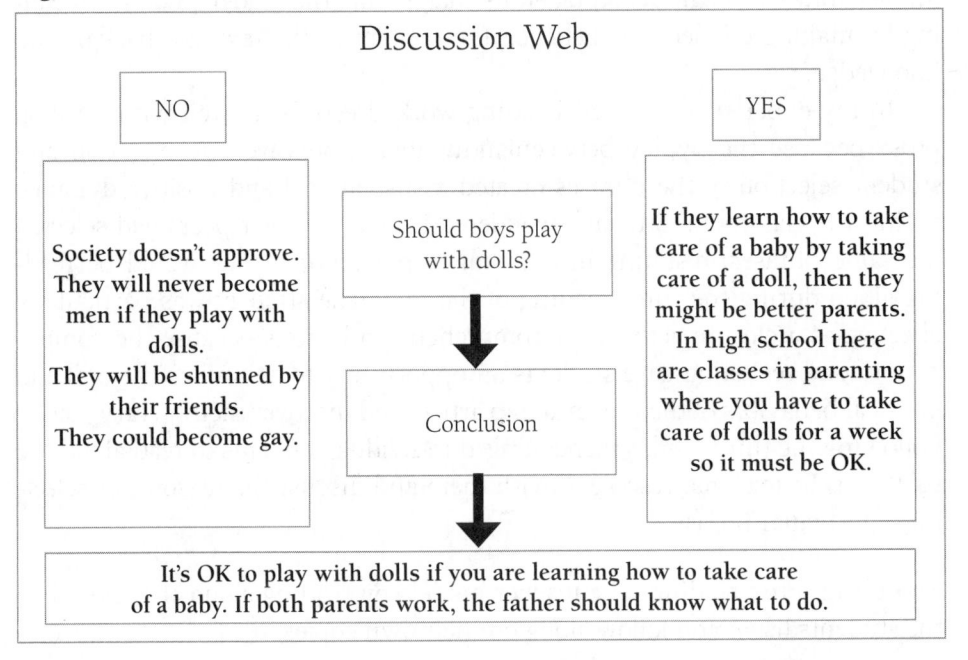

Application. The next day I asked the students to use their previously completed DW graphic organizers to construct individual written responses to the following prompt: What was the father's response to William's grandmother upon learning that she bought William a doll? In extending the DW activity into writing, a context was provided for students' own voices to be heard because the task required them to elaborate and make judgments about the theme, an objective aligned with current NAEP content strands and skills. Thus, regardless of the discussion that occurred during the consensus-building activity of the previous day, students were encouraged to assume individual positions in taking the conversation between William's grandmother and her son to the next level.

Pointed Reading

Here it is appropriate to discuss Pointed Reading (PR; Beers, 2004), a deceptively simple fluency strategy that can be compared with the simpler version of the shared reading approach (Holdaway, 1979) that has enormous implications for fluency training in the middle grades to build comprehension. Fluency not only refers to the "ability to read accurately and quickly" (National Institute of Child Health and Human Development [NICHD], 2003, p. 22) but also implies intact efficient decoding skills that enable the reader to derive meaning by making connections between the content of the text and background knowledge.

In my experience, Pointed Reading worked especially well with hip-hop prose because the byplay between individual expressive interpretation and student selection of the phrases created a suspenseful and positive dynamic within the classroom. Students wondered if many of their peers had selected the same phrases, resulting in a choral response, or if they would be reading alone during the third reading of the text. The strategy was particularly effective as a closure activity for comprehension lessons because the component of oral recitation gave students an opportunity to assimilate the oral and physical behaviors of their favorite rap artists and discover their literary voices. Following the third read, we encouraged individual students to read aloud the part(s) of the text that resonated with them and discuss the reasons for selecting a particular phrase.

Modeling. First reading: The teacher models by reading aloud the text while the students listen and follow along on their own copies.

Guided Practice. Second reading: Students select and highlight six or more phrases with which they connect personally as the teacher reads the text a second time.

Application. Third reading: Students chorally read aloud the portion of the text that they highlighted during the teacher's second reading of the text.

The Transition to Vocabulary Instruction

Using a current research-based supplemental intervention reading program that included a software technology component, the group of struggling middle school readers expanded their knowledge base in reading from a variety of genres on topics including art, natural disasters, world-changing events, survival, sports, and unusual careers, to name a few. To foster independent reading, Ellen agreed that students could self-select books to take home, with the understanding that they would be returned in gently used condition.

Through class discussions, book talks, and students' spontaneous commercials for advertising the best picks, we realized that accurate comprehension of text was frequently compromised when students encountered unfamiliar vocabulary. The students' inclination was to either dismiss unknown words or gather limited information from the context because of their view of dictionary work as one of the more tedious tasks of reading. Although many words can be taught incidentally or through contextual application, the importance of explicit, systematic instruction in vocabulary for developing depth of meaning and improving comprehension has been underscored in the research and in recent legislation (Beck, McKeown, & Kucan, 2002; NICHD, 2003; Richek, 2005).

Because I was familiar with the axiom that struggling readers tended to read less than independent readers, I knew that we needed to arm our students with the appropriate tools for becoming more self-sufficient. We gave them multiple exposures to difficult words and developed depth of meaning for words having several definitions. We instructed them in morphemic analysis (the study of prefixes, suffixes, and roots), context clues, and word expansion through inflectional or derivational endings (affixes).

We used the Concept of Definition (CD; Schwartz, 1988, as cited in Vacca & Vacca, 1999) and Semantic Feature Analysis (SFA; Vacca & Vacca, 2002) strategies to increase student acquisition of vocabulary. The CD strategy, initially used to capture text-based discussions that resulted in a student-friendly definition, ultimately provided students with an interactive format for discovering meanings of unfamiliar words using the dictionary and thesaurus.

Students became adept at integrating the rules of classroom discourse with the multiple cognitive strategies that required them to think and write critically about text. Evidence of higher level thinking was demonstrated orally and in written form as students rendered conclusions about the author's intent in writing a particular piece of prose, drew parallels between their own lives and the lives of the writers, questioned the intent of the author, and incorporated biographic aspects of their lives into their writing.

Concept of Definition

A vocabulary strategy that empowers students to take charge of their vocabulary, Concept of Definition (CD; Schwartz & Raphael, 1988, as cited in Vacca & Vacca, 1999) is both a process and organizational framework used to illustrate unfamiliar concepts, resulting in a user-friendly definition that is easily understood by the student. The vocabulary word to be defined is placed at the center of the graphic organizer; spaces for identifying the classification, properties, examples, and meaningful comparisons of the new term are categorized under the headings of "What is it?" "What is it like?" and "Examples." Critical to the process is the component of modeling so that students can actively participate in the meaning-making activity while learning how to initiate the strategy independently (see Figure 9.6).

The goal of the CD word map is for students to internalize the process of constructing definitions for unfamiliar vocabulary words and to provide them with a strategy for vocabulary acquisition that can be used independently for figuring out unfamiliar words. Though modeling is initially time consuming, the strategy offers students a method to work through the process of defining unfamiliar words that can be generalized to the content areas of math, science, and social studies. As students were involved in the process of constructing definitions for words such as *essence*, *hypocrite*, and *stereotype*, they concluded that one word from the dictionary definition might well contain many synonyms and antonyms in the thesaurus. In teaching the CD as a process for learning new vocabulary, students learned a strategy for uncovering the hidden meanings of words, thereby heightening their conceptual awareness of nontechnical vocabulary. The process of crafting definitions stimulated critical think-

Figure 9.6. Concept of Definition

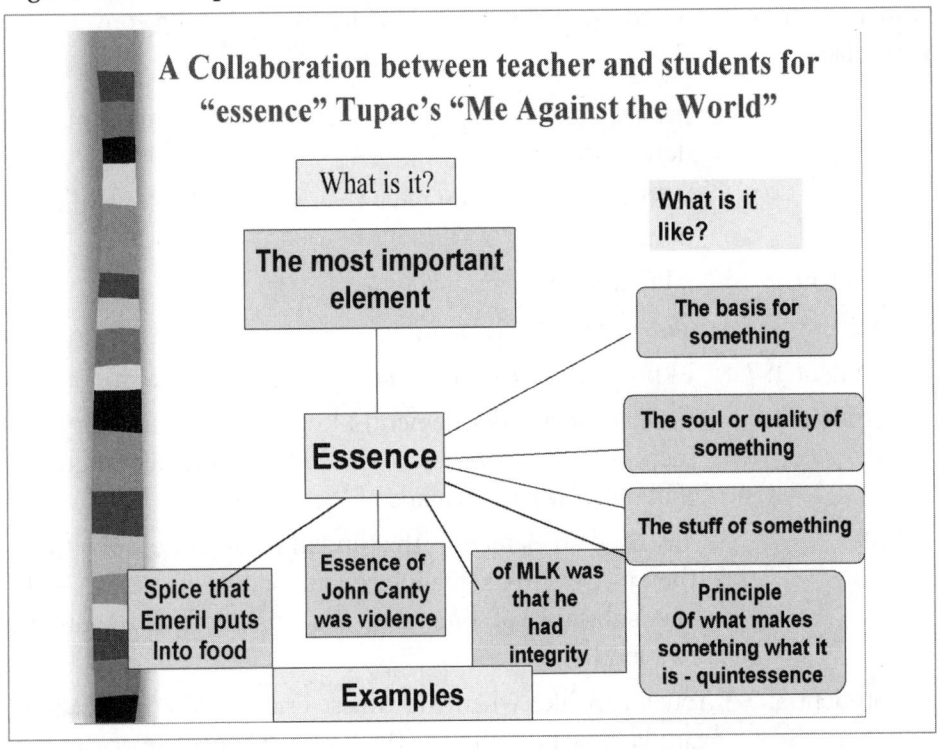

A Collaboration between teacher and students for "essence" Tupac's "Me Against the World"

What is it?

The most important element

What is it like?

The basis for something

Essence

The soul or quality of something

The stuff of something

Spice that Emeril puts Into food

Essence of John Canty was violence

of MLK was that he had integrity

Principle Of what makes something what it is - quintessence

Examples

ing as students evaluated the merit of the synonyms and antonyms that they encountered in choosing which words to include on the CD map.

Vacca and Vacca (2008) caution against misusing the CD word map strategy by having students create definitions for entire lists of words, which is no more efficient than the mundane and antiquated task of writing sentences for vocabulary words. Eventually, students realized the value in being able to use the strategy to decipher the meanings of unfamiliar words in other subjects, and they frequently engaged in construction of CD word maps independently.

Modeling. I directed students to read an excerpt from "Me Against the World" (Shakur, 1998) and to underline the vocabulary words with which they were unfamiliar.

Guided Practice. I divided the class into groups of four, giving each group two dictionaries and two thesauruses. After placing the word *essence* in the center of the transparency of the word map on the overhead projector I asked the students to look the word up in the dictionary, and the following conversation took place:

Student 1:	[*reading from the dictionary*] The most significant element. I don't get it.
Me:	Which word tells you what the term is? Which word is the noun?
Student 1:	...Er...um...element?
Me:	Yes. What's an element?
Student 1:	I know. At least I think I know, but I can't explain.
Student 2:	[*looking up the word* element] I know. It says here that element is a basic substance. The core of something. I guess that mean what it is made of.
Me:	Yes. So if an element is the fundamental part of something, then it refers to its qualities or attributes—its essence—the very substance of something. You might refer to the essence of a food.
Student 3:	You mean like when the tiniest crumbs of a chocolate or vanilla cupcake still have the flavor of chocolate or vanilla?
Me:	[*nodding*] Something like that. Or the essence of someone's character.
Student 4:	Like John Canty's essence was that he was despicable in the *The Prince and the Pauper.*
Me:	Exactly. So what shall I write in this box [*pointing to the first box under the category,* What is it like?]
Student 1:	You should write the stuff that something is made of...the soul of something.
Student 2:	The basis of something.
Student 5:	The part of something that makes it what it is.

We completed the graphic organizer by identifying examples of *essence*. With the story of *The Prince and the Pauper* still fresh in their minds, students decided to use John Canty's character as an example of the essence of violence. All the students knew Emeril as a well-known chef who developed an *essence* that was used to enhance the flavor in meal preparation and therefore chose to use the word *spice* as an example of a type of essence. By the third example, students concluded that if John Canty's character was the essence of violence, then the essence of the character of Martin Luther King, Jr. was integrity. As we worked to complete the CD word map, they realized that they understood the meaning of the phrase *the most important element*, which I wrote as the superordinate category above the focus word of *essence*.

Finally, I showed the students how to construct a student-friendly definition of the word *essence* by transferring the fragmented information from the graphic organizer to a written paragraph that extends and elaborates on the phrases to form sentences that convey the meaning of the word. I pointed to the word *essence* in the middle of the word map, then strategically pointed upward toward the "What is it" category. Subsequently, I continued my oral explanation by identifying properties under the category of "What is it like?" Transferring the language from the graphic organizer to a written paragraph, the homespun definition for the word *essence* read as follows:

> Essence is the most important element. It is the basis, the quality, or the soul of something. It is the stuff of something, and it is the something that makes it what is, like the small part of something. Examples of essence are the spice that Emeril puts into food. The essence of someone's character could be John Canty's violent nature in *The Prince and the Pauper.* The essence of Martin Luther King, Jr. was his integrity.

Independent Practice. Next I asked the students to identify another word from either of the texts with which they were unfamiliar. Here they applied the process of constructing meaning using both the dictionary and the thesaurus as Ellen and I circulated through the room, offering help where needed.

Semantic Feature Analysis

Semantic Feature Analysis (SFA; Vacca & Vacca, 1999) was used to help students build vocabulary through semantically similar definitions of previously known words. In SFA, the dictionary and thesaurus are used once again to increase word awareness of synonyms and antonyms in relationship to the characteristics of a person, determined through a character's actions in a story.

Characters, events, concepts, or terminology inherent in content area text are compared and contrasted in the SFA strategy (Vacca & Vacca, 1999), which requires the student to examine the similarities and differences of individual features that are written at the top of a grid. Items to be analyzed are written on the left side of the grid. Students conclude whether a concept or character illustrates the written feature and indicate their choice by placing either a "yes" or "no" or a plus or minus symbol in each square of the grid to indicate agreement or disagreement, as demonstrated in Figure 9.7. The strategy provides an excellent basis for establishing talking points within small- or large-group discussion formats, and can easily be adapted for writing a comparison essay of the concepts and features of a topic. Finally, it is an interactive vocabulary strategy where the teacher can introduce new terminology through connections to familiar words.

Modeling. Once again using the graphic novel version of *The Prince and the Pauper* (Clemens, 2005), I asked students to list the names of the main characters in the story, which I wrote down on the left side of the grid. Then I asked the students to list a character trait for each of the characters. After talking about the actions and behaviors of the characters in partnerships, I encouraged the students to publicly share their discussions, whereupon they came to consensus in identifying an attribute that was correlated with the character's behavior and placed one in each of the boxes at the top of the grid. They agreed that John Canty was cruel not only because he beat his wife and his son but because he also killed the gentle priest. We put the word *cruel* at the top of the grid. We proceeded in a similar way until the students chose character traits for each of the characters based upon the character's actions in the story. All attributes were written at the top of the grid.

Guided practice—Day 1. I wanted the students to acquire additional synonyms for the mundane vocabulary words that had already been listed on the

Figure 9.7. Semantic Feature Analysis for *The Prince and the Pauper*

	Cruel bloodthirsty	Honorable noble	Generous magnanimous	Kind sympathetic	Teacher enlightened
John Canty	+	−	−	−	−
Tom Canty	−	+	+	+	+
Prince	−	+	+	+	−
Miles Hendon	−	+	+	+	−
Humphrey "Whipping Boy"	−	+	+	+	−
Father Andrew	−	+	+	+	+

grid, so I again divided the class into groups of four and distributed thesauruses and dictionaries in a procedure similar to the one used for the CD activity (Schwartz & Raphael, 1985, as cited in Vacca & Vacca, 1999). This time I instructed them to find a synonym for *cruel*, a term that would enable the reader to visualize the extent of John Canty's miserable character. They determined that the word *bloodthirsty* was a synonym for the word *cruel*, so both words were placed in the same box on the grid. Now both words could be referenced for meaning, one familiar term paired with one new vocabulary word. Next I asked the students to find a synonym for the word *noble*, which generated a list of other words including *moral*, *aristocratic*, and *virtuous*. Students selected the word *honorable* to be placed next to the word *noble* on the grid. We proceeded in this fashion until students were able to select synonyms on their own. The completed grid included at least two synonyms in each box that the students would be able to reference and use interchangeably.

Guided practice—Day 2. After synonyms were listed for each character trait, I continued by having the students determine whether each character possessed the trait that had been established for another. The students concluded that none of the main characters, including Tom Canty, the Prince, Miles Hendon, the whipping boy, or Father Andrew, was cruel or bloodthirsty. Determinations were coded using the plus sign to indicate that John Canty was *bloodthirsty* and *cruel* and the minus sign to indicate that these traits could not be attributed to the other characters in the story. I followed this procedure until the students were able to carry it out independently.

Independent Practice. Once students understood the process, I directed them to complete the grid by requiring them to cite evidence for their assertions. They alternated among arguing respectfully within their groups, conceding when they could not prove their statements, and coming to consensus in establishing the presence or absence of an attribute. Ellen and I circulated within the groups to ensure meaningful participation and to eavesdrop on student conversations.

Application. The students were already familiar with the concepts of comparison and contrast, so I told them to think of the SFA as a format for analyzing the characters and events through writing. Directing their attention to the first feature written on the grid, I facilitated a discussion of the ways that John Canty proved that he was *cruel* or *bloodthirsty:*

Me:	How did John Canty show his cruelty?
Student 1:	He killed Father Andrew.
Me:	He certainly did. What else did he do?
Student 2:	He beat up his son when he came home with nothing in his pocket or any food to eat. He wanted him to steal.
Me:	What do you want me to write?
Student 1:	There were several examples of John Canty's cruelty in *The Prince and the Pauper.*
Student 2:	When his son came home without food or money his father beat him.
Student 3:	Don't forget that he killed Father Andrew.
Me:	So what shall I write?
Student 3:	Write down that Father Andrew died from the blow that he received from John Canty.
Me:	[*after scribing the sentences*] How shall we show the transition from our statement that John Canty is cruel to the pieces of evidence that proved what kind of person he was?
Student 3:	We could say, First of all.
Me:	Yes, we could. Nice work.

The Link to Writing From Graphic Organizers

Both the CD and SFA were used as springboards for writing because the details, concepts, and events were perceived in a logical sequence that permitted the easy flow of ideas. In CD, the transition to writing occurred with an explanation of the concept and in providing examples of the concept to be defined. In SFA, the transformation from oral discussion to print occurred following our conversation about how John Canty demonstrated his cruelty. Subsequently, students constructed their own paragraphs, proving opinions and statements with evidence from the story. An example of a collaborative paragraph about John Canty's character follows:

> John Canty was cruel and volatile in *The Prince and the Pauper.* There were several examples of cruelty in the story. First of all, when his son, Tom, came home without food or money, John beat him. He also beat his wife. He struck Father Andrew, the

gentle priest who taught Tom how to read. Then Father Andrew died. No one else could compare with the despicable character of John Canty.

Lessons Learned

Did students improve their ability to think at higher levels of comprehension? Samples of student work confirmed that questions posed to them pushed their ability to reason rather than summarize; responses were evaluated on a 0–2 scale through student-friendly rubrics that reflected state rubrics for open-ended response to text. If improvements in higher level thinking can be attributed to the quality and quantity of student writing, increased motivation to participate in literacy and literary activities, and eagerness to publish and share original work, then the attitudinal changes indicated that students were well on their way to the internalization of the literacy practices of independent readers.

One English-language learner wrote,

> I want to thank you for helping us this year. You taught us how to be better readers and how to make reading easier and fun. You taught us that asking questions is okay—no one will make fun of us because they probably want to ask the same question. That is why I want to thank you and I think I never read more than 8 books before this year.

A Jamaican student whose schooling had oftentimes been interrupted before coming to the United States wrote,

> Thank you for everything you have done for me. I must admit I have been learning a lot during the past few months about how to fix up strategies and refocus. I learned why meaning breaks down and what I can do about it. Example: brain distraction. I also learned how to put things into my own words. Thank you for making me a better reader.

Another student commented,

> Every time you come to our class I learn something new. I enjoy monitoring comprehension. I liked the *William's Doll* lesson. But the ones that I enjoyed the most were the Rap and Hip Hop Lessons.

And one student wrote this,

> Thank you, Mrs. Waters for coming to our class and helping us learn strategies that will help us read better—like the reread strategy...when you read a paragraph or a story and you don't understand it the first time you read it—you keep reading it until you

understand it. You also taught us to never give up when something is too hard you keep trying. You energized me to see what I can do and don't forget about that 2 Pac paper. If you were not there I probably would not know I can write like that in my life.... If you were not here I don't know what I would do to help myself find out more strategies.

By the end of the year student engagement in authentic discussion was a commonplace occurrence in the classroom. Students referenced the criteria charts that were posted on the walls of the room for fix-up strategies in dealing with the stumbling blocks related to structural and morphemic analysis, or meaning, vocabulary, or comprehension, before soliciting the teacher's help. Students' contributions to oral discussion were significant and reflected in the quality and quantity of their writing. Students became more independent as they practiced the strategies that helped them to acquire proficiency in processing multiple genres of text.

The experience of connecting with a group of disenfranchised youngsters with whom I laughed, cried, and yes, learned, is one that I will forever cherish as a cathartic highlight of my career. In using the lyrics, music, and hip-hop culture of our students as opportunities to teach literacy lessons, I helped to create an environment where my students felt they were valued and respected members of an academic and cultural community. Students learned much more than the layers of comprehension strategies that are designed to meet curriculum objectives, especially because instruction tugged at the life experiences that defined students' characters. Strategy instruction integrated with a socially relevant and responsive curriculum through classic literature, poetry, student news magazines, content-specific books, and hip-hop prose places students at the confluence of a powerful context for tapping—and honing—students' raw potential in reading and writing.

ACTION PLAN

To try the strategies described in this chapter, use your existing curriculum resources or a unit with which you are familiar and the following template for lesson development that draws from the release of responsibility theory: Modeling, Guided Practice, Application.

Do not underestimate the importance of mediated dialogue in the classroom. Discourse by any name is not only a means by which students practice to acquire skills that are mandated through curriculum and legislation, but it is also the context for building foundational skills that will enable students to become contributing members of a social community.

Classroom experience has taught me that, regardless of the label, classroom talk is the medium by which students become better comprehenders. Classroom discussion is difficult to implement without adequate preparation, and many teachers are reticent to free themselves from the traditional modes that have served them well for so many years.

So as you begin to try these strategies in the classroom, remember that robust conversation should precede and accompany the implementation of any new strategy. First establish a supportive atmosphere for your students. It is important to encourage discussions about books, magazines, and any reading material that students find interesting. The following is a listing of tips for starting and maintaining positive discussions that lead to deeper comprehension. Pick a topic or text that excites your students, select a strategy to pique interest, and watch the discussion unfold!

- Treat classroom dialogue as a skill that can help students perceive subtle meanings, resolve controversies, and respect alternative viewpoints. Reinforce these points at every opportunity.
- Model effective conversations. Brainstorm with a colleague who may have experience in facilitating classroom discussion.
- Scaffold instruction and provide explicit instruction whenever necessary.
- Immerse students in a variety of genres to discover what interests them.
- Ask open-ended questions to stimulate thinking and encourage students to elaborate on their ideas.
- Be prepared for students to show emotional response.
- Create an environment in which all students respect one another and feel comfortable.
- Don't be afraid to use items from popular culture as an entry point. In my experience, rap music provided that entry point; for you, it may be a popular movie based on a book, a graphic novel, or even a television adaptation of a classic story.

QUESTIONS FOR STUDY
AND REFLECTION

1. Use what you have: Consider the materials, resources, and units of study that are available and familiar to you—ones that you currently use regularly in your classroom. In Book Study with your colleagues, think about the objectives within your local curriculum that drive your daily instruction. Perhaps your annual units on realism, conflict, or the causes of the American Revolution could use a boost of vitality. Any of these topics might yield rich classroom discussion and a deep sense of meaning. Which of the strategies in this chapter might be adapted for specific classroom use to accomplish familiar objectives that would generate student interest *and* spark conversation that could be extended into the realm of writing?

2. Four for the price of one: Perhaps each member of your grade-level or curriculum development team could select a different strategy that has specific application to an existing unit or topic of study in your classroom. Develop a lesson plan around the concept that you wish to teach using one of the strategies in the chapter, using either your own template or the lesson plan model provided in the chapter. Each teacher on the team makes a copy of an original lesson plan that is distributed to all the members of the team. The effort isn't duplicated when everyone shares in the workload, and the process provides team members with discussion points for refinement of the process and next steps for implementation.

3. Collaboration and professional development go hand-in-hand: Videotape yourself conducting a lesson using one of the strategies in this chapter. The video recording can serve as the basis for shared self-reflection and inquiry through discussion with your colleagues at a subsequent study team meeting. Use the recording to evaluate the extent to which you have maintained integrity to your lesson, the protocol for strategy implementation, and the level of classroom participation. Data obtained from videotapes can be used to shape the course of professional development in enhancing one's practice. I know that this activity sounds somewhat intimidating, but the corpus of research on the effects of collegial interaction in solving problems of practice to enhance one's instructional expertise is profound! For example, I videotaped myself implementing Story Impressions, and I still see room for improvement in providing wait time for students to respond.

REFERENCES

Alvermann, D. (1991). The discussion web: A graphic aid for learning across the curriculum. *The Reading Teacher, 45*(2), 92–99.

Beck, I.L., McKeown, M.G., & Kucan, L. (2002). *Bringing words to life: Robust vocabulary instruction.* New York: Guilford.

Beers, K. (2003). *When kids can't read: What teachers can do: A guide for teachers 6–12.* Portsmouth, NH: Heinemann.

Beers, K. (2004, June). *Comprehension in the middle and secondary schools.* Presentation sponsored by Yale Child Center, New Haven, CT.

Calkins, L.M. (2001). *The art of teaching reading.* New York: Addison-Wesley.

Cazden, C.B. (2001). *Classroom discourse: The language of teaching and learning.* Portsmouth, NH: Heinemann.

Chinn, C.A., & Anderson, R.C. (1998). The structure of discussions that promote reasoning. *Teachers College Record, 100*(2), 315–368.

Coulter, D. (2001). Teaching as communicative action: Habermas and education. In V. Richardson (Ed.), *Handbook of research on teaching* (4th ed., pp. 90–98). Washington, DC: American Educational Research Association.

Connecticut State Department of Education. (2006). *Connecticut English Language Arts curriculum framework: A guide for the development of prekindergarten to grade 12 literacy.* Hartford: Author. Retrieved July 10, 2008, from www.sde.ct.gov/sde/cwp/view.asp?a=2618&q=320866

Damico, J.S. (2005). Multiple dimensions of literacy and conceptions of readers: Toward a more expansive view of accountability. *The Reading Teacher, 58*(7), 644–652. doi:10.1598/RT.58.7.5

Denner, P.R., McGinley, W.J., & Brown, E. (1989). Effects of story impressions as a prereading/writing activity on story comprehension. *The Journal of Educational Research, 82*(4), 320–326.

Desai, S.R., & Marsh, T. (2005). Weaving multiple dialects in the classroom discourse: Poetry and spoken word as a critical teaching tool. *Taboo: The Journal of Culture and Education, 9*(2), 71–90.

Franklin, D. (2005). Beyond test prep: Making a case for extended responses to reading. *Illinois Reading Council Journal, 33*(1), 39–50.

Goldenberg, C. (1993). Instructional conversations: Promoting comprehension through discussion. *The Reading Teacher, 46*(4), 316–326.

Harvey, S., & Goudvis, A. (2005). *The comprehension toolkit: Language and lessons for active literacy.* Portsmouth, NH: Heinemann.

Holdaway, D. (1979). *The foundations of literacy.* Portsmouth, NH: Heinemann.

McVittie, J. (2005). Discourse communities, student selves and learning. *Language and Education, 18*(6), 488–503.

National Institute of Child Health and Human Development. (2000). *Report of the National Reading Panel. Teaching children to read: An evidence-based assessment of the scientific research literature on reading and its implications for reading instruction* (NIH Publication No. 00-4769). Washington, DC: U.S. Government Printing Office.

Nichols, M. (2006). *Comprehension through conversation: The power of purposeful talk in the reading workshop.* Portsmouth, NH: Heinemann.

Palincsar, A.S., & Brown, A. (1984). Reciprocal teaching of comprehension-fostering and comprehension-monitoring activities *Cognition and Instruction, 1*(2), 117–175. doi:10.1207/s1532690xci0102_1

Resnick, L.B. (1999, June 16). Making America smarter. *Education Week Century Series, 18*(40), 38–40. Retrieved August 9, 2007, from ifl.lrdc.pitt.edu/ifl/index.php?section=articles

Richek, M.A. (2005). Words are wonderful: Interactive, time-efficient strategies to teach meaning vocabulary. *The Reading Teacher, 58*(5), 414–423. doi:10.1598/RT.58.5.1

Rosenblatt, L. (1978). *The reader, the text, the poem: The transactional theory of the* literary work. Carbondale: Southern Illinois University Press.

Vacca, R., & Vacca, J. (1999). *Content area reading: Literacy and learning across the curriculum* (7th ed.). Boston: Allyn & Bacon.

Vacca, R., & Vacca, J. (2002). *Content area reading: Literacy and learning across the curriculum* (8th ed.). Boston: Allyn & Bacon.

Vacca, R., & Vacca, J. (2008). *Content area reading: Literacy and learning across the curriculum* (9th ed.). Boston: Allyn & Bacon.

LITERATURE CITED

Boyne, J. (2006). *The boy in the striped pajamas.* New York: Random House.

Clemens, S. (2005). *The prince and the pauper.* Irvine, CA: Saddleback.

Dunbar, P.S. (1899). *Sympathy.* Retrieved October 12, 2008, from project1.caryacademy.org/echoes/03-04/Paul_Laurence_DunbarSamplepoems(Paul_Laurence_Dunbar).htm

Eric B. & Rakim. (1987). Paid in full. On *Paid in full* [CD]. New York: MCA/Universal Records.

Hutchinson, E. (1998). *The red badge of courage. Abridged. Original work by Stephen Crane.* Topeka, KS: Topeka Bindery.

Keyes, A. (2001). Caged bird. On *Songs in A minor* [CD]. New York: J. Records.

Kweli, T., & Def, M. (1998). Respiration. On *Black star.* New York: Rawkus Records.

Masoff, J. (2000a). *American Revolution.* New York: Scholastic.

Masoff, J. (2000b). *Colonial times.* New York: Scholastic.

Notorious B.I.G. (1994). Juicy. On *Ready to die* [CD]. New York: Bad Boy Records.

Polacco, P. (1994). *Thank you, Mr. Falker.* New York: Penguin.

Shakur, T. (1998). Me against the world. On *Me against the world* [CD]. Los Angeles: Death Row Records.

Silverstein, S. (1996). Haunted. In *Falling up* (p. 94). New York: HarperCollins.

Spinelli, J. (1990). *Maniac Magee.* New York: Scholastic.

Zolotow, C. (1972). *William's doll.* Scranton, PA: Harper and Row.

CHAPTER 10

Literacy Initiatives in the Urban Setting That Promote Higher Level Thinking

Karen C. Waters

As a fledgling teacher in 1973 earning a mere US$8,745 annually, I had intended to stay in the inner city just long enough to acquire some experience—then I was planning to head straight for the suburbs. Thirty-one years later, I realized that I spent my entire career in the same district, characterized by the usual urban demographics—over-crowded classrooms in 100-year-old buildings where resources and materials were scarce, and where low student achievement prevailed. Like most of my colleagues, I regularly used part of my salary to purchase pencils, notebooks, cookies, crayons, markers, art supplies, and socks for the students. Most of our students came from single-parent families living in tenements, whose everyday lives were filled with disillusionment and unfulfilled dreams brought on by extreme poverty and unstable lifestyles. Those were the days before controversial legislation focused on ushering students to the forefront of literacy instruction, before federal programs enabled inner-city schools to implement breakfast and lunch programs, and before we realized that teaching higher level thinking with standards-based lessons meant that curriculum reform applied to those of us in the urban setting, too.

I was named the director of literacy for the district. Led by a new superintendent whose vision included a three-year district partnership with a nationally recognized university with expertise in working with urban districts, the administration was expected to collaborate with teachers on the problems that constituted their daily work. In a district that had traditionally allowed the reading department to shoulder the three-part burden of reading curriculum, instruction, and assessment, the issue of literacy instruction now became a hierarchical responsibility to be shared and divided among district constituents:

From *Building Struggling Students' Higher Level Literacy: Practical Ideas, Powerful Solutions* edited by James L. Collins and Thomas G. Gunning. Copyright 2010 by the International Reading Association.

central office administration, school principals, reading specialists, and classroom teachers. This break with tradition was reinforced through monthly six-hour professional development training sessions that principals and reading personnel were required to attend—and then *deliver* to classroom teachers. What followed was a pedagogical overhaul of traditional practices that ultimately led to a revised curriculum embedded with activities emphasizing higher level thinking, data-driven decision making, learning walks focusing on rigorous thinking within standards-based lessons, and a heightened sense of community awareness of the interdisciplinary nature of literacy as a critical entity whose tributaries extended beyond the classroom—all of which were initially accompanied with a certain level of push-back.

I had assumed that the superintendent's well-articulated plan would naturally entice eager participation by principals and teachers alike, because now literacy would be thrust to the top of the priority list of district initiatives and would automatically result in overall enhanced academic achievement. I secretly felt vindicated for the many years that I had implemented instructional conversations (Goldenberg, 1993) as a format for helping students to think at deeper levels of comprehension when the concept of accountable talk (Resnick, 1999) was introduced as both a district mandate and a legitimate strategy for text-based classroom discussion. I anticipated that a collaborative commitment to improved literacy achievement would naturally result in a more literate district.

I had a lot to learn.

This chapter will describe some of the challenges I encountered as a newly appointed literacy director in the context of a culturally diverse urban community whose traditional views of professional development, curriculum, and literacy instruction would be transformed under the leadership of a new superintendent with a vision of collaboration, cohesiveness, and common language among high-ranking district administrators at the central office and principals and teachers at the school sites. I will discuss how we faced the obstacles and summarize the lessons learned from persevering together in spite of unpredictable administrative changes, stringent legislation, and curriculum reform.

Drawing strength from the superintendent's position on staff development, curriculum, literacy instruction, and research-proven strategies, I ultimately viewed my role in the district as an intermediary in translating the principles of modern-day theorists into relevant and functional classroom practices that would be embraced by the teachers. I was fortunate to be able to work with a dedicated and committed staff of curriculum consultants and literacy coaches to create a sustainable and coherent professional development plan in literacy. Our plan involved an analysis of formative and summative district data in the context of the most current research in literacy. A philosophical merge between mentor texts and the principles of learning (Resnick, 1999) completed a comprehensive roadmap that governed our work in addressing the standards through revision in curriculum, instruction, and assessment. The principles of learning (Resnick, 1999), ostensibly reminiscent of the teachings of the constructivist theorists Vygotsky (1978), Dewey (1933), and Bruner (1960), were implemented within a scaffolded and social context emphasizing structured and deliberate guidance that gradually waned as students began to assume responsibility for their own learning.

First, we distributed a teacher-efficacy survey to a representative sample of approximately 200 teachers who were asked to rate their comfort level on a scale from 1 to 7 in the instructional delivery of phonics, phonemic awareness, fluency, comprehension, vocabulary, and assessments (see Figure 10.1). Results showed that although between 84 and 91% of the respondents rated themselves at a 5 or better in teaching the five pillars of literacy instruction, there was a significant gap between student achievement and teachers' perceptions about their teaching abilities. Additionally, 34% of the teachers did not feel comfortable teaching fluency, and 44% of the teachers were not confident in assessing their students' reading achievement.

Thus, teachers generally tended to rate themselves higher than the results of student achievement data indicated. When presented with the results of the survey as contrasted with the data, teachers were astounded, humbly acknowledging that they needed to deepen their knowledge in the teaching of reading by adopting an approach that effectively balanced the components of modeled, shared, guided, and independent reading (Fountas & Pinnell, 1996). In visiting most of the classrooms during my first year on the job, I realized that teachers wanted to be effective in their instructional practices but appeared to lack the necessary tools.

During the next couple of years, we immersed ourselves in the language of literacy as we began to assimilate a common lexicon among the teachers for the components of the literacy block. At that time mentor texts and documents included the work of Fountas and Pinnell (1996, 2000), Keene and Zimmermann (1997), and Taberski (2000). The Connecticut English Language Arts Curriculum Framework (Connecticut State Department of Education, 2003), Harvey and Goudvis (2000), and Put Reading First (National Institute

Figure 10.1. Teacher Efficacy Survey

Level of Use	Please rate your comfort level in teaching each component of a comprehensive literacy program.	Phonological Awareness	Phonics	Vocabulary	Fluency	Comprehension	Explicit Small-Group Instruction	Assessment
0 **Isolation** I use the strategies that I know and am comfortable using!	I presently do not use/model effective strategies in this component. I do what I have always done because I am comfortable with traditional modes of instruction. I know my students, and I have success in the modes of instruction that I use during the instructional day.							
1 **Foundation** That looks interesting!	I am building a foundation of new knowledge and am learning about a variety of new strategies. It seems overwhelming but interesting. I'm still not sure about how to proceed.							
2 **Emergent** I'll use that strategy and let's see what happens.	I have tried out a strategy or two and am still not sure of the implementation procedure, but I am willing to keep learning and trying.							
3 **Procedural Application** There is an awful lot to remember!	I am using/modeling effective strategies on a regular basis in this component. I find that it takes a lot of time and effort because I am not yet comfortable and flexible with the strategies. I know how to interpret data from assessments but may not be skilled in how to differentiate instruction.							

(continued)

Figure 10.1. Teacher Efficacy Survey (*continued*)

Level of Use	Please rate your comfort level in teaching each component of a comprehensive literacy program.	Phonological Awareness	Phonics	Vocabulary	Fluency	Comprehension	Explicit Small-Group Instruction	Assessment
4 **Automation** It's getting a little easier...	I am becoming comfortable with implementing strategies in this component because I have had opportunities to practice and acquire experience in these areas. I am beginning to integrate them into the daily and weekly literacy routines in the classroom. I know how to interpret data from assessments and use this data to inform instruction in the classroom to address the needs of my students.							
5 **Advancement** Wow! Using the data really helps to impact instruction.	I am very comfortable with the effective strategies in this component and have found ways to modify them to increase their effectiveness with students. I differentiate instruction and analyze the impact of that instruction on student performance in my classroom.							
6 **Assimilation** I think I've got it!	I have learned to integrate the strategies with other disciplines such as science, math, and social studies. I am an expert on using data to differentiate instruction to improve the performance of all students.							
7 **Regeneration** And I can also do it this way!	I can invent new strategies to improve the overall approach to early literacy in my school							

of Child Health and Human Development, 2003) initially provided procedural guidance for curriculum revision and corresponding pacing guides in Kindergarten through grade 6. We pondered the three tiers of vocabulary (Beck, McKeown, & Kucan, 2002) in providing explicit teaching of vocabulary with struggling readers and English-language learners at the elementary levels. We read about instructional conversations (Goldenberg, 1993) to acquire depth and context for the principle of accountable talk (Resnick, 1999), which we used in tandem with research-based instructional strategies (Marzano, 2003), and we used data to drive instruction (Reeves, 2004). Grant funds allowed us to purchase several books for study groups that included school principals and literacy coaches so they could hone their skills in content and process as they undertook their roles as staff developers and evaluators, respectively, in the implementation and evaluation of literacy in the classroom (Booth & Rowsell, 2002).

Fortified with a foundation of current research, we prepared ourselves to meet many challenges, including the need to revise a 10-year-old curriculum that was the last vestige of a previous regime, using fragmented editions of assorted basal reading programs that were even older. Understandably, poor test scores spoke to an irrelevant and amorphous staff development plan that was as understaffed as it was ill planned, and certainly not used in conjunction with student data. Additionally, there were approximately 1,000 teachers in kindergarten through grade 6 whose perceptions of literacy instruction were as varied as the texts they used. A new curriculum would require the delineation of the characteristics of effective reading instruction while embedding the concept of higher level thinking for all grades.

The cycle of the district and school improvement plans had changed little over the years: Plans were resurrected from the previous year's file in the opening months of the school year only to be recrafted and reshelved after the documents were resubmitted to the central office where they would gather dust until the following September. Back then, an erroneous perception of accountability implied that the school action plan was developed by a few, signed by all, and submitted on time so that the business of daily instruction could proceed without further interruption. The concept of holistic or student-centered accountability (Reeves, 2004), a system of supports ensuring that best practices in curriculum, teaching, and leadership advanced individual, rather than group, achievement, would be introduced later on.

Reading Specialist as Literacy Coach

For years, like many of their counterparts across the country, district reading specialists practiced the "pull-out" model in working with small groups of students to increase reading achievement. As literacy coaches working under a revised job description, they were required to provide assistance to teachers and principals in a whole-school reform model that placed literacy at the forefront. Thus, their daily work consisted of conducting in-classroom demonstration lessons, presiding over the collaborative assessment or standards-based protocols for looking at student work, designing and providing staff development, lending expertise to school administration in the development of the school action plan, ordering program materials, training paraprofessionals, overseeing intervention programs, and running family literacy workshops at the school site after the end of the instructional day.

Providing the 55 literacy coaches with the knowledge and skills of the trade was a priority. We contracted with national and local experts to work with our staff on the integration of content of literacy and the process of coaching. One day each month was set aside to discuss their practices in the context of research-based literacy strategies, analyze videotapes, participate in coaching conversations, reflect on their coaching styles, and network. The coaches talked about the scenarios that immediately impacted student learning and aired their concerns about working with veteran teachers who were reluctant to grant them access to their classrooms. They considered adult learning theory in their work with the teaching staff and acquired strategies that would encourage teachers to try out new techniques in risk-free environments that respected all learners. The coaches debated the finer points of guided reading and presented arguments for the implementation of a program in writing instruction for all district teachers.

During this time our state had begun to implement two-day literacy modules including explicit, small-group instruction of phonological awareness, phonics, fluency, comprehension, and vocabulary to be "rolled out" to literacy coaches in the 17 priority districts across our state, with the understanding that the literacy coaches from each district would then impart the content of the training to teachers in their districts. The problem was that the number of literacy coaches identified to participate in training was limited to 30 per district. As stated previously, our district had 55 literacy coaches.

Through state funding targeted for early literacy, we paid for all literacy coaches to acquire the training so that everyone would receive the same content and materials. The expectation was clear: All coaches would deliver the content of the training at several levels of staff development—through districtwide and schoolwide professional development, at grade-level meetings at each coach's school, and through in-classroom modeling that involved modeling, coteaching, observation, feedback, and reflection for both the teacher and the literacy coach at every phase of the lesson. A three-tiered approach to staff development would enable district teachers to be recipients of the training several times before being expected to assimilate new practices into their instructional repertoire. Please note, all students quoted in this chapter represent composites of actual classroom dialogue. These are not students' actual names nor direct quotes.

The Problem With Accountable Talk

Accountable talk (Resnick, 1999) is a principle of learning involving a format for text-based classroom conversation that requires the student to actively listen to his or her peers while garnering evidence from more than one source to support a claim.

Initially, while teachers endeavored to implement the principle of accountable talk, they simply did not know how to raise the level of student involvement in linking one student's ideas with another in making the transition to authentic conversation. Reliance on the use of an artificial construct of statement stems seemed to inhibit, rather than elicit, authentic student response. Using cookie-cutter starters to conversation, such as the statements "I agree with _____; This reminds me of _____; I am confused about _____; It surprised me when _____; or I agree/disagree with _____," almost resulted in a misinterpretation of a worthwhile concept—at first. The politeness of scripted conversation did not give way to a burgeoning of ideas—at first. During the initial stages of accountable talk (Resnick, 1999), teachers did not have the tools to weave students' ideas into the intricacies of rich community discourse.

It occurred to me that the first step in the reading process is to summarize the content; the literacy process must precede the literary experience. Focused discussion presumed initial understanding, a necessary precondition for discourse to occur. After all, the goal of discussion is not merely to summarize an author's main ideas; it is to cultivate one's own (Calkins, 2001; Nichols, 2006). I would eventually come to the realization that discourse is neither an end product nor a concrete goal; rather, it is a nonlinear procedural and interactive forum that begins with a logical stopping point in the text. The teacher's subsequent query—"So, what do you think?"—or directive—"Turn and talk to your partner!"—are the first steps in the community building of ideas.

Over time we observed the evolution of classroom conversation from rudimentary, stilted conversation through refinement that eventually resulted in authentic dialogue. As the speaker took responsibility for building on what had been previously stated through explicit references to textual evidence, tentative talk eventually gave way to dialogic conversation in rigorous text-based lessons at deep levels of comprehension.

We noted distinct teacher moves, actions that extended and linked students' ideas during the course of classroom conversation that determined the success of the procedure or the level of rigor of the lesson. Examples of this kind of talk included, "Can anyone add on to what _____ said? Say more about that. Do you agree with _____?" (Wolf, Crosson, & Resnick, 2005, p. 8). Over the course of two years we noted the subtleties in the level of sophistication of classroom conversation and realized that a high degree of expertise was required for the teacher to be able to connect, build, and extend ideas from one student to another (Chinn & Anderson, 1998).

Thus, accountable talk (Resnick, 1999) became the principle around which text-based discussion was sanctioned; accountability to accurate knowledge (Resnick, 1999) demanded reader retrieval of factual information in citing evidence from the text to support a claim, a skill that was justifiably reinforced because it was measured directly on state and national assessments. Intuitively, we realized that in requiring students to prove theories or opinions, we were preparing them for high-stakes assessments. Still, the principle of accountable talk (Resnick, 1999) itself was as elusive as it was critical, and our teachers begged for procedural structures in the implementation of this worthy concept.

Promoting the Concept of Higher Level Thinking at All Grade Levels

To promote higher level thinking embedded with the principle of accountable talk (Resnick, 1999), we offered training on the use of Junior Great Books (Great Books Foundation, 2002) at the local Holiday Inn to teachers in grades 1–8, with the understanding that they would receive classroom materials if they chose to participate. Teachers willingly relinquished their Saturday with the promise of new materials—and stipends—to compensate them for their time. Providing breakfast and lunch in a comfortable setting was a small price to pay to send the message that teachers' work was valued and they were respected as professionals. In providing the teachers with the necessary tools to get the job done, we succeeded in enhancing their performance so that they could, in turn, raise the level of achievement of their students.

The shared inquiry approach as delineated in the Junior Great Books program (Great Books Foundation, 2002) provided a procedure with which to facilitate classroom discussion that would ensure student understanding at deep levels of comprehension. As with other forms of dialogic conversation, the teacher's pivotal role as discussion manager is best described as establishing the foundation from which positions are clarified and arguments are built. This creates an environment that is conducive to social interaction and community learning because as the students gain independence in verbalizing their arguments, the teacher's role is simultaneously diminished, transitioning from facilitator to participant and then from participant to observer.

The shared inquiry procedure encouraged students to negotiate meaning while rehearsing new vocabulary, building a reservoir of ideas, and persisting in a line of inquiry about just one idea. It allowed the English-language learner who was grappling with vocabulary acquisition and adjusting to life in a new country to have multiple authentic opportunities to interact with his peers *and* his teacher, and to practice oral language in a supportive environment that encouraged risk-taking, allowed for mistakes in syntax, and increased understanding of semantics. It pushed students' thinking in cultivating one's own ideas, interpreting characters' actions, and engaging in self-reflection of personal ideals and beliefs rather than merely summarizing or reporting on an author's main points at the literal level. In general, teachers realized that talk was the medium by which students became better comprehenders.

Students learned to listen to one another, generate ideas, explore one idea, challenge one another, build upon one another's thoughts, and apply hermeneutics in acknowledging another's point of view on a continuum of inquiry. The teachers learned to link, merge, and extend students' ideas to build understanding of overarching concepts. As an observer in the classroom, I was captivated by the teachers whose influence intentionally faded in the process of accountable talk (Resnick, 1999) as they adapted their position from interrogator to moderator.

After giving time for the principles of shared inquiry to take hold in the classroom, teachers reported that the procedures were generalized into the disciplines of science and social studies and used with text other than the program materials. Finally, embedded within the approach are procedural and tactful strategies for handling both the reluctant participant and overzealous enthusiast who always has to be the first respondent.

A re-creation of a third-grade conversation follows, as an experienced teacher guides students in a discussion of *The Empty Pot* (Demi, 1990), the story of the aging Chinese emperor who searches among the kingdom's children for a successor to the throne and the young boy named Ping who is sure that his unsuccessful attempts to grow a beautiful flower will cause him to be disgraced. In the story the emperor gives seeds to all the children of the kingdom with the directive that they will return in a year's time with evidence of their best efforts. After repotting the seeds several times during the year, Ping, ashamed, brings back an empty pot to show the emperor his best effort, while the other children produce big beautiful flowers as evidence of their superior gardening skills.

As the students are sitting in seminar configuration, the teacher begins:

Teacher:	Before we read the story of *The Empty Pot*, we discussed the concept of integrity. What is integrity?
Arthur:	It's honesty. When you tell the truth. Like, honesty is the best policy.
Hector:	It's being truthful and honorable. If you tell the truth it is better. Otherwise you have to remember all the times you lied.
Teacher :	[*jotting down names of the students who have responded*] Exactly. And how does the word *integrity* connect with the story of *The Empty Pot*?

There is silence for about five seconds as the teacher gives wait time.

Isabel:	Well, [*deliberating*] Ping had integrity because when he couldn't grow a beautiful flower he kept trying. He put the seeds into a bigger pot with better soil. He waited. He could have done what the other children did.
Nadine:	Yeah. The other children just went out and bought big beautiful flowers to give to the emperor because they wanted to be the next emperor.
Marshall:	And they probably didn't water them [the flowers] all year either. That's not right. The children did not have integrity....
Teacher:	Because...

Marshall:	[*interrupting*] Because they were dishonest! They didn't grow the flowers that they brought for the emperor. They wanted the emperor to think that they spent *all year* growing the flowers.
Teacher:	What was the emperor looking for?
Jose:	He was looking for an empty pot because he knew that the person with an empty pot was being honest. So when he saw Ping with his empty pot....
Nadine:	He knew that Ping had integrity!
Jose:	But what I don't understand is...I don't think the emperor had integrity....
Teacher:	Why not?
Jose:	Well...didn't he lie to the children when he didn't tell them he was giving them cooked seeds? He knew that the seeds wouldn't grow. I don't think that the emperor had integrity.

There is a tenuous quality in the perception of classroom discourse that makes good discourse difficult to attain. Like a piece of delicate porcelain, discourse that is mishandled will succumb under pressure, and the only remedy is to start the process of construction all over again. In a millisecond an innocent remark that is misconstrued can truncate response, diminish enthusiasm, compromise self-esteem, and marginalize a participant. Lastly, discourse and fragile porcelain alike must be handled with care, lest they break. Therefore, the process of discourse, through which democratic, respectful, and lively conversations occur, requires the expertise of a facilitator (teacher) who has had the benefit of specialized training. Implementation of discourse necessitates professional development at the outset so that the teacher learns how to intuit when and how to respond, revoice a student's response, link to other students' ideas, challenge a student's thinking, dignify a reluctant participant's response, or say nothing at all.

Evidence of several important discussion principles was demonstrated during this conversation. First of all, in the initiation of the discussion following the reading of the text, the teacher reviewed the concept of *integrity,* which was not a vocabulary word within the text itself but nevertheless represented the theme. Second, it is interesting to note that the teacher paused for a full five seconds so that the students could think about the question, "How does the concept of integrity connect to the story of *The Empty Pot?*"

So often, I have observed teachers react to an unexpected silence by immediately rephrasing or restating a question because it is assumed that students require further clarification. Having the time to process the teacher's question allowed the students the luxury of thinking about how the idea fit into their understanding of the theme as they formulated their responses. Though silences of this nature can be uncomfortable, the teacher intuited correctly about when to pause, which gave the students ample time to think through their answers before responding orally. It is interesting to note that the teacher actually spoke very little during each of the four times that she participated in the conversation. Rather, the questions that she posed were designed to solicit student assumptions and interpretations about the events of the story and how they related to the theme. As a result, Jose took a risk in stating that the emperor did not have integrity. Jose went beyond the text, which, in turn, gave everyone else (including the teacher) something new to think about!

Ultimately, more talk led to more writing. Questions posed during class discussion were extended into writing prompts that used the tools of holistic scoring, using both student-friendly and official state rubrics for open-ended response to literature and incorporating both formative and summative evaluation for the integration of reading and writing instruction. The next day students were asked to respond to the prompt, "Who do you know who has integrity?"

One female student wrote,

> Someone in my life that has integrity is my mom. She is special to me because once we went to the mall and my mom bought herself a shirt and me a shirt. In that store the cash register lady gave us $30 back. That was too much money. So my mom gave the money back because she didn't want to feel bad. Then she taught me how to act just like her, or should I say she taught me how to have integrity. I really enjoyed learning from my mom.

A male student wrote,

> I have a friend who has integrity and his name is Greg. He is special because he shows me he can be good. When he forgets his homework he always tells the truth. He doesn't lie so he doesn't get into trouble.

And another male student wrote,

> A person I know who has integrity is my friend Rocco. Even when he did it he took the punishment and when he got a lot of money he went back and gave some money back. That's how he has honesty and integrity inside his heart.

The Benefits of Classroom Conversation

During classroom conversation students were nudged into thinking critically about the theme through questions for which there was no one correct answer. Responses were amplified and connected through instructional scaffolding that wove student talk into "connected discourse" (Goldenberg, 1993, p. 319). Goldenberg (1993) asserts that discussion is the precursor for any writing activity. Calkins (2001) reaffirms the notion that students need to talk to write; however, student writing should not be a replication of a book talk discussion. The activities that followed the discussion of the story of *The Empty Pot* (Demi, 1990) confirmed the link between classroom conversation, reading comprehension, and student writing, which was an intentional byproduct of student discourse.

When a struggling district is immersed in initiatives from the top down and bottom up, it is difficult to analyze which ones have had the most impact, unless of course each one has been evaluated through a deliberate empirical design. However, a fusion of purpose and process that acknowledged the recursive nature of change helped to imbue intuition within the district about how best to improve student learning. In the section that follows, I discuss the influences that forever changed the way we regarded professional development, curriculum reform, student achievement, and our roles as educational leaders in the community.

A Confluence of Purpose: Learning Walks, Curriculum Revision, a New Writing Program, and Online Assessments

Learning Walks

Teams consisting of teachers, literacy coaches, administrators, and teachers' union officials were created to conduct weekly "walk-throughs" in schools on a rotating basis to offer constructive feedback to principals, teachers, and coaches about the types of higher level thinking that occurred in the classrooms. Following criteria for what constituted rigorous lessons, we observed teachers' actions that encouraged students to elaborate on their ideas by citing evidence for their reasoning—and deep thinking. It was during these learning walks that we began to observe classroom discourse as a constructivist tool for meaning making, metacognitive reflection, and community building.

The Transformation From Outdated Curriculum to Comprehensive Literacy Plan

Over time, accountable talk (Resnick, 1999) became commonplace within the district, even though some teachers were more adept at facilitating authentic discussion than others. We had made the transition from teacher awareness to action around talk in the classroom and thus laid the groundwork for curriculum revision that considered classroom dialogue a necessary condition for student learning.

We solicited teachers, administrators, and parents to form a curriculum team to develop a comprehensive literacy plan as a roadmap for staff development, make explicit connections to the standards, and provide clear expectations for student performance. Pedagogical procedures, schedules, strategies, assessments, pacing guides, and portfolio requirements were delineated. The school board approved a one-year plan for rolling out the curriculum to district teachers in kindergarten through grade 8, which was put into place via the literacy coaches and a standardized training package that included modeling, lesson plans, and videos for classroom literacy instruction. The curriculum included research-based strategies, pacing guides, a scope and sequence of skills, and differentiated instruction through assured experiences for all students.

The district comprehensive literacy plan became a resource for teachers in the implementation of classroom literacy instruction, a manual for principals in monitoring and in evaluating the literacy program at each school, a guide for the small percentage of parents who opted to home-school their children, and a document that outside consultants could reference when they came to work with us in the district.

No One Uniform Method to Teach Writing in the Classroom

About a year after we implemented the district comprehensive literacy plan, we asked our teachers what else they needed to increase student achievement. Their voices reverberated from each school in the district: We need a uniform writing program—everyone teaches writing differently! Our test scores reflected the myriad writing programs that had come and gone over the years. We contracted with experts in the field who embedded this writing into the teaching of reading. The consultants worked with us to create a four-year implementation plan that would provide training in writing instruction to teachers in kindergarten through grade 8. For the first time in many years, the teachers in the district began to feel comfortable with teaching students the art of expressive writing.

The writing program not only empowered the teachers in giving them a common language for teaching writing in a variety of genres but also fortified student acquisition of expressive writing, even at the kindergarten level where the methodology proceeded with interactive writing. More important, as a district whose turnover for new teachers hovered at approximately 50% for many years, the program would be accessible for new teachers regardless of when they entered the district. Methodology for implementation mirrored state test requirements for the direct assessment of writing, which students were able to generalize in the other disciplines.

Here again, teachers learned that discussion, brainstorming, and idea gathering were essential antecedents for good writing to occur, and they assimilated procedures of the program for helping students to craft quality pieces of original writing. In the middle and upper grades, teachers learned how to assist students in developing thesis and antithesis statements, a cumulative process that helped students think more deeply. As a result of an incremental plan that provided training to teachers at all levels, including the seventh- and eighth-grade social studies teachers, the number of students achieving proficiency on state writing assessments rose by 10% the first year and 20% the second year. Several years later, scores continue to rise and are maintained because the district adopted a common approach to writing instruction.

Online Assessments That Mirrored the State Assessment

As with many districts across the state and nation during the first few years of the new millennium, our district attempted to make sense of imposing legislation while preparing for the eventuality that all students would be assessed from grades 3–8. The inception of the No Child Left Behind Act of 2001 meant that we could no longer view the annual state assessment as simply a practical measure for shaping professional development or customizing instruction. Results of the assessments were not published in a timely fashion, nor could the data from a summative assessment be used to create sensible intervention plans that might advance the achievement of individual students. We needed a formative assessment system that would evaluate student reading achievement efficiently and accurately and provide the teachers and district administrators with immediate feedback so there would be ample time for progress monitoring of discrete skills or strands that required reinforcement.

Thus began the pilot of a quarterly online assessment system and gradual participation of schools and grades within the district through a carefully designed phase-in process. Grant funding provided for an additional district reading consultant to create assessments that would target the skill strands of the high-stakes assessments in a continuum that became increasingly more complex as the year progressed. The new assessment system triggered the need to provide additional literacy training in the strategies that addressed the skills of the strands. Achieving the delicate balance between test preparation and skill instruction using an integrated approach that supported the learner had to be negotiated judiciously.

Stringent federal and state mandates have subsequently created the need to institute an ad hoc curriculum—test preparation for high-stakes assessments that has greatly influenced classroom reading instruction (Higgins, Miller, & Wegmann, 2006). With an emphasis on test taking, students can be deprived of rich learning experiences that result in the internalization of the skills and knowledge needed for future course work and in life (Langer, 2002). Farstrup (2006) states, "Teaching to the test has become a driving factor, effectively constricting the curriculum" (p. 22), forcing teachers to acquiesce to instructional constraints because they fear the consequences of poor test scores. Further, the difference between teaching a content strand or skill and providing students with the tools necessary to construct their own knowledge is a set of tasks to guide and engage students in active learning (Langer, 2002).

I felt that if students were fortified with content knowledge rather than test-preparation skills, they might be better served if they actually knew the difference between amphibians and crustaceans (for example), as measured by a multiple-choice question on a state assessment. If given structured opportunities in the classroom to compare and contrast the phylum of animals through discussion, would this not constitute the background knowledge to which the reading experts and test makers refer? Once again, the reading department, in partnership with the educational technology department, provided training for teachers in grades 3–8 in the strategies to teach the skills that the assessments measured.

We began to look at student data as a set of possibilities. Once an annual grim reality in the district, we began to realize that the concept of data might be within our control. With the help of a state-funded accountability initiative in partnership with the Center for Performance Assessment (Reeves, 2002) to assist the priority districts in using data to drive instruction, schools were challenged to form site-based data teams that would function in a leadership capacity in developing common assessments for the progress monitoring of skills that had been identified as deficiencies on school action plans.

It Didn't Take a Village (Just an Entire District)

When I left the district in 2006 to take a full-time position at a local university, more changes had occurred in the last 7 years than in the previous 25! Through the vision of many hard-working people including superintendents, assistant superintendents, grant coordinators, principals, department supervisors, curriculum specialists, classroom teachers, parents, and representatives from the state department of education, the district rose from obscurity within the state to national recognition, with a nomination in 2 consecutive years for the Broad Prize for Urban Education. (The Broad Foundation honors urban districts that demonstrate greatest overall performance and improvement in student achievement while reducing achievement gaps among ethnic groups and between high- and low-income students.)

Retired Supreme Court Justice Sandra Day O'Connor (n.d.) describes my feelings eloquently with her statement, "We don't accomplish anything in this world alone...and whatever happens is the result of the whole tapestry of one's life and all the weavings of individual threads from one to another that creates something" (n.p.). Since my departure from the district I have kept in touch with colleagues who report that the district is still in a state of upward transition because of the work of many who have continued the commitment to a cycle of ongoing reflective professional development that has been successful in making student learning a priority. Multilevel supports between the central office and the schools have promoted and expanded literacy initiatives that are no longer considered to be "new-think" and are as self-sustaining as they are evolving in a district whose mission is to arm its high school students with the tools to be college ready.

Members of this educational community ascribe to a creed that acknowledges incremental successes, celebrates mightily but briefly, and then goes back to work.

ACTION PLAN

When teachers participate in shared self-reflection and collaborative problem-solving, student achievement increases (Dearman & Alber, 2005; DuFour, 2004; Graham, 2007; Kinnucan-Welsch, Rosemary, & Grogan, 2006; LeFever-Davis, 2002; Servage, 2008; Wood, 2007). There were a number of structured protocols that were used within the district to engender reflective conversation with the focus on student achievement, including the Collaborative Assessment Conference (developed by Harvard's Project Zero), the Standards in Practice, and the Tuning Protocol (Allen & McDonald, 2003).

A comprehensive action plan for systemic change would require much more space than is allocated for this section. Instead, what follows is a list of online resources for reflective practice.

- National School Reform Faculty (www.nsrfharmony.org/protocol/doc/cac .pdf) offers a variety of common protocols, definitions, and implementation procedures for the most common structures for school and district collaborative work.

- Coalition of Essential Schools CES National Web (www.essentialschools .org) offers free access to resources including protocols for looking at student work and ready-to-use surveys for parents, teachers, administrators, and students.

- Looking at Student Work (www.lasw.org) offers many resources related to the Chicago Learning Collaborative (est. 1998), whose mission is to relate analysis of student work to increased teacher learning and student achievement.

- Education World (www.education-world.com/a_curr/curr246.shtml) provides links to the most popular organizations for looking at student work, including the Annenberg Institute, Coalition of Essential Schools, and Harvard's Project Zero.

- Facilitating Use of Protocols (www.dodea.edu/instruction/support/profdev/ studentwork/lsw.doc) presents a generic step-by-step implementation plan for looking at student work.

QUESTIONS FOR STUDY AND REFLECTION

According to the author, the institution of accountable talk (Resnick, 1999) became a foothold for changing instruction within the district. In this chapter the author demonstrated how classroom conversation enabled a student to discern that the theme of a text precluded the main character from having integrity. If the teacher had not nudged the students into thinking critically about the content of the story, that student may not have come to the conclusion that the emperor's position did not absolve him from telling the truth.

1. How can your study team collaborate with other school resource personnel (the school psychologist, media specialist, literacy coach) to identify other texts whose themes have the potential to spark meaty classroom discussions, allow students to explore multiple themes within a text, and acknowledge that "readers and authors are influenced by individual, social, cultural, and historical contexts" (Connecticut State Department of Education, 2006, p. 5)? Finally, how does classroom discourse lead to social change?

2. Professional development is no longer the singular burden of administrators and directors at the central office. Rather, the transformative definition of staff development has come to mean rich opportunities for principals and teachers to build communities of practice and discuss how best to meet the instructional challenges that govern their daily work. How does your school make time to study student assessment data and design intervention plans that will meet the needs of diverse students?

3. How does the classroom teacher use data to inform daily practice and how can a focus on student learning result in increased student achievement? Do teachers at your school have regular opportunities to work collaboratively to solve problems of practice? What role does the literacy coach play in supporting the whole-school reading program, including teachers' efforts to improve instructional delivery?

REFERENCES

Allen, D., & McDonald, J. (2003). *The Tuning Protocol: A process for reflection on teacher and student work.* Retrieved September 23, 2009, from www.essentialschools.org/cs/resources/view/ces_res/54

Beck, I.L., McKeown, M.G., & Kucan, L. (2002). *Bringing words to life: Robust vocabulary instruction.* New York: Guilford.

Booth, D.W., & Rowsell, J. (2002). *The literacy principal: Leading, supporting, and assessing* reading and writing initiatives. Markham, ON: Pembroke.

Bruner, J. (1960). *The process of education.* Cambridge, MA: Harvard University Press.

Calkins, L.M. (2001). *The art of teaching reading.* New York: Addison-Wesley.

Chinn, C.A., & Anderson, R.C. (1998). The structure of discussions that promote reasoning. *Teachers College Record, 100*(2), 315–368.

Connecticut State Department of Education. (2003). *Connecticut English Language Arts curriculum framework: A guide for the development of prekindergarten to grade 12.* Hartford: Author. Retrieved July 10, 2008 from www.sde.ct.gov/sde/cwp/view.asp?a=2618&q=320866

Dearman, C.C., & Alber, S.R. (2005). The changing face of education: Teachers cope with challenges through collaboration and reflective study. *The Reading Teacher, 58*(7), 634–640.

Dewey, J. (1933). *How we think.* Chicago: Gateway.

DuFour, R. (2004). The best staff development is in the workplace, not in a workshop. *Journal of Staff Development, 25*(2), 63–64. Retrieved September 11, 2009, from www.nsdc.org/news/getDocument.cfm?articleID=305

Farstrup, A.E. (2006). NCLB, RF, HQT, SBR, AYP: ASAP? *Reading Today, 23*(5), 22–23.

Fountas, I.C., & Pinnell, G.S. (1996). *Guided reading: Good first teaching for all children.* Portsmouth, NH: Heinemann.

Fountas, I.C., & Pinnell, G.S. (2000). *Guiding readers and writers grades 3–6: Teaching comprehension, genre, and content literacy.* Portsmouth, NH: Heinemann.

Goldenberg, C. (1993). Instructional conversations: Promoting comprehension through discussion. *The Reading Teacher, 46*(4), 316–326.

Graham, P. (2007). Improving teacher effectiveness through structured collaboration: A case study of a professional learning community. *Research in Middle Level Education, 31*(1), 1–17.

Great Books Foundation. (2002, December). *Junior Great Books training.* Seminar provided in Bridgeport, CT.

Harvey, S., & Goudvis, A. (2000). *Strategies that work: Language and lessons for active literacy.* Portsmouth, NH: Heinemann.

Higgins, B., Miller, M., & Wegmann, S. (2006). Teaching to the test...not! Balancing best practice and testing requirements in writing. *The Reading Teacher, 60*(4), 310–318. doi:10.1598/RT.60.4.1

Keene, E.O., & Zimmermann, S. (1997). *Mosaic of thought.* Portsmouth, NH: Heinemann.

Kinnucan-Welsch, K., Rosemary, C.A., Grogan, P.R. (2006). Accountability by design in literacy professional development. *The Reading Teacher, 59*(5), 426–435.

Langer, J.A. (2002). *Effective literacy instruction: Building successful reading and writing programs.* Urbana, IL: National Council of Teachers of English.

LeFever-Davis, S. (2002). The preparation of tomorrow's reading teachers. *The Reading Teacher, 56*(2), 196–197.

Marzano, R.J. (2003). *What works in schools: Translating research into action.* Alexandria, VA: Association for Supervision and Curriculum Development.

National Institute of Child Health and Human Development. (2001). *Put reading first: Helping your child learn to read.* Washington, DC: U.S. Government Printing Office.

Nichols, M. (2006). *Comprehension through conversation: The power of purposeful talk in the reading workshop.* Portsmouth, NH: Heinemann.

O'Connor, S.D. (n.d.). *Discussion quote collection.* Retrieved September 30, 2007, from www.choiceliteracy.com/public/448.cfm

Reeves, D.B. (2004). *Accountability for learning: How teachers and school leaders can take charge.* Alexandria, VA: Association for Supervision and Curriculum Development.

Resnick, L.B. (1999, June 16). Making America smarter. *Education Week Century Series, 18*(40), 38–40. Retrieved August 9, 2007, from ifl.lrdc.Pitt.edu/ifl

Servage, L. (2008). Critical and transformative practices in professional learning communities. *Teacher Education Quarterly, 35*(1), 63–77.

Taberski, S. (2000). *On solid ground: Strategies for teaching reading K–3.* Portsmouth, NH: Heinemann.

Vygotsky, L.S. (1978). *Mind in society: The development of higher psychological processes* (M. Cole, V. John-Steiner, S. Scribner, & E. Souberman, Eds. & Trans.). Cambridge, MA: Harvard University Press.

Wolf, M.K., Crosson, A.C., & Resnick, L.B. (2005). *Accountable talk in reading comprehension* (CSE Tech. Rep. 670). Los Angeles: University of California, Los Angeles, Center for the Study of Evaluation.

Wood, D. (2007). Professional learning communities: Teachers, knowledge, and knowing. *Theory Into Practice, 46*(4), 281–290.

LITERATURE CITED

Demi. (1990). *The empty pot.* New York: Henry Holt.

CHAPTER 11

School, Home, and Community: A Symbiosis for a Literacy Partnership

Karen C. Waters

My son, Dino, roared with laughter each time we came to the line "His mother called him 'Wild Thing!' and Max said, 'I'LL EAT YOU UP!'" during each of the 43 separate readings of *Where the Wild Things Are* (Sendak, 1963) over the course of a year. Even at the tender age of 5, he understood the power struggle between mother and son, and although he could neither define nor spell the word *empathy*, he could easily make a text-to-self connection (Keene & Zimmermann, 1997) that transcended the simple story of a naughty child sent to bed without dinner. In truth, he was the main character of his own narrative and had effectively assimilated the monstrous attributes of the "wild things" in Sendak's award-winning book, which he executed spontaneously in all of their unabashed authenticity whenever he perceived that yet another parental demand was brewing. His response to any such demand, inevitably punctuated with an "I'LL EAT YOU UP!" was simultaneously accompanied with renewed giggles and a growing sense of independence.

As the director of literacy in one of the largest urban districts in my state, I prepared for family literacy events in my town by reflecting on the routines that I had long established for bedtime reading with my son that elicited reactions similar to the one described above. I wondered if my homespun methods could make the transition from mother's intuition to best practices within the community as I began to use monthly interactive read-alouds (Barrantine, 1996) as the format for district family literacy events. Consequently, my experiences as the parent of a school-aged child were used as the basis for working with district parents during my tenure as director of literacy.

From *Building Struggling Students' Higher Level Literacy: Practical Ideas, Powerful Solutions* edited by James L. Collins and Thomas G. Gunning. Copyright 2010 by the International Reading Association.

In this chapter, I describe what happened when at-home literacy experiences provided the themes for a family literacy partnership between the school and community. I believed that fertile ground for a literate environment was created through a combination of oral language, ancestral anecdotes, read-alouds, and other best practices in early literacy. I knew it was possible to connect home and school communities if personal stories were publicized, traditions were honored, standards were maintained, and the context for literacy learning was broadened. Mutual respect among parents, teachers, students, and administration results when the most personal parts of our lives are made public; our heritage is dignified and preserved through retellings of familial stories that engender life lessons and shape the values, beliefs, and superstitions of our heritage.

As an educator for well over 30 years, I have had opportunities to talk with parents whose tumultuous and unstable lifestyles have precluded regular home reading and the reinforcement of skills taught at school. Those parents admitted that their own schooling had oftentimes been interrupted by the problems of living in a city rife with poverty, crime, and unemployment. Yet, according to Padak and Rasinski (2006), all parents want their children to learn to read, and most parents want to help their children but are unsure about how to proceed. I wanted to align the literacy goals of the district with home literacy practices to develop a user-friendly model that would enable our families to support the literacy learning of their children. A successful plan for parent involvement meant that the framework had to be based on the most current research, which included strategies that could easily be replicated in the home.

Some strategies easily made the transition from the daily literacy block to family literacy practices as we adapted procedures for implementing interactive read-alouds, shared reading, and Readers Theatre. During shared reading, we demonstrated the critical role of fluency to parents and children as we read familiar chants that would encourage the audience to read along. A modified definition of fluency has included the ability to use phonics to decode words precisely, automatically, and with the kind of prosodic expression that infers meaning (National Institute of Child Health and Human Development [NICHD], 2003; Pikulski & Chard, 2005). Fluent readers depend on their fund of sight words and efficient decoding strategies to read rapidly while getting the meaning, as opposed to readers whose comprehension is compromised because they labor in decoding unfamiliar words (NICHD, 2003). Repeated reading of the same text has shown to be effective in improving fluency (NICHD, 2003; Rasinski, 2003) and is inherent in a variety of fluency strategies, including student-adult reading, choral reading, tape-assisted reading, partner reading and Readers Theatre.

District Family Literacy Night

Through a combination of funds from Title I and state early literacy grants, we purchased several hundred copies of a "Book of the Month" to distribute at family literacy events. Each month we used a different trade book to demonstrate a particular reading strategy. For example, the texts *The Big Block of Chocolate* (Redhead, 1985) and *Something From Nothing* (Gilman, 1994) were used to model shared reading, while *Chicken Sunday* (Polacco, 1992) easily lent itself to an interactive read-aloud (Barrantine, 1996) using the "turn and talk" strategy (Calkins, 2001; Harvey & Goudvis, 2005). Parents were invited to attend the monthly "Dinner and a Book Series," when the lobby at the district central office was transformed into a reading restaurant, replete with tablecloths, inexpensive centerpieces, and handouts (simple poems and songs) at each table. Notification of the meetings was done via electronic and regular mail, as well as telephone reminders and flyers that were distributed to the children in 22 schools. My staff and I served a simple catered dinner to everyone, which usually consisted of pasta, chicken tenders, salad, and chocolate chip cookies.

To help the parents to feel as if they were part of an extended family invited to Sunday dinner, we stood behind chafing dishes in the meeting room and dished out the portions ourselves. Then we circulated from table to table, welcoming them as everyone ate dinner. Contrary to the principle of not serving refreshments before the program began, dinner was served first—and no one left after dinner. Why? Because the distribution of books—the real lure of the meetings—always took place at the end of the evening. In a district where parent attendance was a concern, we played host to over 150 parents and children at each family literacy event.

In collaboration with the bilingual department, we provided onsite audio interpretation in several languages to parents whose dominant language was not English. The range of topics at the reading restaurant included phonological awareness, an explanation of the benchmark assessment system used to track and teach students at their instructional reading levels, the state reading assessment, and the district curriculum—all without the jargon of literacy-speak, presented in terms that could be understood by the parents. We modeled the research-based strategies delineated within the district's comprehensive literacy curriculum that correlated with classroom practices.

Instead of sending them off to supervised care, the students were invited to participate at each session because they were already familiar with most of the strategies from their daily literacy block. In fact, they were delighted at the prospect of helping to scaffold learning for the parents. This was especially true when we implemented the concepts of interactive read-alouds and shared reading experiences through picture books, or sang favorite songs including "Willaby, Wallaby," "Apples and Bananas," and "Down by the Bay" (Yopp & Yopp, 2003), which the students greeted as old friends, and which teachers regarded as critical to developing phonemic awareness skills in the primary grades. In any case, parents sang right along with their children while we explained the importance of using phoneme manipulation in a lyrical format that included rhythm, rhyme, and repetition and predictability of text. An explanation and procedural adaptation for the implementation of the concepts of interactive read-alouds, shared reading, and Readers Theatre follows.

Interactive Read-Alouds

Reading aloud to children has long been recognized as the single most important activity to promote children's sense of story, vocabulary, and higher level thinking (Barrantine, 1996; Rog, 2001). An interactive read-aloud includes a rich introduction that sets the scene for the narrative and allows time for students to process their thoughts through spirited interactions with the teacher or with a peer. During the reading of the story, the teacher stops at several predetermined junctures to model thinking aloud to arrive at a conclusion that has not been explicitly stated or to encourage students to turn and talk to a partner (Calkins, 2001) about predictions and connections as the events of a story unfold.·

At district family literacy events, each page of the selected text was scanned, presented, and read aloud using PowerPoint projection software so that both the text and the illustrations could be accessible to the crowd of parents and children. Observing the protocol for an interactive read-aloud, we stopped at various places in the story to encourage parents and children to share their thoughts, predictions, and connections. The room was abuzz with intergenerational conversations at each of the stopping points. Later on, parents remarked that this was an activity that they could easily do at home. Books such as *Big Al* (Clements, 1997) and *Thank You, Mr. Falker* (Polacco, 1994) easily lent themselves to the themes of friendship and acceptance, while *A Bad Case of Stripes* (Shannon, 1998) focused on the importance of retaining one's own identity and the problems associated with being a nonconformist. Parents and children alike shared their real-life connections to the events and characters in the narratives at junctures in the stories. Sometimes they spent a few minutes to recount the stories of their lives and took turns at the microphone sharing personal anecdotes with one another. This helped to create a context for trust, common understanding, shared experiences, and ultimately friendship within the parent community.

One year we did an author study on Patricia Polacco. A state-funded grant targeting early reading stipulated that a certain percentage of the funding be used for parent involvement, thus enabling us to purchase several titles for interactive read-alouds, including *Babushka's Doll* (Polacco, 1995), *Chicken Sunday* (Polacco, 1992), *Thank You, Mr. Falker* (Polacco, 1994), *The Keeping Quilt* (Polacco, 2001), and others.

The format for family literacy events was always similar: an interactive read-aloud followed by provocative questions that sparked in-depth conversations between children and parents that were oftentimes captured in written form as well. At each juncture in the story, we stopped to encourage parents and children to engage in conversation that focused on drawing conclusions about the story's lessons, inferring meaning, discussing character traits through the character's actions, supporting opinions through information garnered from the text, and connecting with timeless themes. After reading *The Keeping Quilt* (Polacco, 2001), a tender story about tradition and the passing of a keepsake quilted blanket from one generation to another, we gave the parents and children the option of constructing a personal memoir or writing in collaboration, as the following excerpts, which were recorded during an open mic night, will demonstrate.

One parent demonstrated a comprehensive understanding of the theme of the text in the following letter to her daughter:

> I want to write about my life, so one day you can read it to your children. I was born into a big family.... We grew up on a farm with a lot of cows, horses, chickens, dogs and cats. My mother was a very lovely person. She used to bake a cake for every brother and sister on our birthdays. Our house was like a kindergarten with six children. We played a lot with simple toys. At Christmastime we didn't give out presents. We used to make the nativity set together, put [up] the tree and make a lot of food and eat together. My mother loved to write and read. She wrote many poems and some were dedicated to me. Some day I will write [them] to you. The only thing is that they are written in Spanish. That is why I want you learn my language so you can understand better.

Another family collaborated in the telling of the following memory:

> We are writing about the red cake. Every Christmas my great-grandmother who I've never met would always make the red cake. The recipe was passed down to my grandmother, who up until a few years ago, had made it. Now last Christmas, it was myself, my mom, and my brother baking the red cake.

One family made an explicit text-to-text connection:

> My mom made me and my brother and sisters quilts to put on our beds. She learned how to make them from her grandmother. My mom says that when we leave the house and move out, we can take the quilts with us.

A 6-year-old boy recounted his memory of his first day of school to his mother:

> In kindergarten I didn't like to go to school. I thought we had a mean teacher. Then I learned to live with it. I also remember that we had snack. Now I like school.

A first-grade girl wrote this entry in emergent writing following the reading of *Babushka's Doll* in response to the prompt "Tell about a time you were naughty":

> One time when I was nawty I did't lisn to my mom and I got grati. I codit wash tv for five mitins. Al becz I jmpd on the cwch.
> (One time when I was naughty I didn't listen to my mom and I got grounded. I couldn't watch TV for five minutes. All because I jumped on the couch.)

Through the interactive read-aloud, parents understood the value of extended conversation and writing about the themes of their lives. They experienced the modeled literacy practices as compatible with at-home activities that could facilitate skill development in their children. They came to regard the mundane homemaking tasks of cooking, shopping, and cleaning as rich opportunities to increase vocabulary and extend language. In bridging a rigorous curriculum with the practical functions of everyday life, the parents became our partners in developing children's literacy learning. Next I will describe how we modified the concept of shared reading to provide practical home applications at bath time, bedtime, family celebrations, walks in the park, or rides in the car.

Shared Reading

Here again, as in the interactive read-aloud procedure, the entire text was scanned for a PowerPoint presentation. Sometimes we used the choral reading of a poem as an icebreaker to promote interaction between parents and children. The purpose of shared reading (Holdaway, 1979) is to increase fluency and accuracy in oral reading using text that is characterized by rhythm, rhyme, repetition and predictability of phrases, vocabulary, and story, and is generally used in the primary classroom. Lessons are built in succession over a period of several days in scaffolded instruction that shifts the responsibility of reading from the teacher to the student. During our limited time with the families we did not have the luxury of repeated readings; nevertheless, we were able to engage them in choral reading and offer similar applications for the continuation of the activity at home.

On one occasion we used the text *Something From Nothing* (Gilman, 1994), a lyrical Jewish folk tale about the efforts of a persistent young child to save a beloved and tattered blanket despite his mother's pleas to "throw it out," a popular theme with which everyone could instantly connect. The story contained rich repetitive language that easily lent itself to my best imitation of my great-grandmother's Yiddish accent. By the end of the story everyone enthusiastically read the refrain with fluency and accuracy:

> But as Joseph grew older, the wonderful (blanket, jacket, vest, handkerchief, etc.) grew older, too...Joseph said, "Grandpa can fix it." He turned it round and round. His scissors went snip, snip, snip and his needle flew in and out and in and out and in and out. (pp. 6–9)

In responding to this story parents and children busily wrote and shared their stories about time-worn raggedy, beloved stuffed animals and the shredded "blankeys" that had been boxed up and put into the attic for posterity. One 7-year-old who was obviously skilled in making text-to-self connections wrote in fond remembrance of his earliest recollection of the friendship with his teddy bear:

> My tdy iz lk Crdry. Crdry didt hav a butn. My tdy didt hav a lg. My dg bit hs lg of. Mom put a bndge. He wz my frend.
> (My teddy is like Corduroy. Corduroy didn't have a button. My teddy didn't have a leg. My dog bit his leg off. Mom put a bandage [on it]. He was my friend.)

Sometimes a piece of literature elicits a heart-wrenching confession for which there is no appropriate response. The following statement, dictated by a 7-year-old to his mother, illustrates a child's sad memory of his parents' divorce:

I had a blanket with a big red strawberry on it. I gave it to Dad before he left so that he would remember me. I don't know where my blanket is now and I don't see Dad.

One evening the city's public library graciously offered to host our family literacy meeting, and we used *The Big Block of Chocolate* (Redhead, 1985) in a shared reading activity in bringing together parents, children, and teachers. We nibbled chocolates and repeated the rhyming phrases: "Just the very sight of it brings back the taste delight of it. I'll savor every bite of it. But later, secretly" (Redhead, 1985, p. 3).

The children's head librarian, Eileen, a colleague and friend for over 30 years, greeted the families with library cards, spoke about storytime in the children's room, and explained how she could help parents find books for their children at the level in which they were being instructed in the classroom. The evening concluded when each parent received a copy of the text that was used in shared reading and a list of other books that could be used for shared reading activities in the home.

Readers Theatre

Readers Theatre was a popular strategy at family literacy events because it gave the students an opportunity to showcase their combined literacy and dramatic talents. Readers Theatre is generally used as an opportunity for students to work cooperatively in assuming the roles of characters in a play that has been adapted from a folk tale or familiar story (NICHD, 2003). Students acquire fluency in oral reading as they rehearse their respective parts and perform the finished product for everyone's viewing pleasure. We obtained scripts from websites that we distributed to all the families so that they could replicate the activities at home. Favorites included *Whose Shoes Are These?* (Roy, 1988) and *Where the Wild Things Are* (Sendak, 1963). The websites www.teachingheart.net/readerstheater.htm and www.readinga-z.com were extremely helpful in providing appropriate leveled scripts that corresponded to children's Developmental Reading Assessment (DRA, 1999) levels, which will be explained further in the next section. The poem "Easy Solutions" (author unknown) was used as both an echo and a shared reading activity between parents and children that elicited much dramatic interpretation from them (see Table 11.1).

Table 11.1. "Easy Solutions" Read-Aloud

Child's complaint	Parent's solution
Gee, I'm hungry!	Have a sandwich!
Gee, I'm angry!	Calm down.
Gee, I'm sleepy!	Take a nap.
Gee, it's chilly in here!	Put on a sweater.
Gee, it's hot in here!	Open a window.
I've got the hiccups!	Drink some water.
My nose itches!	Scratch it.
My feet hurt!	Sit down for a while.
My shoes are tight!	Take them off.
I have a toothache!	Go to the dentist.
I have a headache!	Take an aspirin.
I'm lonely!	Call a friend.
I'm bored!	Read a book!

Continuing the Partnership With the Public Library

At one meeting we presented an explanation of the DRA so that the parents could understand how their children were grouped for explicit, small-group instruction in the classroom. The DRA is a criterion-referenced tool designed to document students' reading progress over time through teachers' systematic administration of running records in leveled text to measure students' oral reading behaviors, and it is mandated by state legislation for priority school districts within our state.

With the continued support of the children's librarian, we compiled a list of trade books available at the public library with text features that correlated with the benchmark books for students' reading levels on the DRA. Additionally, we provided each parent with at least three books that were related to their children's DRA level: one at, one above, and one below the DRA level, so that parents could practice reading with their children at home.

Functional Strategies to Address the State Assessment

Parents were concerned about the state assessments and wanted to know how to help their children increase their reading achievement at home. I wanted them to understand that there were probably many literacy-based activities with which they were already involved that needed only minimal modification to be useful. I developed PowerPoint presentations that included humorous graphics to show how open dialogue, questioning, and listening to children about their daily activities facilitated vocabulary building and oral language development in the primary grades.

Three strategies that easily transferred from the classroom to the home included Somebody–Wanted–But–So–And (Beers, 2003); a variation of this strategy for nonfiction texts, Who–What–When–Where–Why; and Read-A-Paragraph (RAP; Katims & Harris, 1997). Each of these strategies is aligned with the current National Assessment of Educational Progress (NAEP) strand of Locate and Recall (Lee, Grigg, & Donahue, 2007) and provides a format for deconstructing as well as summarizing text.

Somebody–Wanted–But–So–And

I showed the parents how frameworks for summarizing fiction and nonfiction text could be used to depict the sequence of events in a text or main ideas of a story. Using "Cinderella" as an example of a narrative, we used the Somebody–Wanted–But–So–And strategy (adapted from Beers, 2003) to summarize the events of the story. With the framework projected onto a screen, we applied the story grammar terminology to parts of the story to construct a sentence that captured the essence of the story: *somebody*—Cinderella; *wanted*—to go to the ball; *but*—her stepmother wouldn't let her; *so*—her fairy godmother made it possible for her to go by waving her magic wand; *and*—she went to the ball with the understanding that she would be home at midnight. We guided the parents through the process of constructing summary statements using the framework and gave them opportunities to discuss how the strategy could be used with other fictional text selections (see Figure 11.1).

Who–What–When–Where–Why

In a similar fashion, I showed them how to summarize nonfiction using a vertical pattern of who, what, when, where, why (5 Ws) to depict the main events of the reading selection. Using an actual news story that appeared in a local newspaper, I correlated each of the segments of the lead paragraph to one of the 5 Ws (see Figure 11.2), and we constructed a main idea sentence from a synthesis of who, what, when, where, and why. As the parents worked to develop summary

Figure 11.1. Somebody–Wanted–But–So–And Chart

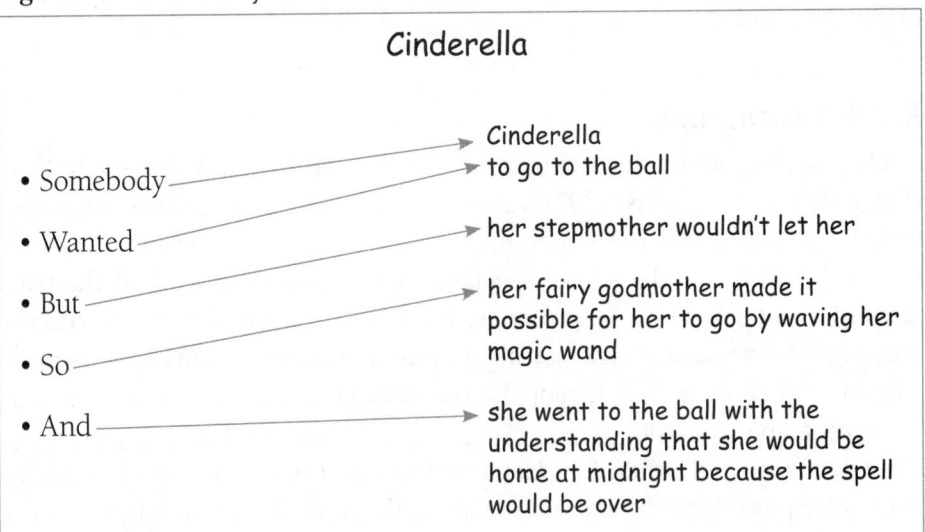

Figure 11.2. Who–What–When–Where–Why Chart

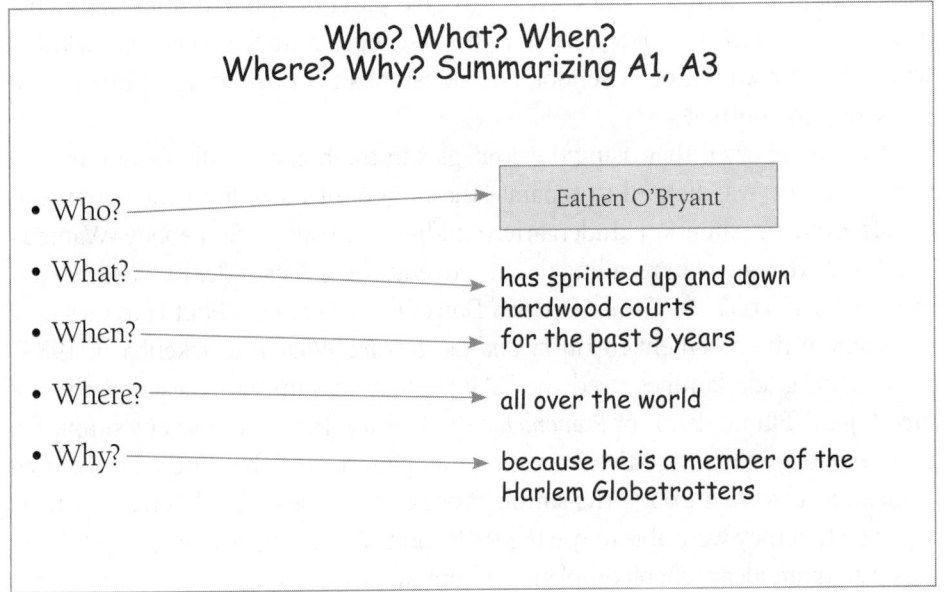

sentences, they could see how this strategy could be applied to reading sections of the newspaper.

Read-A-Paragraph

Another strategy for summarizing nonfiction text is the Read-A-Paragraph (RAP) strategy (Katims & Harris, 1997), a simple format for helping students paraphrase main ideas and distill the important information from the details. Originally designed to help middle school special needs students comprehend the main ideas of a text selection, the procedure has been determined to be an effective metacognitive strategy in synthesizing the most important information for general education students as well. Essentially, the strategy consists of a two-line format: This paragraph is about _____. It tells me that _____. The topic is entered in the first blank and repeated in the second blank, along with descriptive details that are listed about the topic. Simple and fun to use, it requires the student to focus on the main idea or theme and is especially useful in processing nonfiction text. The parents easily transferred the parts of the text to the appropriate lines to sift out the main parts of the reading selection.

After modeling the RAP strategy at one of our family literacy nights, I subsequently urged the parents to try it out at home and share the results at future family literacy nights. All of these summarizing strategies were referenced throughout our family literacy events to give parents opportunities to discuss how they adapted the strategies for at-home use, to reinforce their use at times when children were not in school, and to establish continuity from one parent workshop to another.

Parents reported that using the strategies in the home to talk about narrative story structure was helpful to separate the important ideas from the extraneous details. Even the parents of kindergarten children tried out the Somebody–Wanted–But–So–And strategy in recalling the misadventures of Alexander in *Alexander and the Terrible, Horrible, No Good, Very Bad Day* (Viorst, 1972) or about Harry's fear of monsters in the basement in *Harry and the Terrible Whatzit* (Gackenbach, 1984). Some third-grade families used the RAP strategy to summarize each chapter of *Freckle Juice* (Blume, 1971) or *Ramona the Pest* (Cleary, 1968). Almost any simple fiction story follows the narrative story grammar pattern, and the pattern can be used to glean its essence through the simple process of synthesis. Additionally, parents reported that they were able to use the RAP and 5 Ws strategies in helping children establish main ideas when completing a homework assignment.

The Family and the District: A Sociocultural Partnership

What better way is there to immortalize an original story of a child's first day of school, a stay in the hospital, or an argument with your mother-in-law than by writing it down, adding it to the collection of stored memories, and using it as the text from which a child reads and rereads during the beginning stages of reading? One of my son's favorite stories, *Chocolate Bunnies and Pork for Passover* (Waters, 2003), is my own anecdote of an argument between a wife and her mother-in-law in a two-religion family about Easter Sunday's menu when it just happened to coincide with the first day of the Jewish holiday of Passover. The result was a nontraditional blend of ham and *charoses* (pronounced cha-rō´-sis, a fruit compote made of chopped apples, walnuts, and grape juice served at the Passover dinner), and a reconciliation of both holidays that to this day still elicits giggles from one side of the family and grimaces from the other. This anecdote, one of many that provided hours of happy reading for my son during the emergent stages of literacy, was one that I shared with the families to demonstrate the powerful nature of writing down the memories that constitute the fiber of our families.

To dignify home literacy learning is to pay homage to the recollections of memorable experiences that propel us to main character status in our personal lives. Dialoguing or dramatizing a past event with someone else enhances self-esteem, produces instant authorship, and validates the learner as a writer, all of which are critical factors in literacy development. A spontaneous yarn that approximates reality can aid in the development of oral language and the acquisition of vocabulary in promoting conditions for literacy learning and the idea that every new experience is captured in a lexicon of content-experiential terminology. Consequently, when intergenerational sharing of stories and humorous anecdotes provides the context for skill reinforcement, there is a melding of strategies and stories and the creation of a literate partnership between home and school (Shockley, Michalove, & Allen, 1995). And finally, when stories are shared through social networking, there is reassurance in acknowledging that our similar experiences actually bind us together as members of the same group.

There is strength in the bonds of trust that are built between the school and the community. The books, stories, and experiences that emanate from a family that makes learning a priority and a district with the mission to provide shared literacy opportunities between parents and children—this is a symbiosis that builds partnerships (Shockley, Michalove, & Allen, 1995). For purposes of promoting family literacy within my district we modified the evidence-based strategies of shared reading and interactive-read-alouds as well as other strategies for summarizing narrative and informational text in a lively format that made learning accessible—and attainable. I encouraged our families to write down time-honored traditions and stories that served as texts from which children could practice and hone their skills. Ultimately, families recognized that they possessed the skills to facilitate reading and writing in their children, and they were imbued and empowered with intuition about how to grow readers.

When a seemingly different cultural literacy is integrated with school-based practices, we realize that we are not so far apart after all. Organic literacy practices can and should be incorporated into a comprehensive literacy program that accepts ethnically diverse preliterate essential understandings from the home. These understandings are inextricably linked with curricular standards, evidence-based strategies, and foundational skills to create a full-service literacy plan that ultimately teaches children to read and write.

ACTION PLAN

To implement the shared reading experience (Holdaway, 1979), choose a book with text that is characterized by rhythm, rhyme, and repetition. Shared reading is usually a five to seven day lesson plan that begins as an interactive read-aloud, but concludes as a story that is read independently by all the students in the class. Acknowledging the time constraints of a family literacy event, the author adapted this strategy so that parents could benefit from participating in an activity that could easily be replicated in the home. Either scan the text and show it as a PowerPoint presentation or read the text aloud to provide easy access by parents. (If you have sufficient funding to purchase the text for the parents, even better!) Then follow the procedure outlined as follows:

- Introduce the book by reading the title and author's name, illustrator, copyright, and dedication, if any. Read the story and pause long enough to encourage participation but not so long as to break continuity. (If time permits, the book can be read twice.)
- Invite the audience to chime in as they become familiar with the text, the language, and the vocabulary.

- Finish the activity by employing oral cloze during the reading, because usually by this point the familiar chant will be internalized by both parents and children. Systematically delete words and have the audience supply the missing words. Pause long enough for the audience to finish the sentences. Ask several parents/children how they knew the words.

- Read the book again and employ written cloze using a pocket chart. Integrate with a phonics element that is contained in the literature. Give children an opportunity to see letter–sound relationships function in print so the phonics lesson can be "extracted" from the piece of literature.

- Response to literature: Children put themselves into the very literature that they are reading. Ask questions related to the book, such as Have you ever had something (blanket, doll, teddy bear) that you would take everywhere with you when you were little? What happened to it? Write a story about what you would do with it. This can take the form of writing a journal entry, a letter, poem, or another story, or engaging in shared or collaborative writing to create an authentic (original) product.

- Independent Reading: Send home a copy of the book in a zip-top bag for independent reading. The book is accompanied by a note from the teacher, such as the following:

> Dear Parents:
> We have been reading (put the title of the text) this week. We have also written stories about what became of things that we once treasured. We would like to share our class story with you. Enjoy your time together.
> Sincerely,
> Ms. Brown

Children's book suggestions for shared reading:

Carle, E. (1992). *Brown bear, brown bear what do you see?* New York: Henry Holt.

Carle, E. (1987). *Do you want to be my friend?* New York: HarperTrophy.

Hall, Z. (1996). *The apple pie tree.* New York: Blue Sky Press.

Martin, B.M., Jr., & Archambault, J. (2000). *Chicka chicka boom boom.* New York: Aladdin.

Other suggested book titles can be found at www.hubbardscupboard.org/Quick_Reference_Shared_Reading_Book_List.PDF

QUESTIONS FOR STUDY AND REFLECTION

1. The effects of parental involvement in their children's education "is profound and undeniable" (Padak & Rasinski, 2006, as cited in Deck, 2009, p. 1). Examine the family involvement component of your school action plan. How do you ensure their participation in meaningful ways that will allow symbiosis of partnership within your school or district?

2. After reading *The Keeping Quilt* (Polacco, 2001) the author invited families to share their personal memories in written and oral formats. What personal memories do you have of your own family that could be publicly shared at a family literacy event to inspire the families at your own school to share their memories? All the entries could be captured in a memory book, a collaborative effort between staff and families.

3. Which of the strategies mentioned in the chapter could be easily adapted to accommodate your own unique needs in conducting family literacy events at your school?

REFERENCES

Barrantine, S.J. (1996). Engaging with reading through interactive read-alouds. *The Reading Teacher, 50*(1), 36–43.

Beers, K. (2003). *When kids can't read: What teachers can do: A guide for teachers 6–12.* Portsmouth, NH: Heinemann.

Calkins, L.M. (2001). *The art of teaching reading.* New York: Addison-Wesley.

Deck, J. (2009). *Effect of summer family literacy training on family literacy practices.* Unpublished doctoral thesis, Walden University.

Harvey, S., & Goudvis, A. (2005). *The comprehension toolkit: Language and lessons for active literacy.* Portsmouth, NH: Heinemann.

Holdaway, D. (1979). *The foundations of literacy.* Portsmouth, NH: Heinemann.

Katims, D.S., & Harris, S. (1997). Improving the reading comprehension of middle school students in inclusive classrooms. *The Reading Teacher, 41*(2), 116–123.

Keene, E.O., & Zimmermann, S. (1997). *Mosaic of thought.* Portsmouth, NH: Heinemann.

Lee, J., Grigg, W., & Donahue, P. (2007). *The nation's report card: Reading 2007* (NCES 2007-496). Washington, DC: U.S. Department of Education, Institute of Education Sciences. Retrieved August 14, 2009, from nces.ed.gov/nationsreportcard/pdf/main2007/2007496.pdf

National Institute of Child Health and Human Development. (2003). *Put reading first. The research building blocks of teaching children to read* (2nd ed.). Center for the Improvement of Early Reading Achievement (CIERA). Washington, DC: U.S. Government Printing Office.

Padak, N., & Rasinski, T.V. (2006). Home-school partnerships in literacy education: From rhetoric to reality. *The Reading Teacher, 60*(3), 292–296. doi:10.1598/RT.60.3.11

Pikulski, J.J., & Chard, D.J. (2005). Fluency: Bridge between decoding and reading comprehension. *The Reading Teacher*, 58(6), 510–519

Rasinski, T.V. (2003). *The fluent reader: Oral reading strategies for building word recognition, fluency, and comprehension*. New York: Scholastic.

Rog, L.J. (2001). *Early literacy instruction in kindergarten*. Newark, DE: International Reading Association.

Shockley, B., Michalove, B., & Allen, J. (1995). *Engaging families: Connecting home and school literacy communities*. Portsmouth, NH: Heinemann.

Waters, K.C. (2003). Chocolate bunnies and pork for passover. *Connecticut Journal of Educational Leadership: Essential Topics of the Day*, 1(3), 10–12.

LITERATURE CITED

Blume, J. (1971). *Freckle juice*. New York: Bantam Doubleday.

Cleary, B. (1968). *Ramona the pest*. New York: Avon.

Clements, A. (1997). *Big Al*. New York: Aladdin.

Gackenbach, D. (1984). *Harry and the terrible whatzit*. New York: Clarion.

Gilman, P. (1994). *Something from nothing*. New York: Scholastic.

Polacco, P. (1992). *Chicken Sunday*. New York: Scholastic.

Polacco, P. (1994). *Thank you, Mr. Falker*. New York: Penguin.

Polacco, P. (1995). *Babushka's doll*. New York: Aladdin.

Polacco, P. (2001). *The keeping quilt*. New York: Aladdin.

Redhead, J.L. (1985). *The big block of chocolate*. New York: Scholastic.

Roy, R. (1988). *Whose shoes are these?* New York: Clarion Books.

Sendak, M. (1963). *Where the wild things are*. New York: HarperCollins.

Shannon, D. (1998). *A bad case of stripes*. New York: Scholastic.

Viorst, J. (1972). *Alexander and the terrible, horrible, no good, very bad day*. New York: Aladdin.

Yopp, H.K., & Yopp, R.H. (2003). *Oo-pples and Boo-noo-noos. Songs and activities for phonemic awareness* (2nd ed.). Orlando, FL: Harcourt.

CHAPTER 12

Next Steps: Implementing a Program of Higher Level Literacy for Struggling Readers and Writers

Thomas G. Gunning

The 11 preceding chapters have explored approaches for assessing and teaching higher level reading and writing skills and strategies. Each chapter was packed with recommendations for fostering higher level literacy. This chapter summarizes the key recommendations of the previous 11 by providing a series of action steps that might be taken to implement a program designed to foster the higher level literacy of struggling students.

Step 1: Establish a Curriculum and Standards

Decide what it is that you want students to learn and to be able to do in terms of higher level literacy skills. You can use the listing of Comprehension Skills/Strategies in Table 12.1 as a starting point, but also consider national, state, and local standards and frameworks. Also include the higher level skills and strategies that your students need now and will need in the future. Translate these into objectives so that you and your students have a clear view of the path ahead.

Step 2: Assess Students

Determine, first of all, students' reading levels. As discussed in Chapter 2, students should be instructed on their reading levels, which for most struggling readers will be lower than their grade levels. Through data from mandated tests, classroom tests, observations, discussions, work samples, and other sources

Table 12.1. Comprehension Skills and Strategies

Cognitive Dimension	Skills/Strategies
Locate and Recall	**Details** Recalling details Locating details Recognizing details that answer questions Locating supporting details Recognizing/determining important details Locating and describing explicit details in narratives, such as plot, setting, characters, story problem Making simple inferences
	Main idea/supporting details Recognizing stated main idea Recognizing implied main idea Constructing main idea (stated) Constructing main idea (implied) Noting supporting details
	Summarizing Retelling Summarizing orally Recognizing best summary Composing written summary Polishing written summary by combining and condensing
Integrate and Interpret	**Inferring/concluding** Recognizing inference Recognizing support for inference Given inference, locating support Given support, making inference Constructing inference and providing support Explaining support Judging inferences and conclusions
	Predicting Using background and text to predict Revising predictions Supporting predictions
	Imaging Constructing partial image Constructing fuller image Constructing concrete image Constructing abstract image

(continued)

Table 12.1. Comprehension Skills and Strategies *(continued)*

Cognitive Dimension	Skills/Strategies
Integrate and Interpret *(continued)*	**Questioning** Constructing general questions Constructing specific questions Constructing literal-level questions Constructing higher level questions
	Comparing/contrasting Noting differences Noting similarities Noting differences and similarities Determining key similarities and differences Comparing texts Comparing ideas across texts
	Connecting Noting general connections Noting key connections Justifying/explaining connections
Critique and Evaluate	**Identifying author's purpose** Identifying stated purpose Identifying implied purpose Identifying dual purpose
	Judging fairness/accuracy Distinguishing between facts and opinions Noting biased language Identifying biased/slanted language Identifying persuasive techniques Identifying assumptions Judging credibility of source
	Judging literary quality Identifying/evaluating elements of author's craft Judging effectiveness of literary techniques

Adapted from Gunning, T. (2008). *Developing higher level literacy in all students: Building reading, reasoning, and responding.* Boston: Allyn & Bacon, and National Assessment Governing Board (2008). *Reading framework for the 2009 National Assessment of Educational Progress.* Washington, DC: Author.

discussed in Chapter 2, assess students' ability to apply higher level literacy skills and strategies. As discussed in Chapter 8, be sure to take a close look at students' attitudes, motivation, and volition. Fill out an Interactive Learner Profile for students who are experiencing difficulty. Analyze the assessment results. Where are students in terms of their grasp of higher level skills and strategies? Make a list of their major needs. Plan a program of instruction in higher level reading and writing. Plan to introduce 6 to 8 key comprehension strategies. That's about the number that can be taught intensively in a year's time.

Step 3: Foster High-Level Talk

A good place to start a program designed to increase students' higher level literacy is with the kind of talk that pervades the school day. Construct an environment that fosters understanding. Make sure that at all times students understand what is going on in the classroom. Encourage questions and answer them fully. Help students see the big picture and ask lots of why questions. Engage students in genuine conversations and discussions. Promote higher level talk. Introduce the kind of vocabulary needed to understand and use higher level talk. Build academic vocabulary. Introduce and explain the vocabulary of thinking: *compare, explain, conclude, imply, infer, analyze.* This is important for all struggling readers but is essential for English learners. Implement a program of quality talk and strategic talk as described in Chapters 3 and 4.

Step 4: Teach Key Higher Level Skills and Strategies

For struggling readers, take a step-by-step approach as is suggested in Chapter 7. Start off using brief, easy materials so students can focus on constructing meaning rather than decoding difficult words. Gradually, move into lengthier, more complex materials, but continue to use materials on the students' reading levels, which are probably still below their grade levels. Embed skills and strategy instruction in discussions of text as recommended in Chapter 4. Also use writing as a means for constructing meaning from text as suggested in Chapter 5. Thinksheets, as explained in Chapter 5, are a research-based approach that has succeeded in bolstering the comprehension of struggling readers. Struggling readers typically have difficulty responding to higher level questions. As recommended in Chapter 6, use answer organizers and frames to build students' capability for responding effectively to higher level questions. In today's era of high-stakes tests, struggling readers need to be able to demonstrate their high-level understanding in writing.

As recommended in Chapter 9, build on students' interests. Engagement fosters increased effort and deeper comprehension. Keeping in mind the importance of personal factors and the learning environment, as explained in Chapter 8, create an environment that is conducive to learning, and build the motivational and volitional skills that enable students to sustain the effort needed to develop higher level literacy.

Step 5: Involve Parents

As discussed in Chapter 11, explain to parents the higher level literacy demands made upon their children. Show parents how they can help develop the higher level literacy of their children, and affirm parents' efforts to help their children.

Step 6: Provide Professional Development

Developing higher level literacy is a complex undertaking. It requires the acquisition and development of new teaching skills. As explained in Chapter 10, an effective way to initiate professional development is to take stock of what is known and build on that. One way of developing needed skills would be to form a study group to discuss this text and provide support for one another as you implement its recommendations.

Higher-Order Questions, which is part of the Psychology of Learning presentation sponsored by the U.S. Department of Education's Doing What Works series, provides in-depth explanations along with practical suggestions and extensive resources for developing higher level literacy at all levels and in all subject matter areas. It also features materials and suggestions for professional development. This outstanding site can be accessed at dww.ed.gov/practice/practice_landing.cfm?PA_ID=9&T_ID=19&P_ID=43.

Getting Started

To get started, respond to the self-assessment in Figure 12.1. Note your current status, needs, and possible action steps. Then take action. You can't do everything at once, so set priorities. Based on test results, observations, work samples, and other sources of information, determine students' most urgent needs and select techniques and approaches that have the most promising payoff. Also build

Figure 12.1. Self-Assessment of Higher Level Literacy Program for Struggling Readers and Writers

Components	Current Status	Needs	Action Steps
Set higher level standards (goals) aligned with state and local standards and with tests.			
Believe that all students are capable of achieving higher level literacy.			
Assess students. Find out what level students are on and how well they can respond to higher level questions.			
Match materials to students' levels.			
Teach higher level reading and responding skills and strategies in-depth (about 20 sessions per strategy). Integrate strategies.			
Develop students' abilities to engage in higher level talk.			
Use quality talk and strategy talk during discussions.			
Use wait time, prompts, and lookbacks to foster responding during discussions.			
Use writing to develop higher level skills.			

(continued)

Figure 12.1. Self-Assessment of Higher Level Literacy Program for Struggling Readers and Writers (*continued*)

Components	Current Status	Needs	Action Steps
Use thinksheets, frames, and other scaffolds.			
Teach reading and writing skills required by higher level tests.			
Build background, vocabulary, and higher level language.			
Develop content area knowledge.			
Read high-quality selections to students.			
Foster wide reading.			
Monitor students' progress. Use the results to reteach and replan.			
Involve home and community.			
Other			

on what students know. Sometimes a minimum of effort results in maximum payoff. Making sure students have materials they can handle improves both discipline and learning. As explained in Chapter 4, by changing the wording of your explanations and questions, you can help students implement effective comprehension strategies. And if you have already set up discussion groups, making some changes in the routines and the way questions are asked and answered can make a significant difference in the effectiveness of the groups.

Chances are you are presenting strategies, conducting discussions, using writing in connection with reading, and making efforts to engage students. Improving struggling readers' higher level literacy might be simply a matter of making adjustments here and there. Try out a new technique or routine for a week or longer, if necessary. Once that additional technique or routine has become a habit, try a new routine or technique. If possible, get a coach to help you. If this is not possible, enlist the assistance of another teacher to observe your efforts and provide feedback. Most important of all, track students' performance over time. If their higher level skills begin to improve and they begin to take charge of their learning and have positive attitudes, you can assume that your efforts are paying off.

REFERENCES

Gunning, T. (2008). *Developing higher level literacy in all students: Building reading, reasoning, and responding.* Boston: Allyn & Bacon.

National Assessment Governing Board (2008). *Reading framework for the 2009 National Assessment of Educational Progress.* Washington, DC: Author.

Tomlinson, C.A., 146
Trabasso, T., 85–86, 146

V

Vacca, J., 249–251, 253, 255
Vacca, R., 249–251, 253, 255
Valencia, S.W., 40, 167, 203–204
van den Broek, P., 85
Vaughn, S., 28
Vesperman, B., 24
Viorst, J., 296
Vygotsky, L.S., 265

W

Wade, S.E., 28–30, 168, 180
Waggoner, M.A., 61
Walpole, S., 85
Walston, J., 2
Washburne, C., 205
Wasson, B.B., 21
Wasson, J.B., 21
Waters, K.C., 297
Webb, N.L., 24
Webb, N.M., 64
Wegerif, R., 64, 72
Wegmann, S., 279

Wells, G., 61
West, J., 2
Wilkinson, I.A.G., 72
Wilkinson, L., 128
Willingham, D.T., 10
Wilson, J., 188
Winograd, P.W., 137
Winters, D., 23, 34, 49
Wixson, K.K., 19
Wolf, M.K., 271
Wolf, W., 9
Wood, D., 281
Woodson, J., 136
Worthy, J., 62

Y

Yopp, H.K., 288
Yopp, R.H., 288
Ysseldyke, J.E., 203
Yuill, N., 33, 92, 178–179

Z

Zimmerman, B.J., 201–202
Zimmermann, S., 137, 265, 285
Zolotow, C., 246

Note. Page numbers followed by *f* and *t* indicate figures or tables, respectively.

HOME-SCHOOL CONNECTIONS, 285–301; and higher
level literacy program, 307

I

ILP. *See* Interactive Learner Profile
IMAGING, 7*t*; instruction in, 183–184
INDEPENDENCE: in higher level skills program,
163–164; as instructional stage, 128;
struggling readers and, 215–217; with
written responses, 133–135
INDEXICAL HYPOTHESIS: of language
comprehension, 171
INFERENCING: instruction in, 178–181; with
what's missing, 33
INFERRING, 7*t*
INFORMAL READING INVENTORIES (IRIs), 13–14, 86
INITIATION, RESPONSE, EVALUATION (IRE), 117
INSTRUCTION: combining writing and reading in,
104–107; elements of, 138; in higher level
literacy program, 306–307; high-quality,
importance of, 156–157; language shift in,
85–101; modes of, 117; with open-ended
questions, 125–161; for struggling readers,
9–10; with thinksheets, 116–121, 118*f*; in
urban classroom, 231–262
INSTRUCTION PLANNING, 52; assessment analysis
and, 14–21; for discussions, 78–79; for
literature response, 139*f*–140*f*; using all
available resources for, 50–51
INSTRUCTIONAL LANGUAGE: models of, 92–98;
preparing, 92; shift in, 85–101
INTEGRATE AND INTERPRET, 6, 7*t*–8*t*, 60, 150, 151*t*,
166*t*–167*t*, 304*t*–305*t*; drilled down layer of,
153–156, 154*t*–156*t*; instruction in, 178–
188; instructional sequence for, 153–153
INTERACTIVE LEARNER PROFILE (ILP): application
of, 206–209; data summary on, 209–211;
development of, 204; on external variables,
209; on internal variables, 207–208;
and personalizing instruction, 199–229;
sample, 223*f*–229*f*
INTERNAL VARIABLES: interaction with externals,
211–217; in Interactive Learner Profile, 205;
observation of, 207–208; struggling readers
and, 215
INVENTORIES: group, 19–20, 35–36, 35*f*;
informal, 13–14, 86

INVERTED PASSAGES, 180–181; think-alouds with,
29–30
IRE. *See* Initiation, Response, Evaluation
IRIs. *See* informal reading inventories
IT SAYS-I SAY-AND SO CHART, 181, 181*f*
ITEM ANALYSIS, 23

J

JOURNALS: for assessment, 36–37

K

KNOWLEDGE TRANSFORMATION MODEL, 109, 120

L

LANGUAGE: in higher level skills program, 164;
judging, 188–190; using with care, 192–
193. *See also* instructional language
LEARNER CHARACTERISTICS, 201–204; data
summary on, 209–211; diversity in, 206;
interaction of, 211–217; model of, 204–206
LEARNING DISABILITIES, STUDENTS WITH:
characteristics of, 201. *See also* struggling
readers
LEARNING WALKS, 276
LESSON PLANNING. *See* instruction planning
LIBRARIES: and family practice, 292–293
LITERACY. *See* higher level literacy
LITERARY QUALITY: judging, 8*t*
LOCATE AND RECALL, 6, 7*t*, 60, 150, 151*t*, 166*t*,
304*t*; drilled down layer of, 153–156,
154*t*–156*t*; instruction in, 168–177;
instructional sequence for, 153–153
LOGS: for assessment, 36–37
LOOKBACK, 168
LOW-ACHIEVING READERS. *See* struggling readers
LOWER LEVEL COMPREHENSION, 60; focus on, 9

M

MACRO CLOZE, 179–180
MACROSTRUCTURE, 4
MAIN IDEA, 7*t*; constructing, 170–171; deriving,
169–170; organizers for, 173–175, 174*f*–175*f*
MANIPULATIVES: for Locate and Recall, 171–173
MAPS: compare-contrast, 186–187, 188*f*;
Concept of Definition, 250–253, 251*f*
MARS. *See* Metacognitive Awareness of
Reading Strategies
MAZE TESTS, 20–21; sample passage for, 20*f*

MENTAL MODEL THEORY, 3–5

METACOGNITIVE AWARENESS OF READING STRATEGIES (MARS), 32

METACOGNITIVE STRATEGY INDEX (MSI), 32, 86

MICROSTRUCTURE, 4

MIDDLE SCHOOL: higher level literacy in, 231–262

MODELING: of deriving main idea, 169–170; of discussion, 79–80; explanation and, 142, 144; in instruction planning, 139*f*, 144; as instructional stage, 128; of making connections, 184–185; of rules for discussions, 74; of think-alouds, 31, 214; of written responses, 130–131

MSI. *See* Metacognitive Strategy Index

MYSTERY PASSAGES, 180–181; think-alouds with, 29–30

N

NATIONAL ASSESSMENT OF EDUCATIONAL PROGRESS (NAEP), 2–3; framework for reading, 3, 23, 60, 165; sample tests from, 22; on strategies/skills, 6, 7*t*–8*t*, 150

NEEDS, IDENTIFICATION OF, 51

NO CHILD LEFT BEHIND ACT, 278

O

OBJECTIVES: drilled down layer of, 153–156, 154*t*–156*t*; in instruction planning, 139*f*, 140–141; logical sequence of, 149–153

OBSERVATION, 35–39; and personalizing instruction, 199–229; recording guide for, 35–36, 35*f*

OBSERVATION SUMMARY: development of, 204; of external variables, 209; of internal variables, 207–208

ONLINE RESOURCES: for maze tests, 20–21; for professional development, 281; for Readers Theatre, 292

OPEN-ENDED QUESTIONS, 125–161; and higher level thinking, 126–127

OPINION: determining, 190–192

ORAL RETELLINGS: as assessment, 15–16; prompting, 16–18; shortcomings of, 18

ORGANIZATIONAL FRAMEWORKS: for struggling readers, 214

ORGANIZE THINKSHEET, 113

P

PARENTS: and higher level literacy program, 307; literacy partnerships with, 285–301

PERSONALIZATION: and higher level skills, 199–229; in higher level skills program, 165

PHYSICAL BASE: in higher level skills program, 164

PLAN THINKSHEET, 113, 112*f*

PLANNING PAGE: examples of, 45*f*–47*f*; use of, 44–48

PLOT: and aesthetics, 193

POETRY: for Readers Theatre, 293*f*

POINTED READING (PR), 233*t*, 248–249

PRACTICE: guided, 132–133; in instruction planning, 139*f*, 145

PREDICTING, 7*t*; instruction in, 181–183

PREDICTION CHART, 182*f*; example supporting, 182*f*

PRESENTATIONAL MODE: of instruction, 117

PREVIEWING, 181–182

PRIOR KNOWLEDGE. *See* background knowledge

PROBABLE PASSAGE, 234*t*, 243–244, 244*f*

PROCESS: struggling readers and, 146–147

PRODUCT: struggling readers and, 146–147

PRODUCTIVE TALK, IN DISCUSSIONS: characteristics of, 64–66; elements of, 64, 65*t*–66*t*; example of, 67*t*

PROFESSIONAL DEVELOPMENT, 263–284; and higher level literacy program, 307

PROMPTS: in guided practice, 145; in retellings, 16; in strategy instruction, 89–90; in think-alouds, 25, 26*t*–27*t*, 28

PROPOSITIONS, 4

PURPOSE FOR READING: struggling readers and, 215

Q

QUALITATIVE READING INVENTORY, 27, 39

QUALITY TALK, 72

QUESTION-ANSWER RELATIONSHIPS (QAR), 33, 179

QUESTIONING, 8*t*

QUESTIONNAIRES, 32–33

QUESTIONS: and family practice, 289; in instruction, 87–88; for making connections, 184; open-ended, 125–161; in productive talk, 64, 65*t*, 74–76

R

RAP. *See* Read-A-Paragraph

RAP LYRICS: in classroom, 238–239, 241–242, 244, 248, 251

READ-ALONGS, 31

READ-ALOUDS: interactive, in family practice, 288–290

READ-A-PARAGRAPH (RAP), 294, 296

READERS THEATRE, 292; poetry for, 293*f*

READING: as strategic, 137–147

READING COMPREHENSION: instructional language and, 85–101; as meaning-making process, 58–60; mental model theory of, 4–5; skills and strategies for, 5–9, 7*t*–8*t*; study of, 57–83, 58*t*; talk and, 69–72

READING SPECIALIST: as literacy coach, 269–270

REASONING WORDS: in productive talk, 64, 66*t*

RECITATION, 61–62

REFERENCES TO TEXT: in productive talk, 64, 65*t*

REFLECTION QUESTIONS: on assessment-based instruction, 52–53; on comprehension theories and instruction, 11; on discussions, 81, 260; on family partnerships, 300; on higher level skills program, 195; on Interactive Learner Profile, 220; on open-ended question responses, 158*f*, 160; on professional development, 282; on shifting instructional language, 100; on thinksheets, 122

RELEASED TESTS, 22

RESPONDING SKILLS, 165

RESPONSE TO INTERVENTION (RTI), 143

RESPONSIVE ELABORATION, 34–35

RETELLINGS: as assessment, 15–16; difficulty with, 168, 207–208; prompting, 16–18; shortcomings of, 18; written, 19

RTI. *See* Response to Intervention

RUBRICS, 37–39; Interactive Learner Profile as, 207; for prompted think-aloud, 28; sensitive, creating, 37–39, 38*f*, 38*t*; for written responses, 148*f*–150*f*

RUNNING RECORDS, 13–14

S

SAMPLE TESTS, 22

SCAFFOLDING, 88; for comparing, 186; in comprehension instruction, 138; and family practice, 288; and instructional language,

95–98; versus product, 116; of written responses, 173–175

SCHOLASTIC READING INVENTORY, 19

SELECT AND CONNECT, 107

SELF-ASSESSMENT: thinksheets and, 48–49

SELF-EDIT THINKSHEET, 113

SELF-TALK: modeling, 214

SEMANTIC FEATURE ANALYSIS (SFA), 234*t*, 249, 253–256, 254*f*

SETTING: and aesthetics, 193

SHARED INQUIRY APPROACH, 272

SHARED READING: in family practice, 287, 290–292, 298–299

SHARING: as instructional stage, 128

SHIFTING INSTRUCTIONAL LANGUAGE, 85–101; procedures for, 91–92

SI. *See* Story Impressions

SILENCE: in discussion, management of, 274–275

SITUATION VARIABLES: sample, 229*f*; struggling readers and, 214

SKILLS, 5–6, 7*t*–8*t*, 166*t*–167*t*, 304*t*–305*t*; key, instruction in, 306–307; presentation of, 165–168

SO WHAT STATEMENT, 187

SOMEBODY-WANTED-BUT-SO-AND, 177, 177*f*, 294, 295*f*

SOURCES: judging, 192

SQ3R, 174

STAR ASSESSMENT, 19

STICKY NOTES: for summarizing, 215; as think-alouds, 31–32

STORY GRAMMAR, 241

STORY GUESS, 242

STORY IMPRESSIONS (SI), 234*t*, 240–243; graphic organizer, 241*f*

STRATEGIES, 5–6, 7*t*–8*t*, 166*t*–167*t*, 304*t*–305*t*; versus background knowledge, 39–40; factors affecting, 199–229; in higher level skills program, 163; institutional scaffold for, 233*t*–234*t*; instructional language and, 85–101; key, instruction in, 306–307; opportunities for, identifying, 91–92; for reading, 137–147; sequence of, 165–168; in urban classroom, 231–262; for writing, 127–136, 140*f*

9744